MW00387481

Fate and fortune in rural China is a major contribution to the study of both the social and population history of late traditional China and that of historical demography in general. Lee and Campbell use the example of Liaoning to demonstrate the interaction between demographic and other social pressures, and to illustrate graphically the nature of social mobility and social organization in rural China over the course of the century from 1774 to 1873. Their conclusion—that social norms, rooted in ideology, determined demographic performance—is supported by a mass of hitherto inaccessible primary data. The authors show how the Chinese state articulated two different principles of social hierarchy—heredity and ability—through two different social organizations: households and banners. These different boundary conditions, each the explicit creation of the state, gave rise to contrasting demographic behavior.

Fate and fortune in rural China

Cambridge Studies in Population, Economy and Society in Past Time 31

Series Editors

ROGER SCHOFIELD

ESRC Cambridge Group for the History of Population and Social Structure

RICHARD SMITH

ESRC Cambridge Group for the History of Population and Social Structure

JAN DE VRIES

University of California at Berkeley

PAUL JOHNSON

London School of Economics and Political Science

Recent work in social, economic and demographic history has revealed much that was previously obscure about societal stability and change in the past. It has also suggested that crossing the conventional boundaries between these branches of history can be very rewarding. This series exemplifies the value of interdisciplinary work of this kind, and includes books on topics such as family, kinship and neighbourhood; welfare provision and social control; work and leisure; migration, urban growth; and legal structures and procedures, as well as more familiar matters. It demonstrates that, for example, anthropology and economics have become as close intellectual neighbours to history as have political philosophy or biography.

For a full list of titles in the series, please see end of book

Fate and fortune in rural China

Social organization and population behavior in Liaoning 1774-1873

JAMES Z. LEE

Humanities and Social Sciences
California Institute of Technology

and

CAMERON D. CAMPBELL

Department of Sociology
University of California, Los Angeles

with contributions by
Chris J. Myers and Yizhuang Ding

CAMBRIDGE
UNIVERSITY PRESS

PUBLISHED BY THE PRESS SYNDICATE OF THE UNIVERSITY OF CAMBRIDGE
The Pitt Building, Trumpington Street, Cambridge CB2 1RP, United Kingdom

CAMBRIDGE UNIVERSITY PRESS
The Edinburgh Building, Cambridge, CB2 2RU, United Kingdom
40 West 20th Street, New York, NY 10011-4211, USA
10 Stamford Road, Oakleigh, Melbourne 3166, Australia

© Cambridge University Press 1997

First published 1997

Printed in the United Kingdom at the University Press, Cambridge

Typeset in Palatino type

A catalogue record for this book is available from the British Library

Library of Congress Cataloguing in Publication data

Lee, James Z., 1952-

Fate and fortune in rural China: social organization and population behavior in Liaoning, 1774–1873 / James Z. Lee and Cameron Campbell.
p.   cm. – (Cambridge studies in population, economy and society in past time : 31)
Includes bibliographical references and index.
ISBN 0 521 58119 2 (hardback)
1. Liaoning Province (China) – Rural conditions.
2. Liaoning Province (China) – Population – History.
3. Social classes – China – Liaoning Province– History.
I. Campbell, Cameron.   II. Title.   III. Series.
HN740.L53L52   1996
306'.095182 — DC20   96-19232   CIP

ISBN 0 521 58119 2 (hardback)

BAC

for
our parents

Contents

ix

Figures

Appendix figures

Maps

Tables

Appendix tables

Acknowledgements

This book has been in gestation for more than twelve years. The first six, from 1982 through 1987, were largely devoted to data acquisition, data entry, and repeated data cleaning. I did not begin to analyze the data in earnest until late 1987, and was fortunate to be joined by Cameron Campbell and Christopher Myers. Cameron and I worked together on an almost daily basis during the 1987 and 1988 academic years, and on a daily basis during the summer of 1990, when we produced most of parts two and three. Chris and I worked during the 1989 and 1990 academic years primarily on part four. In addition to writing the necessary programs to manipulate the data, both Cameron and Christopher made important conceptual and analytic contributions. Both also contributed to the text. Cameron, most especially, participated in the writing and the thinking—reworking in particular chapters 8, 9, and 10 during the summer of 1992, and chapters 3, 4, and 5 during the spring of 1995. Every chapter, indeed virtually every page in the book, contains his prose. His name deservedly follows mine on the spine. Without his and Christopher's help, this would be a thinner and poorer book. It gives me great pleasure to state my gratitude to both co-authors.

Because of our academic schedule, we drafted eleven of these thirteen chapters during the summers of 1988, 1989, 1990, 1992, and 1994, and completed the manuscript in the summer of 1995. Ill-health and other projects intervened all too frequently, delaying completion. Without these other efforts, however, our understanding of Chinese demography and banner society would also be far less complete. We describe the conceptions, presentations, and revisions of each chapter, and acknowledge our intellectual debts, in separate footnotes to these texts. We reserve our thanks here to the people and institutions whose contributions transcend specific chapters.

First, we would like to thank Ju Deyuan, who in 1982 introduced me to the existence of the Liaoning household and population registers, as well as Wu Fusheng and Liu Kuizhi, who in 1982, 1985, and 1987 collected and filmed the specific registers we use here. We are deeply grateful to them and their colleagues at the Liaoning Provincial Archives for their assistance.

Second, we would like to thank the many friends, colleagues, and assistants who helped in the labor-intensive task of data transcription and inscription. Although I personally transcribed the 1774 and 1792 registers, most of the work was done by others. Robert Eng transcribed, with me, the registers for 1780 and 1786. Julie Sun transcribed the registers for 1798 and 1819. Liu Guiping, Wang Yuanqing, and He Ti transcribed the registers for 1855, 1861, and 1864 respectively. Anna Chi transcribed the registers for 1795, 1843, 1846, 1858, and 1873. Alice Suen transcribed all the remaining registers: 1801, 1804, 1810, 1813, 1816, 1822, 1828, 1831, 1837, and 1840. The total process took several thousand hours. Moreover, Anna Chi devoted hundreds of additional hours to help clean the data. We would like to thank all these participants, in particular, Anna Chi and Alice Suen, for their help. Their efforts were heroic.

Third, we would like to thank eleven friends who encouraged and helped us during the progress of this study. Ding Yizhuang and Mark Elliott introduced us to banner history and provided us with vital information on banner sources. Robert Eng introduced us to population history and participated in the initial data transcription and analysis (Lee and Eng 1984). William Lavely put his knowledge of demographic methods and comparative sociology at our disposal. Liu Ts'ui-jung shared her own results from a parallel project of comparable dimensions in Chinese population history (1992), and did much to make us welcome in Taiwan where we completed a significant portion of this book. Wang Feng instructed us in life course and event history analysis. Stephen Lee not only provided critical moral support during a particularly difficult period, but also accompanied me on an almost daily basis during June–July 1994, as did Wang Feng during June–July 1995. Stephen and Wang Feng, moreover, read and commented on virtually every chapter, as did George Alter, Helen Dunstan, Mark Elliott, Morgan Kousser, and John Shepherd, sometimes at considerable inconvenience to their own work. In so doing, they helped transform this book from a demographic monograph to a work of historical sociology.

Finally, we would like to thank the many institutions which provided financial and material support for this project, including the Academia Sinica, Beijing University, the California Institute of Technology, the Durfee Foundation, the Liaoning Population Research Institute, the National Program for Advanced Study and Research in the People's Republic of China, the National Endowment of the Humanities, the National Science Council of the Republic of China, and the Wang Institute of Graduate Studies.

We are particularly grateful to two institutions. The California Institute of Technology not only gave material and financial support, but also provided a nurturing environment where we could learn the demographic and statistical methods necessary for our work and pursue the many calculations necessary for our book. Very few "humanities" faculties would have been so forbearing. The Academia Sinica, especially the Institute of Economics, provided a supportive home away from home where we could calculate and compose free from the distractions of our primary affiliation. Indeed, it was in Taibei during three separate visits in 1989, 1990, and 1991 that we wrote the initial text of half this book.

Barbara Calli's contribution to this book equals that of any individual or institution. She not only typed numerous versions of the tables and text during the processes of calculation and composition, she also typeset the final version of the book itself. Much of the physical elegance of the current volume is her creation.

To all these people and institutions we express our gratitude.

James Z. Lee

Addendum I would also like to express my personal gratitude to the Durfee Foundation, the Thomas J. Watson, Jr. Foundation, and the Population Studies Center of the University of Michigan. The Durfee and Watson foundations provided travel grants to spend a year (1989–1990) in Taibei, Beijing, Shenyang, and Daoyi. That experience was instrumental in convincing me to pursue my interest in Chinese studies, and to continue this and other related research. The Population Studies Center at the University of Michigan, meanwhile, has provided me with an NICHD Postdoctoral Fellowship that has, among other things, allowed me to spend January through July 1995 working on revisions to this book.

Cameron D. Campbell

Part 1

Daoyi village[1]

Prologue

Landscape: a river, a road, a ridge

Three features define the Daoyi landscape. Maps 1.1 and 1.2 locate the village and surrounding communities that are the subject of this book in relation to Shenyang, the capital of modern Liaoning province and of Fengtian Prefecture during the Qing (1644–1911). Figure 1.1 depicts Daoyi village (*Daoyi tun*) today, based on personal visits in 1985, 1987, and 1990, and identifies all three geographic features.[2]

The *river*, called the Pu, divides the village in half. One of many shallow streams that meander through the broad plain of the Liao River valley, it is unnavigable and prone to periodic flooding.[3] Past floods have left scattered ponds in and around the village, as well as several hallows filled with mud. Side creeks have carved deep gullies that are now thick with vegetation. Except for some recent rice paddy, there is little irrigation.[4] The villagers use the Pu for domestic water and little else.

The *road*, which intersects the river, is the major route connecting Shenyang to the provinces of Jilin and Inner Mongolia to the northeast

---

[1] We drafted the prologue in July 1994. Stephen Lee assisted in the composition. Charlotte Furth and John Shepherd read and commented extensively on the manuscript for which we would like to express our thanks.

[2] The first two visits, by Lee in October 1985, and Lee and Campbell in July 1987, were short—just long enough to interview the surviving village leaders from the 1940s and 1950s and to obtain a copy of the 1984 edition of the *Daoyi District Gazetteer* (or *Daoyi xiangzhi*, hereafter *Daoyi XZ*), as well as some contemporary population records. The third visit by Campbell in May 1990 was several weeks long, during which he systematically interviewed all the older residents and resided in the local old age home. We would like to thank Li Lin for helping arrange this third visit.

[3] Average annual precipitation is 680 millimeters (23.6 inches), one-third of which is concentrated in July and August (*Daoyi XZ* 1984, 4).

[4] These paddy occupy what used to be the village graveyard. They were planted largely after 1956 by Korean immigrants who settled in Daoyi during the early twentieth century (*Daoyi XZ* 1984, 12).

1

Figure 1.1. *Daoyi today*

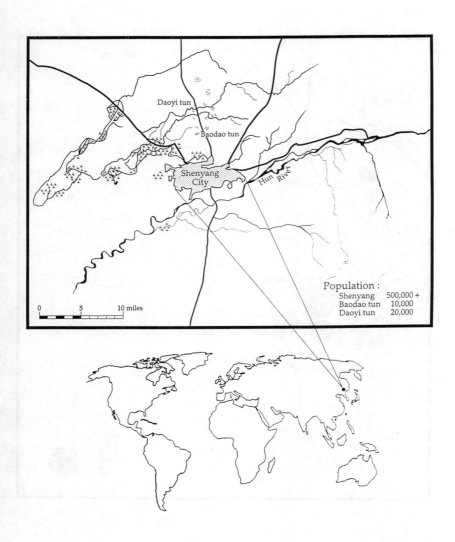

Map 1.1. *Rural Liaoning in global perspective*

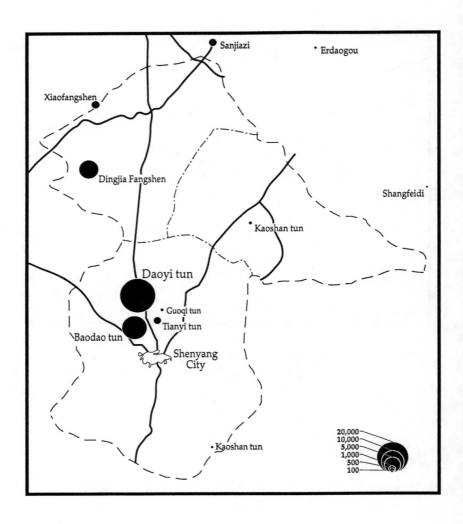

Map 1.2. *Village addresses in Daoyi and surrounding communities: number of individual observations*

and northwest respectively. One of five county highways today, this was an imperial post road during the Qing.[5] While most residential housing is away from the main road, along heavily rutted mud tracks, littered with animal droppings, the road itself is well paved and well maintained, lined with small, colorfully decorated restaurants and inns, as well as other stores and businesses. Traffic is heavy; and villagers go to the city and back frequently since the 18-kilometer trip takes less than an hour.[6]

The *ridge* lies several hundred meters north of the present village. A gentle hill rising perhaps 100 meters from the river basin, this elevation is nevertheless sufficient to provide a commanding view south toward Shenyang. More than a century ago, the village apparently lay at the base of this ridge, along a former riverbed of the Pu. Now, the site is deserted. The sole visible remains date from this century: the ruins of some Japanese fortifications squat on the crest of the ridge, empty pillboxes overlooking fields of grain.

History: a flood and a bridge

The major local historical event during the century from 1774 to 1873 was a change in the course of the Pu River, which forced the village to relocate to its present site. This catastrophe, only partially documented in the district gazetteer, is vividly preserved in local legend. It is said to have occurred in the early nineteenth century during a period of prolonged flooding.[7] According to village elders, local banner soldiers assigned to build a new stone bridge across the river had a formidable foe. Giant tortoises repeatedly came and destroyed whatever they built until the village erected a turtle temple (*wangba miao*) to appease these gods. The final construction, which is recorded in the district gazetteer as the Peace Bridge (*Ping'an qiao*), is reported to have been 30 meters long and 8 meters wide, one of the largest and finest stone bridges in the Shenyang area.[8] Villagers still recall with pride the

---

[5] *Liaoning gonglu jiaotong shi* 1988 provides a detailed history of highway development in Liaoning in general. *Daoyi XZ* 1984, 21, describes recent developments in Daoyi specifically.

[6] Indeed, Daoyi is so close to Shenyang that during the Republican period several well-off villagers with city jobs are said to have commuted back and forth on horseback.

[7] One informant dated the flood to "before 1840." Villagers followed the river since it provided their domestic water supply.

[8] These dimensions, recorded in *Daoyi XZ* 1984, 1, seem exaggerated. The surviving pillars on the south bank of the river are perhaps 4 meters apart. The turtle temple, on the opposite north bank, apparently was also quite small, with a foundation perhaps 2 by 2 meters.

labor required to quarry and transport the stone from Liaonan, 200 kilometers away. Although neither the bridge nor the temple survived the Great Proletarian Cultural Revolution,[9] several village families have preserved photographs of the bridge to commemorate this local achievement.

Otherwise the village history before this century is largely genealogy—family history, not community history. The village name, *tun*, implies that Daoyi was a military farm community during the Qing, a fact corroborated by the Han Army Eight Banner household registers that provide virtually the entire data for this book. While the original settlement may predate the Qing military occupation of Shenyang in 1625, most villagers today trace their ancestry to *bomin*, government settlers who arrived in the seventeenth century, or to *yimin*, voluntary settlers who arrived in increasing numbers from the eighteenth century onwards.[10] Many claim to have come from Shandong; others say they came from Hebei, and a few from as far away as Shanxi.[11]

Whatever their immigrant origins, the peasant population around Shenyang were incorporated by the Qing government as regular "bannermen" (*zhengshen qiren*) under the local Han Army Banners.[12] Their status was accordingly quite different from the peasants around Beijing, whom the Qing state transformed into estate serfs.[13] Although Daoyi peasants were also classified by the Qing government

[9]   When we first visited this site in 1987, it was little more than a pile of rubble since local villagers had cannabalized the stones from the temple and bridge during the Cultural Revolution to build homes and other structures.

[10] Roughly two-thirds of the present-day villagers trace their residence back to the Qing. The remaining third came largely during the Republican and, especially, Manchukuo periods. Few immigrants have settled in Daoyi since 1949, perhaps because of the unavailability of empty land.

[11] All the villagers interviewed claim that their families originally migrated from China proper. Moreover, of the nine village elders who knew the precise location of their ancestral origins, six claim to have come from Shandong in the late seventeenth or early eighteenth century, two claim to have come from Hebei in the middle of the nineteenth century, and one claims to have come from Shanxi in the late nineteenth century. Only two of these families, the Leis and the Mas, both of whom claim to come from Shandong, had even partial documentary evidence from family genealogies in their possession. See Ding and Liu 1988 for a description of immigration to Northeast China during the eighteenth century.

[12] See Li Shutian 1993, 32–39, for a general description of this process and Ding and Liu 1988 for a description of immigration to northeast China.

[13] Huang describes the creation of the Beijing estate serfs (*zhuangding*[a]) and their gradual transformation into commoner farmers (1985:87–89, 95–97). While the process and timing are quite different for the Shenyang bannermen no one has described this specific process in detail. The best account may be scattered through Li Shutian's 1993 reconstruction of the broad national processes (267-363), but see Zheng Chuanshui's pioneering 1981 article as well.

as ethnically Han, most non-bannermen considered the entire banner population to be ethnically Manchu.[14] This aspiration was evidently shared in the eighteenth century by some Daoyi males who even assumed Manchu names.[15] By the mid-nineteenth century, however, almost all had returned to Han names. Today virtually all the residents of Daoyi district declare themselves to be Han.[16]

In any case, Daoyi was state land; and Daoyi inhabitants were hereditary state servants, albeit elite servants. In contrast with the estate serfs around Beijing, however, they were responsible not to estate owners, but to the Qing state itself. Provided with ample land, their principal functions were to provide the state with grain, as well as labor and especially military service.[17] In particular, according to elderly residents, they maintained the Shenyang road and guarded the Pu River bridge. The majority of their time was devoted to farming. Even today, the village has little rural industry.[18] The vast majority of arable land is devoted to cereal production.[19] Only a small fraction is allocated for vegetables: cabbage, carrots, and potatoes.[20] And most of these, until very recently, were for local consumption, not the urban market.

Unfortunately the other qualitative information we have gathered on the economy and society of Daoyi does not extend further back than the 1920s and 1930s, and is hardly representative of village life

[14] Many contemporary Chinese historians agree with this definition, but this issue is complicated. See Crossley 1989, 1990; Ding 1992; Elliott 1993; Fu and Chen 1980; Li 1989; Wakeman 1985; and Wang 1990c for detailed discussions of banner ethnicity.

[15] Most men typically reported several names during their lifetime, depending on their age and aspirations. Together with Mark Elliott, we have, therefore, embarked on a separate study of Han banner ethnicity based on an analysis of naming practices in Daoyi and other Han banner communities.

[16] The vast majority of contemporary village residents no longer consider themselves to be Manchu. In the 1982 census, of the 17,792 people who lived in Daoyi district, 60 declared themselves to be Muslim, 62 to be Mongol, 343 to be Xibo, 563 to be Manchu, 618 to be Korean, and 16,146 to be Han Chinese (*Daoyi XZ* 1984, 6).

[17] In theory, the state initially provided each adult bannerman with the equivalent of 36 *mu*. Moreover, banner land tax assessments were quite light compared with civilian land taxes (Li Shutian 1993).

[18] According to the *Daoyi XZ*, virtually all industrial activity is extremely recent. As late as 1970, there was only one rural factory in the entire district, with just thirty-eight employees producing farm tools (1984, 15–16).

[19] There are 60,000 *mu* of cultivated land in Daoyi today, approximately the same as in 1950. The major food crops in descending order by acreage, used to be soybean, sorghum, and millet. Recently, however, corn (maize) has become the second most common crop (*Daoyi XZ* 1984, 11–12).

[20] The proportion of cultivated land for vegetables was just 5 percent in 1950 and 10 percent as late as 1975. Economic reforms beginning in 1979 have doubled these proportions to over 25 percent (*Daoyi XZ* 1984, 14–15).

in earlier times. This book is an account of Daoyi and surrounding communities identified on maps 1.1 and 1.2 from 1774 to 1873. Our sources are not the oral traditions and family memories of today's population, but rather a series of household and population registers preserved and stored in the Liaoning Provincial Archives, which we also visited three times.[21] By the last visit, we had found and photographed 25 of the 33 triennial registers compiled by the Qing government during this century. [22] We then transcribed the 90,000 individual observations, 10,000 household observations, and 5,000 kin-group observations from these registers into machine-readable form at the California Institute of Technology; and compiled by machine, individual, family, and kin-group histories for some 12,000 people from Daoyi and the surrounding communities. Although our sources and research methods are physically and psychically remote from the contemporary village, they provide an equally vivid, and even more detailed and quantitatively accurate, account of village life in the eighteenth and nineteenth centuries.[23]

For the people of Daoyi, the two historical visions are equally valid: the tracing of ancestors,[24] their vital events, and their household and banner positions, just like the *river, road, ridge,* and *bridge* are

---

[21] These visits by Lee in August 1982, October 1985, and July 1987 were necessary to locate the Daoyi household and population registers, which were unaccessioned, and are stored outside Shenyang far away from the main archival "stacks" in what had been an underground civil defense shelter. Lee obtained the 1774, 1780, 1786, 1792, 1798, 1801. 1804, 1810, 1813, 1816, and 1819 registers during his 1982 visit; the 1822, 1828, 1831, 1837, 1840, 1843, 1846, 1855, 1861, 1864, 1867, and 1873 registers during his 1985 trip; and the 1795 and 1858 registers during his 1987 visit.

[22] Ironically just as we were on the verge of completing this book, copies of all the surviving household and population registers from the Liaoning Provincial Archives, including the registers for Daoyi, became available on film through the Genealogical Society of Utah, an organization of the Church of Jesus Christ and Latter-day Saints. The Society catalogue lists in addition to our twenty-five registers, several other Daoyi registers which we are in the process of obtaining and transcribing for future research. We would like to thank Melvin Thatcher of the Genealogical Society for his gracious help in obtaining these films as well as catalogues of all the Liaoning films available through the Society.

[23] By village life we mean largely male village life since our sources are less informative about rural female society. Nevertheless, because our study focuses on demographic behavior—fertility, nuptiality, and mortality, including female mortality—our account of rural society provides insights into everyday female behavior as well as male behavior in rural late imperial China.

[24] Several of our informants, for example, used photocopies of the registers we made available to them to identify their own ancestors: parents, grandparents, great-grandparents, and great-great-grandparents. They were particulary interested in the characters used to write their ancestors' names since they had few surviving written records of family history.

complementary aspects of their life and heritage.[25] For the contemporary historian, Daoyi provides a unique opportunity to reconstruct the social organization and demography of a rural Chinese community during the late imperial period. And as we shall see, our understanding of social stratification and population behavior in rural Liaoning has important implications for our understanding of social hierarchy and social mobility throughout late imperial China.

[25] Indeed, we discussed our research findings on household structure and demographic behavior with many villagers all of whom were quite open-minded. The same cannot be said for some Chinese historians who refused to believe that infanticide and neglect were commonplace during the late imperial period in Liaoning, or anywhere else in China for that matter. For our evidence, see Chapters 4 and 5 of this book on infanticide among the Liaoning peasantry and Lee, Wang, and Campbell 1994 on infanticide among the Beijing aristocracy.

2

Social organization and social mobility[1]

Sixty years ago, amidst the chaos of warlordism and world war, two of Modern China's most well-known social novelists, Lao She (1899-1966) and Ba Jin (1904-), sought to identify what feature of Chinese society was most responsible for China's crisis. The answer they produced was contradictory. For Lao She, China's crisis was a product of traditional Chinese "selfish Individualism."[2] For Ba Jin, the fault lay rather with China's cultural legacy of "subservient Collectivism."[3]

The reason for their confusion about the nature of Chinese society is that from ancient times, social hierarchy in China has been organized according to two antithetical principles of social mobility: heredity and ability.[4] On the one hand, Chinese believe deeply in ancestral and familial birth rights. On the other hand, Chinese also value strongly individual ability and achievement. Mencius (371-289 BC) recognized the primordial nature of both principles, when he wrote that the two cardinal rules upheld in ancient times by feudal lords were first to

---

[1] We first conceived this chapter in July 1993 from a conversation with Wang Feng, but did not write it until the summer of 1994. Charlotte Furth, Stephen Lee, and John Shepherd commented extensively on the draft. We are very grateful for their assistance.

[2] In his novel, *Luotuo xiangzi*, Lao She concludes, "[Camel Xiangzi] was handsome, ambitious, a dreamer of fine dreams, selfish, individualistic, great . . . An unlucky child of Chinese society's diseased traditions, he was a ghost caught in the blind alley of selfish Individualism." (Lao She, *Rickshaw*, 249)

[3] According to Ba Jin, "[Traditional Chinese thought] is nothing but lessons on how to behave like a slave. Its full of phrases like . . . The son who is unwilling to die at his father's command is not filial." and . . . "Of all virtues filial piety is the best." (Ba Jin, *Family*, 86)

[4] Throughout this text, we use heredity specifically to refer to the principle by which Chinese transferred individual status, such as kin and occupational position, according to parental status. We are accordingly not referring to the genetic-environmental inheritance of personal characteristics, nor to the inheritance of property.

protect the familial lines of succession and to punish unfilial sons; and second to praise and to promote talented men.[5]

Both principles were central tenets of the Confucian canon. Confucius (551–478 BC) himself advocated that familial subordination was the foundation of all social and political hierarchy.[6] At the same time he also insisted that the ideal society was one where an intellectual and moral elite should rule; and where access to such education should be open to all.[7] As a result, the Chinese developed two social myths that on the surface seem contradictory. First, they accepted that their individual *fate* could be beyond their personal control (Lau 1985). Second, they also believed that with ability and achievement they could better their *fortune*. This dichotomy between subservience and success provides a fundamental tension at the core of Chinese society.[8]

Successive Chinese dynasties thereafter, from the Qin (221–206 BC) through the Qing (AD 1644–1911), based their political institutions on these two antithetical principles. Imperial law codes, a good example, were designed to reinforce familial prerogatives over individual personal and property rights. According to the surviving remnants of Qin law, the first imperial legal code, parents had control over their

[5] According to Mencius both principles were articulated as early as the seventh century BC, when, "Duke Huan of Qi (685–643 BC) was the most illustrious of the Five Feudal Leaders. At the meeting he organized at Kui Qiu (in 651 BC), the feudal lords ... swore a written oath ... The first oath was, 'Sons who are not dutiful are to be punished; heirs should not be put aside; concubines should not be elevated to the status of wives.' " The second oath was, "Honor good and wise men and train the talented so to make known the virtuous." ... The fourth oath, was, "Gentlemen should not hold office by heredity. The selection of Gentlemen should be appropriate." (Mencius, 6.2:177).

[6] The Confucian classics are replete with passages on filiality. The most famous collection is undoubtedly the *Classic of Filial Piety,* an apocryphal text from the second century BC ascribed to Zeng Zi, one of Confucius' students. Confucius, like Mencius, stressed the historicity of the principle of filial piety when he quoted from *The Book of History,* a text purportedly about the second millennium BC, "Simply by being a good son and friendly to his brothers a man can exert an influence upon government" (Confucius, 2.21:66). Confucius makes his own support of this principle extremely clear when he states at the very beginning of *The Analects,* "To be a filial son and an obedient young man is the root of virtue. Once roots are established, the Way can grow from them" (Confucius, 1.2:59).

[7] His well-known dictum in *The Analects* is that, "In education, there should be no restrictions" (Confucius, 15:39). Confucius himself claimed, "I have never denied instruction to anyone who, of his own accord, has given me so much as a bundle of dried meat as a present" (Confucius, 7:7).

[8] Some Confucian scholars accordingly felt the need to justify individual ambition as an expression of filiality. Zeng Zi, for example, is supposed to have said, "There are three degrees of filial piety. The highest is to honor our parents [by our achievement]. The second is not to disgrace them [by our failures]. The lowest is just to be able to support them" (*Li Chi* 21, 226).

children's property.[9] They also had authority over their children's bodies.[10] Unfilial behavior was a capital offense.[11] Moreover, such authority extended beyond parents at least to grandparents.[12] Children of all ages, in other words, had no "human rights"; they only had filial obligations.

By the Qing, the last imperial legal code, parental authority over the person and property of "children" had grown to encompass a wide range of kin relations delineated by sex, seniority, and degree of kinship.[13] Qing law required even distant family relationships to be identified in all legal proceedings with rare and incredible precision.[14] Qing criminal case records accordingly reported routinely any family relationship within the "fifth degree" (*wufu*[a]), that is, common great-great-great-grandparents, and occasionally even beyond such spacious boundaries.[15] The definition of many crimes depended as

[9] According to Qin law, for example, "A father stealing from his children is not a case of theft; a stepfather stealing from his step-children is a case of theft" (Hulsewe 1985, 125).

[10] They could, for example, petition to have their children exiled. The surviving Qin code, for example, contains a form entitled "To Banish a Son." This form requires that A, a commoner of X village, should state, "I request to have the feet of my natural son, C, a commoner of the same village, fettered and to have him banished to a border prefecture in Shu, with the injunction that he must not be allowed to leave the place of banishment ... to the end of his life" (Hulsewe 1985, 196).

[11] The surviving Qin code also contains a form for parents to have their children executed. This form entitled, "To Denounce a Son," requires that A, a commoner of X village, should state, "My son, C, a commoner of the same village, is unfilial. I request to have him killed." C, after interrogation, must then acknowledge his guilt and state, "I am A's natural son. I have been truly unfilial to A" before the execution can take place. Execution, in other words, required proof of infiliality. Banishment did not. (Based on Hulsewe 1985, 196).

[12] "Beating one's grandparents is punished by tattooing and being made a wall-builder or grain-pounder" (Hulsewe 1985, 141).

[13] Indeed, according to Boulais, the legal definition of unfiliality, one of the ten abominations, specifically refers to parental property rights, "établir un foyer différent et acquérir des bien qui ne leur sont pas remis." as well as parental corporal rights, "maudire et injurier ses grand-père, grand-mère, père, et mère" (Boulais 1924, 29-30).

[14] In theory, relatives beyond the immediate family should be reported as uncle (*shu* or *bo*) or aunt (*shen* or *gu*) if senior relatives; male cousin (*xiong* or *di*) or female cousin (*jie* or *mei*) if contemporary relatives; nephews or nieces (*zhi* or *zhinü*) if junior relatives, prefaced by the degree of common descent they share: *qin* (common parents), *qi* (common grandparents), *xiaogong* (common great-grandparents), *dagong* (common great-great-grandparents) and *sima* (common great-great-great-grandparents). In reality, the terminology occasionally overlaps and is sometimes obscure, even contradictory. Uncles, for example, are often identified as *qinshu* or *qinbo* rather than *qishu* or *qibo*. See Feng 1937 for a summary of these and other kinship terms.

[15] Terms such as *wufu*[b] (related outside the five degrees of mourning), *zuren* (lineage member), or *tongxing buzong* (same surname if not same lineage), for example, are quite common.

much on the familial relationship between the criminal and the victim,[16] as on the specific act itself. An act of violence committed by an inferior against a superior might be a capital offense. The same act committed by a superior against an inferior might be a misdemeanor or not even a crime. The closer the relationship, the greater, or the lesser, the offense.[17]

At the same time, each successive dynasty also opened political office to the able and accomplished. The Qin and Han (206 BC - AD 221) emperors, for example, routinely recruited men of distinction to serve them (An 1985). The Tang (AD 618-906) and Song (AD 960-1278) emperors established a well-known system of highly competitive formal examinations to select candidates for high office (Chaffee 1985; Miyazaki 1981). The Ming (AD 1368-1644) and Qing extended these principles to other state institutions. The best known example is a system of military examinations, parallel to the system of civil examinations, that tested prowess, as well as skill and strength (Zi 1896). By the late imperial period, similar systems of state tests had become commonplace for low offices as well as high offices. These testing systems persist today, especially in Republican China where in theory bureaucracy has become synonymous with meritocracy.[18] In contrast to the Confucian family, where the individual has no rights, everyone, or at least every man, can rise as high as his ability in the Confucian state. Chinese society in consequence was, and still is, an unusual blend of "open" and "closed" institutions.

Several classic studies have been able to quantify the proportion of late imperial officials who rose through ability or heredity. According to Ping-ti Ho's well-known analysis of 40,000 officials who served during the Ming and Qing dynasties,[19] half of all officials achieved office through competitive examinations, while the other half entered

---

[16] As a result we can identify even very remote family relationships between criminals and victims. Lee 1991 analyzes the patterns of domestic violence during the late imperial period based on the reported kin relations for capital crimes for selected years and provinces during the Qing.

[17] Thus, according to the Qing code, a son who strikes a parent suffers decapitation irrespective of whether or not injury results, while no penalty applies to parents who beat a son, unless the son dies, in which case the punishment is 100 blows of the heavy bamboo, if the beating was provoked by the son's disobedience, and one year of penal servitude plus 60 blows of the heavy bamboo, if the beating was done wantonly (Boulais 1924, 616-617).

[18] In the Republic of China, for example, one of the five executive *yuan*, or policy-making bodies, is the Examination Yuan which supervises more than one hundred different civil service and professional examinations.

[19] These include 14,562 officials who held the highest *jinshi* degree, 23,480 officials who held the *juren* degree, and 5,524 officials who held the *shengyuan* degree.

office through purchase or heredity (Ho 1962). Moreover, many of those who did well in the examination system were from humble origins in the sense that they were not direct descendants of other officials or degree-holders.[20] Even among the highest degree holders, the proportions of men from humble origins were as high as two-thirds during the fifteenth and sixteenth centuries, only to decline during the eighteenth and nineteenth centuries to one-quarter by the early twentieth century. Among the elite, in other words, ability was as important a ladder to success as heredity.

There are no corresponding studies of individual social mobility in late imperial peasant society. When rural social mobility has appeared as a subject of study, it has been at the level of the lineage (Freedman 1966), or the household (Huang 1985, 1990), rather than the individual, in part because rural nominative data were until recently simply not available.[21] Social scientists, especially anthropologists, have focused their energies instead on efforts to define both the formal kin structure and the corresponding system of behavioral norms in traditional rural society. Discussions of individual behavior have therefore been

[20] By close familial ties, Ho meant that neither their father nor grandfather had passed the *juren* examination and achieved entry into what he called the "gentry" class (1962, 107). Recently Hymes, working with Song data from Fuzhou prefecture, has shown that, among the several dozen *jinshi* there, many such "humble" candidates had other more distant relatives who were officials or members of the gentry class (1986, 29-61). He, therefore, concludes that there was "a dense network of connections—agnatic, affinal, scholarly, and personal—joining official and commoner" (1986, 52).

Hymes' conclusion, that Ho's results may be more apparent than real, is well-taken, but is also open to question. To prove his point, he also has to show that the proportion of successful candidates with distant relatives who were officials or gentry was higher than the proportion of the overall population with such relatives. Otherwise there is always a possibility that the range of kinship Hymes includes in his search for officials and gentry members is so wide that randomly selected individuals could be shown to be similarly "connected."

Readers interested in further details on methods for the study of intergenerational mobility are referred to Hout 1983. Interestingly, the approach Ho took in his much earlier work, restricting to comparisons between grandfathers, fathers, and sons, conforms much more closely to methods used by contemporary sociologists.

[21] The lack of such nominative data is a problem not just for the study of social mobility in historical China, but for the study of Chinese peasant history in general. Huang provides a concise summary of the strengths of available Chinese data for the study of elites, and their weakness for the study of peasants: "The study of peasants and villages in Chinese history has been severely limited by the lack of adequate source materials. For the elites, historians have been able to draw on large quantities of official sources, elite writings, and elite genealogies, and for more recent centuries, on the large numbers of elite biographies in local gazetteers for quantitative analysis . . . For the 'little people' of Chinese history, however, we have yet to gain access to the kinds of materials that have informed the best of the recent studies of social history in other countries" (1985, 33).

limited to the description and interpretation of normative practices. The peasant potential for individual agency remains unexplored and unknown.

As a result, it is sometimes assumed that, before this century, individual outcomes in rural China were determined by heredity, not ability.[22] In this conception, an individual's prospects were fixed at birth by the status of his lineage in local society, the relative position of his family within the lineage, and his own relationship to the head of his household. Trades and occupations, routes by which talented individuals might conceivably have overcome disadvantages imposed by their backgrounds, were kept within families.[23] Even positions at the local yamen, intended by the state to be awarded according to ability, were frequently monopolized by specific families and lineages (Chu 1962; Cole 1986). Whatever social mobility an individual experienced in his or her lifetime was usually the product not of personal characteristics, but of generational characteristics, specifically the location of his or her generation in the multi-generation cycle in which household fortunes were believed to rise and fall.[24]

Sources

This study tests these assumptions.[25] Our book is an analysis of social organization and social mobility among the peasants of Daoyi district during the eighteenth and nineteenth centuries. We outline in detail the structure of two types of social organization: a household

---

[22] Olga Lang in certain passages of her classic text on Chinese family and society seems to deny any role at all for individual ability in traditional China. She asks, for example, "Is nepotism really synonymous with inefficiency? After all China did manage to survive for thousands of years although her offices and business enterprises were staffed with relatives appointed regardless of qualifications. The question seems worth raising and often came up in formal and informal conversation with Chinese of all classes" (1946, 146).

[23] In a discussion of who the craftsmen and tradesmen in the village are, Fei states, "Since technical knowledge is usually transmitted through the kinship line, it is often not easily assimilated by the indigenous population" (1939, 141). Lang states "Sons usually inherited their father's trade and seldom left their homes" (1946, 17).

[24] In this cycle, generations born when the household was poor learned to be hard-working and thrifty, so that household circumstances improved during their life-times. Generations born when the household was wealthy learned to be lazy and spendthrift, so that household circumstances deteriorated during their lifetime. See Chapter 11 of Yang 1965 for a description of this process, especially page 132.

[25] These assumptions were the classic consensus of Chinese social scientists. While more recent scholarship has suggested that rural social mobility greatly increased during the late imperial period, these studies depend on qualitative rather than quantitative data (Elvin 1973, Skinner 1976, and Huang 1985).

hierarchy based on familial birth rights, and a banner hierarchy based on individual merit. Accordingly, we show to what extent the population behavior of peasants—marriages, children, mortality—were determined by ability and to what degree they were predetermined by heredity.

Our data are derived from "Household and Population Registers of the Eight Banner Han Chinese Army" (*Hanjun baqi rending hukou ce*) that were compiled in Daoyi on a triennial basis between 1774 and 1873. These registers record at three-year intervals for each person in the entire population the following information in order of appearance: relationship to their household head; name(s); adult banner status; age; animal birth year;[26] lunar birth month, birth day, and birth hour; marriage, death, or emigration, if any during the intercensal period; physical disabilities, if any and if the person is an adult male; name of their kin-group head; banner affiliation; and village of residence. We summarize counts of the recorded population and demographic events in the twenty-five available registers in table 2.1, and describe these sources and their comparative advantages and disadvantages in Appendix A.

The Daoyi registers provide far more comprehensive and accurate demographical and sociological data than the *baojia* household registers common elsewhere in China (Harrell 1987; Skinner 1987; Telford 1990). This is true for the entire northeast which was the Qing homeland and was under special state jurisdiction, distinct from the provincial administration elsewhere. Regimentation of the population actually began as early as 1625, when the Manchus made Shenyang their capital and incorporated the surrounding communities into what became the banner system.[27] By the late eighteenth century, not only was the population registered in remarkable precision and detail, but migration was strictly controlled, not only between northeast China and China proper, but between communities within northeast China as well.[28] Government control over the population was tighter than in almost any other part of China.

---

[26] The Chinese distinguish twelve-year cycles in which each year is identified with a specific animal: rat, ox, tiger, rabbit, dragon, snake, horse, sheep, monkey, chicken, dog, and pig.

[27] For a description of this process, see Zhao Lian (1770-1829), *Xiaoting Zalu* (Beijing: Zhonghua, 1980, 30). Also see Zhou Yuanlian (1981, 1982).

[28] Not only was immigration into the area controlled, but because the state depended on the area's residents for labor, so was emigration from it. As a result, individuals who departed from the area without permission were identified in the registers as "escapees" (*taoding*).

As a result, we are able to recreate the household structure and domestic processes in Daoyi from the banner registers in greater detail than elsewhere. The household (*zhenghu* or *linghu*), defined by common residence (*tongju*) and common consumption (*tongchi*), was the basic unit of banner social structure (Fu Kedong 1983). Banner registers accordingly organized individual records by household beginning with the head, followed by other household members according to their relationship to the head. The ordering principle depended in descending order on degree of kinship, generation, and gender. Children follow immediately after parents. Thus sons, daughters, grandsons, and granddaughters come before brothers, sisters, nephews and nieces, and they in turn come before uncles and cousins. These same principles of hereditary priority underlay the processes of household formation, creating three distinct interest groups within the multiple-family household.

We are also able to recreate the hierarchy of banner ranks and responsibilities in these rural communities. As we will eventually show, the banner system provided significant opportunities for individuals to advance outside the household. Daoyi was state land, and its people were to some extent state servants. Adult males (*ding*) were, therefore, not only liable for military conscription, but also for other labor services as well. The banner registers accordingly record either state service or assessment of fitness for service. Categories of state service include military ranks (soldier, sergeant, captain), artisanal crafts (blacksmith, tailor, tanner), and local offices (runner, scribe, student). Although such servicemen were generally selected for their ability, each profession followed its own distinctive behavioral patterns. Assessments of fitness for service differentiated between "healthy" adult males (*zhuangding*[b]) and infirm (*feiding*) or retired (*tuiding*) adult males.

Finally, we reconstruct the patterns of population behavior—birth, marriage, and death—at the individual level according to changing demographic, household, and banner circumstances. We take, in other words, a "life course" approach to population history and use, in addition to the standard arithmetic of demographic rates, the less transparent mathematics of event history analysis. We accordingly trace all 12,000 individuals from register to register, and transform our latitudinal observations into longitudinal files, with each individual's entire recorded life history at three-year intervals: their demographic events, household and banner positions, and demographic, household, and banner circumstances. We describe these data manipulations in

Table 2.1. *A summary profile of the population registers*

Register	Population			Entrances			Exits			Disappearances		
	Total	Male	Female	Birth	Marriage	Migration	Death	Marriage	Migration	Total	Male	Female
1774	2,192	1,234	958	–	–	–	135	31	–	–	–	–
1780	2,548	1,467	1,081	366	115	266	118	38	2	242	109	133
1786	2,748	1,578	1,170	479	170	226	188	47	32	417	217	200
1792	2,772	1,568	1,204	357	203	60	252	60	8	283	136	147
1795	2,902	1,629	1,273	260	112	24	174	50	29	14	5	9
1798	2,951	1,642	1,309	226	95	42	213	46	7	45	19	26
1801	3,041	1,697	1,317	198	73	14	162	38	14	13	7	6
1804	3,155	1,768	1,387	317	120	22	223	72	17	8	6	2
1810	3,144	1,776	1,368	354	176	37	251	56	16	255	95	160
1813	3,181	1,782	1,399	182	97	33	207	55	8	4	3	1
1816	3,131	1,758	1,373	131	88	4	209	50	3	7	4	3
1819	3,154	1,781	1,373	124	65	11	128	39	11	6	4	2
1822	3,151	1,781	1,370	236	150	24	285	106	2	21	11	10
1828	3,270	1,869	1,401	530	215	38	196	60	15	395	185	210
1831	3,270	1,865	1,405	197	85	6	233	46	0	11	6	5
1837	3,291	1,929	1,362	400	187	17	204	65	6	309	128	181
1840	3,214	1,912	1,302	154	84	2	236	64	1	17	7	10
1843	3,125	1,889	1,236	114	54	2	195	35	2	27	6	21
1846	3,094	1,869	1,225	118	93	1	173	39	3	29	12	17
1855	3,187	1,953	1,234	393	283	28	190	29	6	386	172	214
1858	3,162	1,962	1,200	126	95	7	174	36	14	32	12	20
1861	3,199	1,997	1,202	156	99	3	177	30	3	12	6	6
1864	3,132	1,997	1,155	173	98	32	334	15	1	22	13	9
1867	3,156	2,012	1,144	188	109	31	244	21	8	30	17	13
1873	3,271	2,067	1,204	316	225	35	249	10	4	204	108	96
Total	12,466	6,326	6,140	6,095	3,091	965	5,150	1,138	212	2,789	1,288	1,501

Note 1: The columns under "Population" record the number of people alive at the end of each register period. "Exits" include all the people who are recorded to have departed during the intercensal period through death, marriage, or emigration. "Entrances" list all the new people who appear in the registers for the first time through birth, marriage, or immigration. People who disappear without annotation between the previous and current register are listed under "Disappearances." The number alive in a register is equal to the number alive in the previous register plus the entrances and minus the exits recorded in the current register.

Note 2: Registers were compiled every three years. Most numbers, and all exits, therefore, represent the cumulated events over a three-year intercensal period. Due to missing registers some numbers, however, represent the cumulated events over six years and, in one case, over nine years. To differentiate these numbers we italicize them. Thus the entrances recorded for 1780 represent all people who appear in the 1780 register who were not present in the 1774 register while the disappearances represent largely the people who exited between 1775 and

Appendix A, and these analytical techniques and their comparative advantages and disadvantages in Appendix B.

We use these data to examine how Confucian norms about family organization shaped the distribution of power and privilege in Daoyi, and to demonstrate how individual ability modulated the effects of such norms. In the ideal Chinese household, one organized according to Confucian hierarchical principles, heredity was the primary determinant of individual power and privilege. Status and authority derived from kinship. Households were stratified by generation, with senior generations taking precedence over junior.[29] Members of the same generation were in turn differentiated by chronological age, a proxy for proximity to the patriline.[30] For example, in an extended family in which a head lived with his married brothers and cousins, the head and his family took precedence over his brothers and their families, and they in turn took precedence over cousins and their families.

In rural Liaoning, however, banner organizations provided an opportunity by which peasants could transcend the fate dictated by their domestic circumstances. While household positions in Daoyi were inherited, many banner positions were not. Military ranks were supposed to be recruited and promoted according to their ability and virility. Civil officials were elected or selected for their acumen, aptitude, and honesty. At least in theory, therefore, a talented peasant from an otherwise undistinguished family background should have been able to rise, in Horatio Alger fashion, to a position of wealth and prestige, regardless of where he stood in his household's hierarchy. The problem, of course, is how to measure the relative benefits of banner position versus household position.

---

[29] See Feng 1937 for a classic description of the ordering of status and authority in the Chinese kinship system. He states, "The architectonic structure of the Chinese kinship system is based upon two principles: lineal and collateral differentiation, and generation stratification. The former is a vertical and the latter a horizontal segmentation. Through the interlocking of these two principles every relative is rigidly fixed in the structure of the whole system" (1937, 87). See Baker 1979 and Yang 1959 for more recent analyses of familial hierarchy.

[30] Because marriage was arranged according to seniority—elder brothers married before younger brothers—the oldest members of a given generation tended to be the ones closest to the descent line, which passed through eldest sons. For example, the children of a household head tended to be older than the children of his younger brothers. Given that cousins are the children of the head's father's younger brothers, they tend to be younger than the head and his brothers, and their children tend to be younger than those of the head and his brothers.

Methods

Population rates provide an objective measure of social privilege as well as social behavior in rural China. The rewards of elite success—positions held, titles bought, examinations passed—are well documented for the late imperial period, but there are far fewer visible, let alone quantifiable records of the benefits of such banal triumphs as the succession from son to household head or from farmer to blacksmith. Success, for these peasants, was measured not by the receipt of an imperial title or office, but among other things by the demographic achievements common to peasants everywhere: marriage, many children, and a long life.

Nuptiality and fertility rates are an especially sensitive index of privilege in China because while the desire for marriage and children is on some level universal to all societies, it is particularly acute in Chinese society. The desire for biological perpetuation has been traced back to the prevalence of ancestor worship dating back to the third millennium BC (Ho 1975, 322-327). Numerous texts as early as the first millennium BC articulated the need for marriage and children. The famous saying of Mencius, that of all unfilial deeds none is more serious than the failure to produce male descendants, is perhaps the most direct statement of this belief.[31]

Ethnographic evidence reveals the obsessive concern of Chinese peasants with the production of progeny, in particular, sons. Typically, newlywed couples were congratulated not only by wishing them a long and harmonious marriage (*bainian haohe*), but also the early arrival of a son (*zaosheng guizi*).[32] Folk sayings also reveal a deep concern with marrying and having male children (Zhu 1974, 1989). One common folk saying was "the sooner you can raise children the sooner you have strength; the sooner you plant seedlings the sooner you have roots." In northeast China, where our study is based, a particularly common saying claimed that "Life at forty without sons is as bitter as a medicinal root" (Zhu 1989, 260).

Empirical evidence confirms that Chinese peasants went to great lengths to achieve their goals for family size and sex composition. Polygyny and concubinage, while relatively rare among the peasantry, were two well-known practices which seem to transfix the attention

---

[31] "There are three ways of being a bad son. The most serious is to have no heir" (Mencius, 6.1:127).

[32] Here we only include a few illustrative examples. Chinese is, of course, replete with sayings to express the importance of sons, and to list them all here would be impossible. Many common expressions include "*duozi duofu*" (the more sons, the greater the happiness).

of Westerners (Lee and Wang 1995, 1996). They allowed economically privileged males to translate their wealth directly into reproductive success. The availability of multiple forms of fictive kinship in China, meanwhile, allowed the peasantry to overcome even the limits imposed by human biology. In particular, peasants made use of many different types of male and female adoption as part of their efforts to guarantee the continuation of the male descent line (Waltner 1991; Wolf and Huang 1980).[33] Rich and poor alike practiced female infanticide to adjust the sex composition of their children (Lee, Campbell, and Tan 1992, Lee, Wang, and Campbell 1994).

The chances that an individual couple would achieve their goal for family size and composition, however, depended on their social position. Fertility varied sharply by social background. The better-off not only married earlier; in some cases they also had higher fertility within marriage. The net result was that they had more children than the poor (Harrell 1985, Telford 1992). Fertility varied as well by household position. In Daoyi, the members of the household most closely related to the head tended to marry earlier and have more children (Lee, Campbell, and Tan 1992). Even in the Qing imperial lineage, late imperial China's highest social stratum, there were fertility differentials according to status, so that higher-ranked lineage members had higher fertility than lower-ranked lineage members (Wang, Lee, and Campbell 1995). Demographic behavior consequently reflects social organization.[34]

Power and wealth in late imperial rural China translated into other less quantifiable demographic privileges as well. Death rates, like birth rates, followed class-specific patterns (Telford 1990). This partly reflected differential access to resources. In Daoyi, higher position by sex, seniority, and kinship translated into greater consumption of such daily necessities as food, clothing, and fuel. This was particularly evident at meal times. Men, throughout northeast China, ate first. Women, regardless of their status, ate last (Shirokogoroff 1926). Elderly villagers still recall the rigid rules that decided who slept where on the heated household platform bed (*kang*). Senior relatives slept closest to the flue; junior relatives slept further away.

---

[33] For example, in early twentieth-century Taiwan, variant marriages to adopted sons-in-law or "little" daughters-in-law were as common in some decades as major marriage (Pasternak 1983; Wolf and Huang 1980). Even in an elite population, the Qing imperial lineage, male adoption accounted for an average of 7 or 8 percent of all births, and in some decades rose almost as high as 20 percent (Lai 1994).

[34] This is also true, if to a lesser extent, in modern China. Parish and Whyte (1978, 155-199), for example, demonstrate that higher-class peasants marry earlier than lower-class peasants.

Thus demographic outcomes in a peasant Chinese population, like exam and career outcomes in an elite Chinese population, illuminate the processes of rural social mobility and rural social organization. Length of life, timing of marriage, and number of children, in other words, are among the best indicators of individual privilege in rural China. An analysis which links demographic variables to household context, economic conditions, and occupational circumstances can reveal for the first time how the familial and banner hierarchies interacted. Moreover, we not only can assess the effects of position in the family and banner hierarchies on mortality, nuptiality, and fertility, we also can determine the effects of position in one hierarchy on position in the other.

The results of such a demographic analysis have the potential to reshape our understanding of peasant society in late imperial China. Previously, historical research on rural society was impeded by a paucity of data. Unlike the rural and urban elite, peasants left few published records, and what little information exists was recorded through the flawed lens of elite prejudice. This is less true of demographic data which, we now know, survive in large quantities in China's historical archives.[35] Consisting largely of events whose definitions are simple and constant—birth, marriage, and death—these records provide a more objective window on peasant behavior in the past. Biases and errors may of course persist, but as we describe in Appendix A, they are often systematic, identifiable, and sometimes even correctable. Historical demography, in other words, gives us a new lens through which we can view the past, while demography and data processing provide the tools to shape and calibrate that lens virtually at will.

Outline

Our book is accordingly divided into five parts: two introductory parts on the ecological and demographic setting, two middle parts on household and banner organization, and a concluding part on the larger implications of our findings.

The first part introduces the people of Daoyi District and describes the sociological and ecological conditions under which they lived.

---

[35] The major advances in Chinese historical demography, as in Europe, have been inspired by the discovery and analysis of nominative records. Two types of sources have been especially important. The first are genealogies. The second are household registers. The major repository for both sets of sources are the microfilm holdings of the Genealogical Society of Utah.

We touch, in this chapter, on the constraints imposed on individuals by household and banner organization. We focus in Chapter 3 on the constraints imposed on the entire community by constricted and increasingly limited natural resources.

The second part, on the Liaoning demographic system, summarizes the patterns of fertility, nuptiality and mortality in Daoyi. Specifically, we identify two types of positive check—differential neglect and infanticide—in Chapter 4; and two types of preventive check—delayed marriage and prolonged chastity in Chapter 5. We conclude by demonstrating how registered fertility consequently varied by a wide variety of social and economic circumstances. We reconstruct, in other words, how Chinese peasants could deliberately adjust their demographic behavior according to both their individual household and banner conditions as well as to the changing economic circumstances of the community as a whole.

The third part deals with household formation, household hierarchy, and demographic behavior. First, we establish in Chapter 6 that the vast majority of people lived in a variety of large complex households, and identify their characteristic domestic cycles. Then we demonstrate in Chapter 7 that there was a wide discrepancy in nuptiality, fertility, and even mortality at the individual level depending on household position. Demographic achievement was a consequence of familial status and position. Marriage was awarded according to seniority. So were children.

The fourth part closes with an analysis of banner structure, banner hierarchy, and demographic behavior. We describe in chapter 8 the banner system of kin organization, and military ranks and occupations, and identify two ladders of success: through the banner civil and military occupational hierarchy, and through the banner kin organizational hierarchy. Then, in Chapter 9, we show how different banner positions, much like different household positions, had different demographic characteristics.

We conclude in Chapter 10 with a comparison of the patterns of social mobility in the household and banner hierarchies and their associated demographic behaviors. We show, for example, how household members of low household seniority and high banner position could obtain demographic privileges that their more senior but less accomplished relatives might otherwise have denied them. In so doing, we seek to show to what extent individuals could influence their chances of marriage, the number and sex of their children, the length of their life, and their social position.

Fate and fortune

Our book confirms the importance of the Confucian principles of household organization and individual mobility. Mortality increases and fertility decreases with distance from the line of inheritance. Even the sexual composition and spacing of children depend on household position. The configuration of relationships in the residential household was also important. The more complex the household, the greater the differentiation between the top and bottom. Position at birth, in other words, often determined the number and sequence of life course events.

Given such a context it is hardly surprising that both Confucius and Mencius recognized fate (*ming*) as a central concept in Chinese culture.[36] While the individual is born in the West with a set of "human rights," consisting largely of opportunities to pursue personal fulfillment freely, in China an individual is born with a set of "Confucian rights," made up largely of entitlements and obligations.[37] The most important of these obligations were to parents, the residential household, and the larger kin group. It is these entitlements and obligations which largely determined individual demographic performance. Chinese culture accordingly does not emphasize personal fulfillment through self-maximization, but rather personal contentment through family-maximization.

And yet even in rural China individuals could better their fortune through personal ability and achievement. In rural Liaoning this was principally through advancement in the banner system. Individuals who could not achieve household headship through heredity or division could rise to positions of banner responsibility. Climbing either ladder of success, up the banner hierarchies or up the household hierarchy, led to greater chances of marriage, more children, and a longer life span. Our study quantifies the probability that any individual could climb these ladders, and the rewards associated with each rung. We show that while Daoyi peasants may have been trapped by a fate imposed by household circumstances, they could still seek their individual fortune through the banners. We quantify, in other words, the degree of freedom or self-determination in Liaoning peasant society.

For Chinese historians, the most interesting feature of this study may be our reconstruction of rural peasant society during the late

---

[36] Their position is stated most aptly by Mencius: "A gentleman follows the norms and awaits his Fate" (14:33, 201).

[37] While no one has explored the contrast between Western and Confucian rights in much detail, see Wang Gung-wu 1979 for a preliminary attempt. See too Claude 1976 and Shapiro 1986.

imperial period and of rural banner society "outside the passes." Recent historical advances by American and Chinese scholars have greatly advanced our understanding of banner society "within the passes" (An 1983: Crossley 1990; Ding 1992; Elliott 1993) and even within the forbidden city (Han 1988; Lee and Guo 1994). But there have been virtually no analyses of banner society in northeast China, the so-called Manchu heartland.[38] As a result, we have had to situate this study based on our understanding of late imperial China from "ideal models" of "traditional" Chinese society. There are no comparable studies of pre-twentieth-century Chinese peasant society in northeast China or for that matter any other region of China. And yet, while Daoyi may be the first such community history, it should not be the last. Similar data are plentiful and easily accessible to scholars worldwide.[39]

For demographic historians, the principal significance of this study may be our demonstration of how demography can illuminate our understanding of social structure. Through the analysis of differentials in demographic rates, we now know who was more enfranchised in the rural household and who was more enfranchised in rural society. Through examinations of the distribution of household types, family relationships, and banner occupations, we know what proportions of the population were more privileged, or less privileged, at any given time. Finally, by tracing individuals over time, we uncover the patterns of movement from one of these categories to the other, illuminating for the first time the processes of social mobility in a rural Chinese society before the twentieth century.

For social scientists, however, our main contribution is our proof of how social norms, rooted in ideology and reinforced by state institutions, determined social mobility and in turn demographic performance.[40] Though we have long believed that family relations

---

[38] The only notable exception is the work by Guan Jialu and Tong Yonggong on rural banner estates which is largely confined to compilation and translation of primary Manchu language documents (Guan, Tong and Wang 1987). See, however, Isett 1996 for a preliminary effort to make sense of these materials.

[39] In addition to the 3,000 household registers from the Liaoning Provincial Archives already available on microfilm from the Genealogical Society of Utah, another 2,000 registers from the Heilongjiang Provincial Archives are currently being filmed for the Genealogical Society. Together these registers provide information on demographic and family history for well over one million individuals, largely from the nineteenth century.

[40] William Goode's own evaluation of his *World Revolution and Family Patterns*, for example, was that it was "missing" any analysis of the link between family and social mobility in the past. "As soon as we move from the last two decades of research on mobility . . . into the past, we are once more without any reliable data.

are fundamental in Chinese society, until now we have been unable to appreciate the scope or the intensity of the family's influence on basic life and death decisions. Household structure, domestic formation, and position in the hierarchy jointly determined who could marry and who could not; who could have children and what the sex of these children should be. The analysis of demographic behavior provides us with concrete measures of, not only the influence of the canonical hierarchy on individual lives, but also the degree to which individuals operating within such constraints could compensate for their effects through determination and ability. While everyone adhered to the same basic set of Confucian family values, some individuals were able to rise above the station in life dictated by the familial circumstances of their birth, embodying the parallel Confucian emphasis on individual talent and ability. In so doing, they illustrate the vitality in late imperial China of "Confucian rights," as opposed to human rights, among peasants as well as among elites, and among Manchus as well as among Han.

Consequently, this theoretically important time link of family variables with the stratification system must remain unanalyzed for yet a while." (1970, xviii)

3

Spatial and temporal setting[1]

Fate and fortune in rural Liaoning were subject not only to the broad organizational constraints of the Chinese household and the Manchu banner, but also to the specific ecological setting of the local climate and land. In Chapter 3, we locate the spatial and temporal setting of our population and show how three such ecological circumstances—the seasonal harvest cycle, the annual fluctuation in climate and prices, and a secular trend of rising demographic pressure—defined the boundary conditions of demographic and social behavior in Daoyi and surrounding communities. The demographic response to seasonal cycles and short-term fluctuations consisted of variations in vital rates. The response to the secular trend of rising Malthusian pressure, however, was not just a sum of individual demographic responses, but rather a fundamental transformation of the household and banner systems that radically changed the domestic context of daily life. In Daoyi, in other words, organizational constraints such as the household and banner systems were in turn shaped by ecological conditions.

The harvest cycle

Throughout the world, rural life is dominated by the passing of the seasons. Daoyi is no exception. Its extreme northern location guarantees a short, intense, agricultural season with only one harvest.[2]

[1] We originally composed section II of this chapter for the 1988 JCCS Conference on Chinese History in Economic Perspective (Lee, Campbell, and Tan 1992). Sections I and III are completely new. We completed the analysis and began the writing during the summer of 1990, but did not complete the text until the spring of 1995.

[2] According to *Daoyi XZ* 1984, 4–5, which has a brief summary of climatic conditions in Daoyi, there are only 150 frost-free days a year in the district. For a more general discussion of climatic conditions in Liaoning see *Dongbei qu ziran dili ziliao* 1957, 11–26. We would like to thank Dr. Tai-Loi Ma for bringing this book to our attention.

Spring does not arrive until May, which brings little rain, but more sunlight than any other month of the year. The transition in the weather is rapid. Farmers accordingly have to rush to prepare their fields and plant their crops before the rainy season in July and August. This concentration of activity during the spring planting renews with the autumn harvest in September. Like the spring, the fall is quite brief—often no more than one month long. The winter lull, by contrast, lasts for more than six months, from October through April. During this half-year, the mean temperature is less than $-7°C$. The first frosts come to Daoyi by the beginning of October. By early November, the ponds and rivers are frozen solid; and by late November the ground is frozen solid as well.[3] The topsoil does not thaw until early April. The last ice on the ponds and streams does not melt until late April, and the last snowfall is usually in April as well.

Monthly changes in grain prices reflect the effects of the harvest cycle on food availability. Our data on grain prices come from an empire-wide system to monitor food conditions that began in Liaoning in the late eighteenth century. Thereafter, until well into the twentieth century, county magistrates reported, each week, the price of five major food grains (rice, wheat, husked and unhusked millet, soybean, and sorghum) to the provincial government. The governor, in turn, prepared a brief monthly summary for the central government of the lowest and highest county prices by prefecture. These monthly prefectural summaries provide the bulk of our price data.[4] They only report the extreme prices in each month and do not tell us the precise location of the reported prices. Moreover, some data are missing and have to be derived through a process of interpolation.[5] We consequently cannot calculate an accurate average

[3]   According to *Zhongguo ziran dili tuji* 1984, 103, the top 10 centimeters are frozen from November 29 to March 25; while the next 20 centimeters are frozen from December 12 to April 5.

[4]   To date, we have collected 1,500 of these lunar monthly, summary reports for the Shenyang area (Fengtian prefecture), almost 1,000 of which are from the century between 1774 and 1873. James Lee collected 1,200 of these memorials from the First Historical Archives in Beijing in 1985, 1986, and 1987. Yeh-chien Wang kindly provided the remaining 300 memorials from his own research in the Palace Museum in Taibei. We would like to thank Professor Wang for his gracious assistance to us here and elsewhere. Anna Chi transcribed the material into machine-readable form.

[5]   We do not have prices for one-sixth of the lunar months, including five entire years: 1791, 1815, 1822, 1823, and 1825. The other missing months are distributed largely at random and can be interpolated with some confidence since prices generally fluctuate in accordance with the harvest cycle. The process of interpolation has three steps. First, we convert our data from lunar to solar months to assign each month a seasonal weight. Second, we spline the data according to these weights to estimate missing values. Third, we reconvert the data to lunar years since most of

prefectural price. We can, however, assume that the data do represent general price trends over time.

As we might expect, the agricultural seasons dominated the price calendar. Table 3.1 depicts the average pattern of monthly variation in low and high grain prices.[6] In a typical year, both low and high prices rose from the beginning of spring until the end of the summer, reflecting the depletion of the stocks remaining from the previous harvest. In August and September, when the harvest came in and stocks were replenished, prices stabilized. In the months afterward, they declined rapidly, reaching a trough in December and January, but then rebounded. Prices dropped once more at the beginning of the spring, perhaps because the purchases of spring seed had by then been completed.[7]

Human reproduction followed the same seasonal cycle. Table 3.2 summarizes the monthly distribution of registered births as an index of the monthly average. As is the case in most populations, seasonal variation in fertility was high.[8] In Daoyi, there were more than four times as many births reported in the peak months (the second and third lunar months) as in the trough months (the ninth through eleventh lunar months). Indeed, almost two-thirds of all registered births were concentrated between the second and the sixth lunar month. Human fecundity, in other words, peaked during the warmer months and ebbed during the colder months. The birth dearth in the eleventh lunar month reflects the effects of a reduction in conceptions at the end of the winter and beginning of the spring, while the birth spurt

---

our demographic values are by lunar year. This process produces a series of prices suitable for analysis, although it loses some data and slightly modifies many of the remaining values during the process of conversion. Peter Perdue and Lawrence Anthony assisted in the conversion process. We would like to acknowledge their efforts here.

6   As we do not know the precise locations to which each set of prices relates, we include both sets of prices in this chapter's analysis.

7   There were some years in which prices followed an inverse pattern. In these years, rather than decreasing in the late fall, prices increased. Almost all of the high-price years apparent later in figures 3.1 and 3.2 followed such a pattern. These were apparently years of poor harvest, in which awareness of reduced yields caused prices to rise immediately after the crops had been brought in. In such cases, prices usually remained high until the following fall, at which time a new harvest came in.

8   See Lam and Miron 1991 and 1994 for two recent, comprehensive reviews of findings on seasonal variation in fertility, and attempts to test some of the leading explanations for such variation. They conclude that, while seasonal variation in fertility is apparent in almost all human populations, historical and modern, patterns of variation are remarkably diverse, and no one explanation seems to account for all of them.

Table 3.1. Monthly variation in grain prices in Liaoning (Fengtian Prefecture), 1774-1873

Month	Rice	Low prices in taels per shi				Rice	High prices in taels per shi			
		Wheat	Millet	Sorghum	Soy		Wheat	Millet	Sorghum	Soy
January	1.74	1.40	1.02	0.54	0.59	3.68	2.95	2.34	1.49	1.73
February	1.81	1.44	1.06	0.55	0.60	3.69	2.99	2.38	1.54	1.79
March	1.80	1.46	1.04	0.56	0.60	3.70	3.01	2.37	1.53	1.77
April	1.82	1.45	1.04	0.56	0.61	3.69	3.01	2.32	1.51	1.77
May	1.79	1.45	1.02	0.55	0.60	3.67	3.02	2.32	1.53	1.77
June	1.86	1.47	1.04	0.57	0.63	3.81	3.06	2.41	1.60	1.80
July	1.85	1.46	1.03	0.56	0.63	3.82	2.99	2.41	1.61	1.82
August	1.91	1.46	1.07	0.57	0.63	3.92	3.03	2.51	1.65	1.83
September	1.88	1.46	1.05	0.55	0.62	3.86	2.98	2.45	1.59	1.78
October	1.91	1.47	1.08	0.56	0.62	3.83	2.99	2.48	1.56	1.79
November	1.82	1.43	1.05	0.55	0.61	3.80	2.99	2.40	1.49	1.74
December	1.77	1.42	1.02	0.54	0.59	3.80	3.01	2.41	1.52	1.74
		Percent change from lowest price month					Percent change from lowest price month			
January	0.00	0.00	0.00	0.00	0.00	0.27	0.00	0.86	0.00	0.00
February	4.02	2.86	3.92	1.85	1.69	0.55	1.36	2.59	3.36	3.47
March	3.45	4.29	1.96	3.70	1.69	0.82	2.03	2.16	2.68	2.31
April	4.60	3.57	1.96	3.70	3.39	0.55	2.03	0.00	1.34	2.31
May	2.87	3.57	0.00	1.85	1.69	0.00	2.37	0.00	2.68	2.31
June	6.90	5.00	1.96	5.56	6.78	3.81	3.73	3.88	7.38	4.05
July	6.32	4.29	0.98	3.70	6.78	4.09	1.36	3.88	8.05	5.20
August	9.77	4.29	4.90	5.56	6.78	6.81	2.71	8.19	10.74	5.78
September	8.05	4.29	2.94	1.85	5.08	5.18	1.02	5.60	6.71	2.89
October	9.77	5.00	5.88	3.70	5.08	4.36	1.36	6.90	4.70	3.47
November	4.60	2.14	2.94	1.85	3.39	3.54	1.36	3.45	0.00	0.58
December	1.72	1.43	0.00	0.00	0.00	3.54	2.03	3.88	2.01	0.58

Table 3.2. *Births by reported lunar month of occurrence, 1792-1804*

Lunar month	Corresponding solar months	Implied Solar months of conception	Number of births	Number of births/ average
1	Jan-Feb	April-May	81	0.74
2	Feb-March	May-June	205	1.88
3	March-April	June-July	169	1.55
4	April-May	July-Aug	141	1.29
5	May-June	Aug-Sept	147	1.35
6	June-July	Sept-Oct	143	1.31
7	July-Aug	Oct-Nov	100	0.92
8	Aug-Sept	Nov-Dec	75	0.69
9	Sept-Oct	Dec-Jan	53	0.49
10	Oct-Nov	Jan-Feb	76	0.70
11	Nov-Dec	Feb-March	47	0.43
12	Dec-Jan	March-April	73	0.67
Total			1,310	

during the second lunar month reflects a climax in conceptions during the early summer.

This seasonal cycle, with a peak in births in springtime and a trough in wintertime, is similar to those of such other northern populations as Sweden and England. Between 1737 and 1836, for example, the historical English populations reconstructed by Wrigley and Schofield (1981, 503–524) also exhibit a fertility peak in early springtime, and a trough in the late fall and early winter (Lam and Miron 1994, 64). Detailed analyses of this pattern using European data, however, have failed to identify a simple causal explanation. Lam and Miron (1991) note that the agricultural cycle may have made an important contribution to seasonal variations in fertility in pre-industrial populations, partly by affecting patterns of coital frequency, but the agricultural cycle does not seem to have accounted for all of such variations. Seasonal variation in photoperiod, temperature, and nutritional intake have all been suggested to have direct, biological effects on fecundity, and some of these factors undoubtedly contributed to creating Daoyi's seasonal pattern.

Short-term fluctuations

Rural life was subject not only to the regular and predictable influences of the seasonal cycles, but also to the irregular and unpredictable influences of short-term fluctuations in economic conditions. In Europe, changes in agricultural prices have been shown to have had

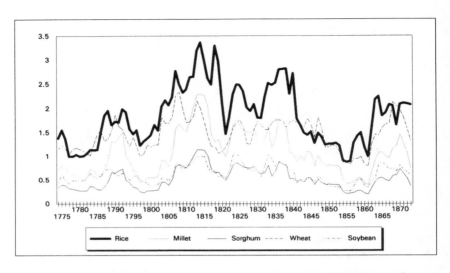

Figure 3.1. *Annual average monthly low grain prices in Fengtian prefecture* (*taels per shi*)

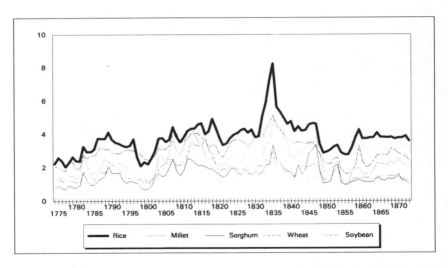

Figure 3.2. *Average annual monthly high grain prices in Fengtian prefecture* (*taels per shi*)

powerful effects on the demographic behavior of peasants (Galloway 1988). Peasant incomes were especially vulnerable to changes in price, especially ones caused by a failed harvest, because the positive effects of being able to sell at a higher price were usually more than offset by the negative effects of having less to sell.[9] Even individuals not directly dependent on the land, such as craftsmen and small merchants, were affected by price fluctuations because their usual customers had less disposable income. Typically, only the large producers and grain traders benefited from high prices.

Short-term variations in agricultural prices were just as important a determinant of peasant well-being in rural Liaoning. According to the recollection of elderly residents of Daoyi, before the middle of the twentieth century, there was very little commercial activity in the village that was not directly related to agriculture, except for a few households running small sideline businesses selling basic goods, and some inns along the main road. Although we know from the household registers that some village residents held banner occupations and civil offices, their number, while large enough to have an impact on local society, was not large enough to impact on the local economy.[10]

Grain price data demonstrate the scale of short-term fluctuations in the agrarian economy in rural Liaoning with which peasants in Daoyi had to contend. Figures 3.1 and 3.2 illustrate the annual average monthly low and high prices of all five grains in taels of silver per *shi* of grain.[11] In almost every case, prices moved quite volatilely, usually in tandem, and occasionally by as much as a factor of two or three within just one or two years. Rice was usually the most expensive grain, followed by wheat, millet, sorghum, and soybean, a function of food availability and market demand. Prices of expensive grains such as rice varied less than prices of common grains, a reflection perhaps of the fact that markets for such premium grains were integrated over a wider area.

A recent study by Wang Shaowu of the climate and harvest history of Manchuria indicates that fluctuations in summer temperature were responsible for changes in harvest yields that caused many of the price fluctuations in figures 3.1 and 3.2. In northeast China, summer

---

[9] Agricultural prices were such an important determinant of peasant well-being that many studies of historical Europe use them as proxies for peasant income. See, for example, Galloway 1988 and Wrigley and Schofield 1981.

[10] See Chapters 8, 9, and 10.

[11] A tael is a unit of weight equivalent to 38 grams. A *shi* is a unit of volume equivalent to 103.5 liters. Weight varied by type of grain. According to Chuan and Kraus 1975, one *shi* of milled rice roughly equaled 84 kilograms (79–98).

temperature is an important determinant of crop yield.[12] Even in this century, low summer temperatures in 1954, 1957, 1969, 1972, and 1976 reduced harvest yields by as much as one-third. According to Wang, there were at least twenty-six similarly cold summers between 1774 and 1873, concentrated in the 1780s, 1810s, and 1830s.[13] Given the low level of agricultural technology in the late eighteenth and early nineteenth century, the impact of these low temperatures on harvest must have been even more severe than in the twentieth century.[14] In fact, an examination of figures 3.1 and 3.2 reveals that these three decades were characterized by rapid price increases.[15]

Prices fluctuated, however, not only in response to changes in climate, but also to market conditions and state interventions. Although information on the commercial economy in Liaoning is extremely sparse, we do know that by the early nineteenth century, Liaoning was regularly exporting large quantities of grain, especially millet, sorghum, and soybean, to north China and the lower Yangzi (Guo Songyi 1982; Wu Chengming 1985). Moreover, the Qing state occasionally intervened in this trade, either to make large purchases of its own for the state granaries in Zhili and Beijing,[16] or to ban the export trade to protect local food supplies.[17] Prices accordingly fell

---

[12] Wang Shaowu 1988 reconstructs the temperature history of Manchuria by using a time series of floral germination records from the Japanese island of Hokkaido which he explains was dominated by the same pressure system and therefore subject to the same large-scale fluctuations in temperature. See Feng Peizhi, Li Cuijin *et al.* 1985, 110–116 for a detailed analysis of "cold summers" in northeastern China.

[13] According to Wang Shaowu 1988, these unusually cold summers were 1774, 1776, 1778, 1782, 1783, 1785, 1786, 1789, 1793, 1813, 1815, 1825, 1830, 1831, 1832, 1833, 1835, 1836, 1837, 1838, 1841, 1846, 1856, 1857, 1866 and 1869.

[14] For example, again according to Wang Shaowu 1988, a mean summer temperature just 1.5–2°C below normal in 1902 and 1913 resulted in 50 and 80 percent reductions in harvest yield respectively, compared in each case with the average yield of the five previous years.

[15] We are fortunate to have more than 160 climate and harvest reports for the Shenyang area (Fengtian Prefecture) in our possession and would like to thank Zhang Peiyuan, Zhang Jinrong, and Gong Gaofa for making these data available to us. According to these reports, there were unusually poor harvests evaluated as *shaolian* or *lianbo* in 1788, 1789, 1802, 1807, and 1815 as well as unusually good harvests graded as *jiaohao*, *fengnian, fengshou*, and even *shenhao* in 1794, 1795, 1796, 1797, 1798 1799, 1801, 1804, 1816, 1818, 1820, 1822, 1825, 1826, 1846, 1864, and 1873.

[16] According to *Fengtian Tongzhi* (hereafter *Fengtian TZ*) 1934/1982, 40.800, 803, 809, 41.827, 830, the Qing government purchased (*caimai*) large quantities of Liaoning grain in 1853, 1854, 1855, 1862, and 1863. According to the *Donghua lu*, the emperor personally ordered on March 22, 1862, the transfer of 200,000 *shi* of grain from Liaoning to Beijing.

[17] *Fengtian TZ* 1934/1982, 38.753, reprints a government edict dated March 2, 1822 banning the private ocean export trade in grain. The state, however, apparently did not prohibit government grain purchases until 1824 when another edict, dated Jan-

precipitously in 1822 when the provincial government intervened in the local grain trade and quickly rebounded in 1825 when the ban was rescinded. Fluctuations in grain prices were therefore sometimes a function of harvest supply, and sometimes a function of export demand, a reflection of the complexities of the late imperial grain trade.

Short-term fluctuations in climate and agricultural prices were important determinants of demographic behavior in Europe before this century (Galloway 1988, 1994). Increases in European agricultural prices were associated with lowered fertility, delayed first marriage, and increased mortality.[18] A variety of social and economic mechanisms have been proposed by which price fluctuations caused such demographic responses. By reducing peasant incomes, increased grain prices forced young adults to delay or even cancel plans for marriage.[19] By spurring individuals to migrate in search of work or famine relief, price increases could separate married couples, reducing their coital frequency and thus their fertility. Even couples that remained together may have had reduced fertility, either because they used traditional methods of contraception to delay their next birth, or because maternal malnutrition caused an increase in intrauterine mortality.[20] By increasing the prevalence

uary 31, specifically halted government purchases of millet (*Fengtian TZ* 1934/1982, 38.757).

[18] Galloway (1988, 288-291), found that fluctuations in grain prices in Europe before this century accounted for 40 to 60 percent of the variance in fertility, and 20 to 40 percent of the variance in non-infant mortality. Prices and non-infant mortality together accounted for between 20 (France, Prussia, and Denmark) and 70 (Austria, Belgium) percent of the variance in nuptiality.

[19] Simultaneous increases in mortality may also have disturbed the marriage market, causing the death of prospective spouses and requiring the initiation of new searches for partners. See also Feeney and Hamano 1990, as well as the papers in Bengtsson et al. 1984.

[20] Pebley *et al.* 1985 found that in Matlab, Bangladesh, intrauterine mortality was inversely related to the mother's nutritional status, measured either by her preconception weight, or by her weight gain within the previous month. Reduced fecundity, supposedly caused by malnutrition, has also been suggested to have played roles in reducing fertility during times of reduced nutritional intake (Frisch 1975, 1978), but this view has not held up under closer scrutiny. Empirical investigations have revealed that, for the most part, malnutrition has an effect on fecundity and fertility only when it is severe enough to amount to starvation. Bongaarts and Potter (1983, 14) state: "The current consensus is that moderate chronic malnutrition such as prevails in many poor developing countries has only a minor influence on fertility. On the other hand, the acute starvation found in famines caused a substantial reduction in fertility. The weak effect of chronic malnutrition apparently operates primarily through two of the proximate variables: the age at marriage as affected by the timing of menarche, and the duration of postpartum

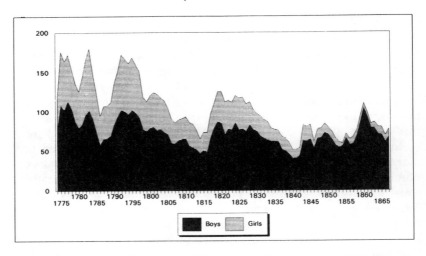

Figure 3.3. *Annual births per thousand married women aged 16–35 sui*
(three-year moving average)

of malnutrition, which reduced resistance to infection, and by trig-
gering population movements, which increased exposure to infection,
price rises could increase mortality.[21]

In China before this century, the positive, mortality-based checks
are usually assumed to have been the most important demographic
response to short-term increases in pressure. Norms favoring early
and universal marriage, supported by an extended family system that
permitted young adults to marry without regard for current economic
circumstances, are supposed to have precluded the possibility that
marriage could be delayed in response to a short-term deterioration in economic conditions.[22] A deeply rooted preoccupation with

infecundability." See also Bongaarts 1980, Gray 1983, and Menken *et al.*, 1981.

[21] Climatic fluctuations could also have direct effects on vital rates, especially mortality
(Galloway 1994, 9–12). In general, temperature seems to work by affecting death
rates from specific causes. For example, stroke incidence increases during cold
weather.

[22] This view began with Malthus himself: "The population which has arisen naturally
from the fertility of the soil, and the encouragements to agriculture, may be considered as genuine and desirable, but all that has been added by the encouragements
to marriage has not only been an addition of so much pure misery in itself, but has
completely interrupted the happiness which the rest might have enjoyed" (Malthus
1872, 105). The notion that extended family systems are incompatible with the operation of variations in age at marriage as a preventive check form a key component
of such influential analyses as Davis 1955 and Hajnal 1982.

Table 3.3. *Crude vital rates in the male population (per 1000)*

| Interval | Increase | Entrances | | Death† | Exits | Legal |
		Birth	Immigration		Illegal	
1774-1780	28.8	28.9	18.8	19.7	20.1	0.2
1780-1786	12.2	31.5	14.8	30.4	3.4	0.0
1786-1792	-1.1	23.1	2.9	27.3	0.8	0.0
1792-1795	12.7	34.2	2.5	18.1	3.5	0.0
1795-1798	2.6	26.7	1.8	27.7	1.2	0.8
1798-1801	11.0	25.2	1.6	13.0	0.8	0.0
1801-1804	13.7	38.3	2.5	23.7	1.9	0.0
1804-1810	0.8	19.8	2.2	20.0	1.4	0.0
1810-1813	1.1	22.1	2.6	22.3	1.3	0.9
1813-1816	4.1	17.5	0.6	21.5	0.6	0.0
1816-1819	4.1	16.2	0.9	11.5	1.9	0.0
1819-1822	-0.2	30.9	2.6	33.3	0.4	0.0
1822-1828	8.0	32.1	2.1	24.8	1.3	0.0
1828-1831	-0.7	23.2	0.9	25.0	0.0	0.2
1831-1837	5.6	24.1	0.9	18.8	0.4	0.0
1837-1840	-3.0	19.8	0.2	22.6	0.2	0.0
1840-1843	4.0	16.5	0.2	19.8	0.2	0.0
1843-1846	-3.5	16.1	0.2	19.5	0.5	0.0
1846-1855	4.9	19.4	0.4	15.4	0.3	0.0
1855-1858	1.5	19.6	0.5	16.5	0.3	0.0
1858-1861	5.9	23.9	0.2	17.5	0.2	0.0
1861-1864	-3.4	27.2	1.7	33.2	0.2	0.0
1864-1867	5.8	29.4	1.5	24.1	0.5	0.0
1867-1873	4.7	22.3	1.4	19.2	0.2	0.0
1774-1804	12.0	29.1	8.1	23.8	1.6	0.1
1804-1873	2.3	22.5	1.1	20.8	0.6	0.0

†Includes disappearances.

having a large number of children, especially male ones, supposedly guaranteed that fertility within marriage would always be high and uncontrolled, ruling out the possibility that births could be deferred until times were better.[23] The death rate was the only demographic variable that could vary, thus if short-term fluctuations in conditions had any effect on demographic behavior, they would have done so by affecting mortality. All other rates are assumed to be invariant.

In Daoyi, there was more short-term variation in vital rates than these traditional models of China's population dynamics would predict. All three vital rates—fertility, nuptiality, and mortality—varied by factors of two to three, sometimes within the space of only a few

[23] See, for example, pages 5 and 6 of the introduction to Hanley and Wolf 1985.

years.[24] In figure 3.3, male birth rates ranged from 50 to 100.[25] According to tables 3.3 and 3.4, crude death rates, the number of deaths per 1,000 people alive, ranged from 11.5 to 33.2 for men, and from 16.5 to 38.8 for women.[26] In table 3.5 male marriage rates, calculated as the number of marriages to men aged 16 to 35 *sui* per 1,000 unmarried men that age, ranged from 37.4 to 117.2. The remarriage rates of widowers fluctuated considerably as well, ranging from 9.6 to 62.3.

These fluctuations indicate that both preventive and positive checks were operating in Daoyi: correlations between vital rates and average annual grain prices, presented in table 3.6, reveal that demographic rates were associated with prices. The extended family system and the alleged desire for large families were not, as is often supposed, proof against the demographic effects of short-term variations in economic conditions. As was the case in historical Europe, grain prices showed a strong positive correlation with mortality, and extremely strong negative correlations with nuptiality and fertility. In other words, marriages and births declined when food prices were

[24] Our demographic data suffer from limitations that prevent the construction of time series of vital rates as precise as those for grain prices. We cannot calculate reliable birth or death rates for several years due to missing registers. Moreover, birth and death rates in the years for which data are available may be underestimated because some children died before they ever appeared in the registers. Due to the triennial nature of the registration system, we can only compute marriage and death rates averaged over three-year intercensal periods. Because we cannot compute annual marriage and death rates, our nuptiality and mortality statistics are deceptively stable. Given the incompleteness of the vital data we should therefore anticipate that any linkages between prices and population behavior will be weaker on paper than they were in reality. See Appendix A for more details.

[25] Rates were computed by dividing the number of births in each year by the number of married women aged 16 to 35 in that year. Births were assigned to specific years by subtracting age (in *sui*) at first appearance from the register year of first appearance, then adding one year.

[26] In tables 3.3 and 3.4, annual rates of increase were computed for each intercensal period by dividing the net change in the number of recorded males during the interval by the estimated number of males in the population at the midpoint of the period, and then dividing the result by the length of the period in years. The population at the midpoint of the time interval was estimated by averaging the population sizes at the beginning and end of the interval. Crude birth rates were computed by dividing the number of new children registered in each intercensal period by the length of the intercensal period and the estimated size of the population at the midpoint of the period—note that this procedure is based on year of entrance into the registration system, not calculated year of birth. Population size at the midpoint of the period was estimated by averaging the sizes of the populations at risk at the beginning and end of the period. Similar procedures were used to calculate death rates, marriage rates (tables 3.4 and 3.5), immigration rates, and internal migration rates (tables 3.4 and 3.5). In the case of male death rates, both deaths and disappearances were included in the numerator.

high and increased when prices were low. Conversely, deaths increased when prices were high and declined when prices were low, reflecting the presence of short-term positive checks as well. Visual inspection of prices in figures 3.1 and 3.2 and vital rates in figure 3.3, and tables 3.3, 3.4, and 3.5 confirms these findings: troughs in marriage and birth rates coincide with sustained peaks in grain prices, most prominently during the 1810s. Peaks in marriage and birth rates, meanwhile, usually coincide with troughs in grain prices, most prominently during the 1790s.

In Daoyi, as in Europe, evidence is insufficient to identify precisely the causal mechanisms by which the short-term checks operated, but because the population was closed to emigration, at least some of the mechanisms hypothesized for Europe can be ruled out. While reductions in fertility may have been partly due to reductions in coital frequency, such behavior was not the byproduct of spousal separation and spousal migration. Reductions in fertility had to have come about through deliberate reductions in coital frequency, the application of pre-modern methods of contraception, increases in intrauterine mortality, or increases in the proportion of unregistered births. Similarly, increases in mortality during periods of high prices cannot have been the result of disease outbreaks triggered by population movements. The rise in mortality had to have been due either to reductions in resistance induced by malnutrition, increased exposure to disease as a result of lower quality food, or, when price increases were due to climatic fluctuations, the direct effects of changes in the weather.

Long-term change and the structural transformation of society

In pre-industrial societies such as Daoyi, long-term Malthusian pressures generated by imbalances between population and resources were superimposed on the transitory effects of seasonal cycles and short-term fluctuations. Studies of European countries have already found evidence of preventive and positive checks which over the long term helped keep population in balance with resources.[27] In studies

---

[27] See Lee 1987 for a review of the evidence on homeostasis—density dependencies in population growth that lead to equilibria in population size—in human and animal populations. Lee concludes that the evidence for homeostasis in historical Europe is strong. For Europe as a whole, the elasticity of real wages with respect to detrended population size, a proxy for density, was -1.6 (a 10 percent increase in detrended population reduced wages by 16 percent). The elasticity of fertility with respect to population density was between 0 and -0.3, while the elasticity of the net reproduction rate was approximately -0.25. See also Chapter 11 of Wrigley and Schofield 1981.

Table 3.4. *Crude vital rates in the female population (per 1000)*

Interval	Increase	Birth	Entrances		Death	Marriage	Exits		Disappearance
			Marriage	Immigration			Illegal departure	Emigration	
1792-95	18.6	25.6	30.4	2.4	23.4	13.5	0.0	0.3	2.2
1795-98	9.3	22.2	24.5	1.6	20.7	10.3	0.8	1.0	6.7
1798-01	2.0	17.3	17.8	1.0	22.9	9.7	0.0	0.0	1.5
1801-04	17.3	28.6	29.3	2.2	24.7	17.0	0.7	0.3	0.5
1810-13	7.5	15.4	23.4	3.6	21.2	11.6	1.9	0.2	0.2
1813-16	-5.6	8.7	21.2	0.2	23.1	9.4	2.6	0.0	0.7
1816-19	0.5	9.0	15.5	1.0	26.5	9.0	0.5	0.0	0.5
1819-22	-0.7	16.0	36.2	2.4	27.5	21.9	3.4	4.0	2.4
1828-31	1.0	15.4	20.2	0.2	22.8	9.5	1.2	0.0	1.2
1837-40	-15.0	9.8	20.8	0.0	27.3	15.3	0.8	0.0	2.5
1840-43	-17.0	5.3	14.2	0.3	22.6	8.9	0.3	0.0	5.5
1843-46	-3.0	7.3	25.2	0.0	20.3	9.8	0.8	0.0	4.6
1855-58	-9.6	2.5	26.0	0.6	23.3	8.2	1.6	0.0	5.5
1858-61	1.1	3.9	27.5	0.3	21.1	8.1	0.3	0.0	1.4
1861-64	-13.6	2.8	27.7	1.4	38.8	2.5	1.7	0.0	2.0
1864-67	-3.2	3.5	31.0	1.5	29.0	3.5	2.3	0.0	3.8

Table 3.5. *Other demographic indices: internal migration and marriage*

Interval	Internal migration rate	First marriage rate (per 1000)†		Widower remarriage rate‡ (per 1000)	Age At first marriage (in *sui*)		Percentage 36-40 *sui* never married	
		M	F		M	F	M	F
1774-80	-	71.3	59.3	28.6	22.4	20.9	19.3	0.0
1780-86	-	85.0	86.6	32.8	23.2	21.7	14.0	0.0
1786-92	-	94.9	88.7	43.0	22.3	20.8	13.2	0.0
1792-95	18.4	128.8	212.3	23.9	22.3	20.8	13.2	0.0
1795-98	17.2	88.6	170.4	61.1	20.9	19.4	14.5	0.0
1798-01	8.5	67.5	136.6	29.8	21.8	20.3	11.4	0.0
1801-04	17.6	100.7	277.4	62.3	21.4	19.9	8.5	0.0
1804-10	13.0	79.7	56.7	34.0	20.5	19.0	11.7	0.0
1810-13	21.6	79.7	148.5	26.5	21.1	19.6	16.6	0.0
1813-16	9.2	64.1	10.1	34.3	22.3	20.8	20.1	0.0
1816-19	5.7	36.0	83.3	36.0	20.8	19.3	18.2	0.0
1819-22	4.6	115.6	250.0	33.3	22.3	20.8	17.3	0.0
1822-28	1.7	90.2	90.3	27.5	22.0	20.5	17.3	0.0
1828-31	1.9	86.8	137.6	18.8	20.8	19.3	15.5	0.0
1831-37	0.3	90.9	71.6	22.7	20.9	19.4	17.6	0.0
1837-40	7.2	74.8	232.1	22.2	19.2	17.7	18.1	0.0
1840-43	6.9	46.6	163.5	9.6	21.2	19.7	16.1	0.0
1843-46	3.3	70.4	145.5	22.7	21.7	20.2	15.8	0.0
1846-55	0.6	66.3	26.1	18.8	22.0	20.5	17.1	0.0
1855-58	0.3	65.2	207.8	16.3	21.5	20.0	22.3	0.0
1858-61	1.1	70.9	339.9	19.3	20.4	18.9	27.7	0.0
1861-64	0.2	59.3	116.7	24.3	20.6	19.1	25.8	0.0
1864-67	0.0	68.3	166.7	34.3	22.3	20.8	18.9	0.0
1867-73	2.1	24.6	88.9	15.4	19.8	18.3	20.5	0.0
1774-04	15.4	88.8	126.6	38.6	22.2	20.7	14.0	0.0
1804-73	4.3	75.1	121.1	24.0	21.2	19.7	18.2	0.0

†Annual marriages to never-married men (women) aged 16-35 *sui* per 1,000 never-married men (women) aged 16-35 *sui*.

‡Annual marriages to widowed men, all ages, per 1,000 widowed men, all ages.

Table 3.6. *Correlations of grain prices and death and birth rates in Daoyi, 1774-1873*

	Household death rate All		Household birth rate All		Complex†		Simple‡	
Grain	Female	Male	Female	Male	Female	Male	Female	Male
Rice								
High	-	-	-0.62	-	-0.46*	-	-0.46*	-0.36
Low	-	-	-0.60	-0.37*	-0.48	-	-0.54	-0.46
Millet								
High	-	-	-0.65	-0.37	-0.55	-0.33*	-0.50*	-0.56
Low	-	0.32	-0.49	-	-0.42*	-	-	-0.45
Sorghum								
High	-	-	-0.57	-	-0.46*	-0.33*	-0.39*	-0.39
Low	-	0.26	-0.58	-0.40*	-0.54	-	-0.46*	-0.49
Wheat								
High	-	-	-0.68	-	-0.36*	-	-0.54	-0.34
Low	-	0.43	-0.44	-0.38*	-0.48	-	-	-0.39
Soybean								
High	-	-	-0.45*	-	-0.63	-	-	-0.51
Low	-	0.39	-0.57	-0.40*	-0.36	-	-0.40*	-0.47

Note: All correlations have a significance of 0.001 unless marked with an asterisk, in which case the significance is 0.01. Correlations with a significance of less than 0.01 have been omitted. Our calculations begin from 1774 for all households and from 1789 for the breakdown by simple and complex households, and end in 1840 for female births and in 1873 for male births. The prices are adjusted annual averages from Fengtian prefecture; the birth and death rates are annual rates from Daoyi.

†Households with two or more conjugal units.
‡Households with only one conjugal family unit.

of Western Europe, the preventive check was especially prominent. Population growth decreased as population density increased because fertility rates were positively related to real wages, and real wages were inversely related to population density. Thus the regulating mechanisms in this system were the labor markets, which translated increases in population density into decreases in real wages, and the marriage market, which translated decreases in real wages into increases in the mean ages of marriage and first birth.

In China, the positive check—mortality—is usually assumed to have been solely responsible for keeping population and resources in balance over the long term, just as it has been assumed to be responsible for most of the demographic response to short-term fluctuations. The logic is essentially the same: not only did the allocation of resources within the extended family system protect age at marriage against the effects of short-term fluctuations, it also shielded the age at marriage against the effects of secular trends of increasing pressure on resources. Similarly, the primordial desire for large families that allegedly prevented couples from delaying births in response to short-term fluctuations also prevented them from reducing family size in response to a long-term worsening in economic circumstances. Thus as population pressure increased, only mortality could fluctuate, and it did so, with disastrous consequences,[28] the most commonly cited example of which is the perceived Malthusian crisis in China from the late eighteenth through the late nineteenth century.[29]

In the late eighteenth century, when our population data begin, neither positive nor preventive checks were likely to have been operating with much force in Daoyi and surrounding communities. Pressure on resources was still light. In the previous century, Liaoning had been virtually emptied by the devastations of the Ming–Qing transition. The Qing had moved most of the region's original residents into the Chinese interior as garrison troops and organized the remainder into state farms. By the middle of the seventeenth century only 2 percent of the registered land in Liaoning was in private hands: 2.7 million *mu*

---

[28] For example, Huang states that "If the above speculations [on the nature of China's demographic system in historical times] are valid, they suggest that China's demographic change was driven by alterations in the mortality rate, not in the fertility rate as in early modern Europe" (1990, 329). For an important opposing view, however, see Li Bozhong 1994.

[29] While (Ho 1959, 270–278), may be the classic example of such views, they have recently been reinvigorated by Harrell's 1995 reevaluation of Chinese mortality rates (7–9, 14). Harrell's findings, however, are based solely on highly flawed retrospective reconstructions of specific eighteenth- and nineteenth-century populations by Chinese genealogists during the very late nineteenth century and twentieth century.

of banner land versus only 50,000 *mu* of private land (Wang et al. 1991, 331). The state policy was to continue expanding the state farms, more than doubling the Liaoning banner lands to 7 million *mu* by 1693 and 8.2 million *mu* by 1727. To work these farms, the state had to rely on government settlers brought in from the Chinese interior. Interviews with elderly residents of Daoyi revealed that many families in the district trace their ancestry to these eighteenth-century settlers.

In Daoyi, however, the 1810s were a watershed that marked the beginning of a prolonged period of intensified Malthusian pressures. The intensification of pressure is most apparent in figures 3.1 and 3.2 as a series of prolonged periods of high grain prices, beginning in the 1810s. Prefectural high and low prices for all five grains had been on the rise since the turn of the century, reaching peaks in the 1810s. Increases in the price of millet, one of the most important grains in the district, were especially pronounced. With the exception of a brief respite during the 1820s, prices remained at high levels until the 1840s. After another respite during the 1850s, they rose again during the 1860s. The peasants of Daoyi, in other words, spent much of the nineteenth century enduring the effects of an agrarian price crisis.

Institutional pressure on peasants, in the form of demands for service imposed by the state, was also on the rise, a reflection of the deterioration of the banner system and the increasing fiscal desperation of the state. It is now common knowledge that in China proper the Eight Banner system deteriorated considerably during the eighteenth century.[30] In Liaoning, this process began in the middle of the nineteenth century and continued until the early twentieth century (Zheng Chuanshui 1981). We have very little specific information for Daoyi, but internal evidence from the registers themselves suggests that state demand for corvée labor from Daoyi peasants increased dramatically over time. In table 3.7, the proportion of adult men that the state was willing to classify as disabled (*feiding* or *chen*) and exempt from service requirements declined steadily over time.[31] Initially, roughly one-third of the men between the ages of 16 and 55 *sui* were classified as disabled or were annotated as having a specific disability (for example, *laozheng*–tuberculosis), but by 1873 less than

---

[30] The two best books are probably Elliott 1993 in English and especially Ding 1992 in Chinese. But see too Chen 1985 and Li Qiao, 1985.

[31] By contrast, the proportion of disabled and elderly among the banner population "within the passes" increased, demonstrating the distinctive character of banner populations "outside the passes." (Ding Yizhuang personal communication October 19, 1995).

Table 3.7. *Percentage of males 16-55 sui by reported banner occupation*

Register year	No occupation*	Banner occupation		Old, retired	Disabled†	Total (N)
		Healthy adult males‡	Soldiers, artisans, officials			
1774	5.9	51.5	16.2	1.3	25.1	746
1780	6.6	54.9	13.9	1.3	23.4	864
1786	6.9	44.4	11.1	1.9	35.7	930
1792	5.5	49.8	5.7	2.4	36.7	968
1795	5.5	53.1	5.5	1.4	34.5	983
1798	3.9	51.2	5.6	2.4	36.9	1,022
1801	3.8	52.1	5.7	1.8	36.6	1,037
1804	5.3	49.8	5.2	1.1	38.7	1,047
1810	7.3	53.6	4.5	1.5	33.1	1,099
1813	5.0	56.7	4.9	1.2	32.2	1,140
1816	5.7	59.0	5.0	1.6	28.7	1,160
1819	7.0	59.0	5.4	1.9	26.7	1,194
1822	6.5	62.4	4.7	2.1	24.3	1,165
1828	5.2	71.0	4.9	1.5	17.4	1,102
1831	4.0	74.7	4.2	1.9	15.1	1,084
1837	2.7	82.3	5.0	1.3	8.6	1,132
1840	6.8	80.1	4.5	1.4	7.2	1,168
1843	6.3	82.0	5.2	0.7	5.7	1,206
1846	5.6	85.0	5.1	0.4	3.9	1,226
1855	5.1	87.9	5.0	1.4	0.6	1,187
1858	6.2	87.8	4.9	0.9	0.3	1,160
1861	8.5	84.4	4.8	2.0	0.3	1,159
1864	4.9	87.6	5.2	2.2	0.1	1,155
1867	4.2	87.6	4.7	3.0	0.5	1,171
1873	5.0	87.3	5.1	1.9	0.7	1,212

* Almost all of these individuals are adolescent males.
†Includes individuals whose banner occupational status are originally recorded as disabled (*feiding* and *chen*), as well as individuals not recorded as disabled, but who are annotated as having a specific disability (for example *laozheng* - tuberculosis).
‡Included individuals annotated as young (*you*) and new (*chu*).

1 percent were so identified. Even the aged were increasingly less likely to be exempted from labor exaction. In table 3.8, the proportion of men aged 56 *sui* and above who were still classified as healthy adult males rose steadily over time, from less than one-tenth in the earliest registers, to almost one-half in the last few registers.

A sharp decline in immigration into Daoyi, and a cessation of internal migration, suggest that the district itself "filled up" sometime

Table 3.8. *Percentage of males 56 sui and above by reported banner occupation*

Register year	Healthy adult males	Soldiers, artisans, officials	Banner occupation		Retired adult males†	Old males‡	Total (N)
			Other	Disabled*			
1774	11.0	10.5	29.1	19.8	19.8	9.9	172
1780	13.0	8.7	47.1	17.3	8.7	5.3	208
1786	7.6	4.3	42.2	35.1	9.2	1.6	185
1792	10.2	1.6	4.3	37.6	4.8	41.4	186
1795	7.3	3.1	0.5	44.8	7.3	37.0	192
1798	3.7	3.7	2.6	33.7	4.2	52.1	190
1801	6.9	3.4	2.5	26.0	25.5	35.8	204
1804	9.5	4.2	0.0	26.3	38.4	21.6	190
1810	8.9	6.3	0.0	33.2	30.5	21.1	190
1813	11.9	4.6	0.0	32.5	36.6	14.4	194
1816	13.8	4.4	0.0	32.5	39.4	9.9	203
1819	13.6	4.2	0.0	32.6	38.1	11.4	236
1822	19.3	5.2	0.0	34.4	30.7	10.4	212
1828	26.9	4.8	0.5	26.4	31.7	9.6	208
1831	27.5	6.3	0.0	27.1	31.4	7.7	207
1837	25.3	4.1	1.4	11.8	40.3	17.2	221
1840	19.2	3.1	0.9	11.8	47.6	17.5	229
1843	31.3	1.3	0.0	13.4	27.7	26.3	224
1846	39.2	1.4	0.0	14.4	27.9	17.1	222
1855	32.0	5.5	3.4	2.2	32.9	24.0	325
1858	38.3	4.7	0.3	2.3	29.2	25.1	342
1861	45.6	4.4	0.0	3.8	31.1	15.0	366
1864	41.2	4.9	2.6	1.6	40.8	8.8	306
1867	39.6	6.3	1.1	0.5	6.7	46.3	270
1873	58.3	5.9	1.2	0.7	6.3	28.3	254

* Includes individuals whose banner occupational status was originally recorded as disabled (*feiding* and *chen*), as well as individuals not recorded as disabled, but annotated as having a specific disability (for example, *laozheng* - tuberculosis).

†Retired consists of men recorded as *tuiding*, (*chen*) *tui*, and *tuijia*, or recorded as having retired from a specific occupation.

‡Old consists of men recorded as *laoding* and *laotui*.

around the beginning of the nineteenth century, creating direct pressures on resources, most obviously the availability of land. Immigration into the district was the first to be affected. According to table 3.3, the male immigration rate was between 18.8 and 14.8 per 1000 in the 1770s and early 1780s, but below 3 per 1,000 in all subsequent registers. Internal migration, in which peasants changed villages but remained within the district, continued for a few more decades, with rates above 10 per 1,000 in every intercensal period before 1813–1816 but one (table 3.5). By the late 1810s, however, even this form of migration began to be curtailed. Internal migration rates in subsequent years were all close to zero. As a result of the reduction in internal movement, only 16 percent of the 981 people who changed villages during the century under observation did so in the 63 years after 1810.[32] Increasingly,

Daoyi bannermen were forced to reside solely in the community of their birth place. The closing of this migration valve greatly increased demographic pressures.

Daoyi was by no means the only part of China in which such pressure appears to have been on the increase during the nineteenth century. Thus its experiences during this period may have paralleled those of the nation as a whole. Throughout the country, social and economic conditions appear to have been deteriorating. The country as a whole is believed to have been overpopulated, in the sense of having more people than the land could support properly given available agricultural technology (Ho 1959). The resulting pressure on resources has not only been used to explain the increased frequency of famines during the nineteenth century (Li 1982), but also to help explain the social disorders of the period, most notably the Taiping Rebellion. State power, meanwhile, was on the wane, as the Qing government came under pressure from a variety of sources. During the nineteenth century, the state was not only in the midst of a process of institutional decay, it was confronted with the need to deal with both internal threats, posed by social and economic disturbances such as the Taiping, and external threats, posed by foreign powers.

In Daoyi, secular increases in pressure led to a permanent reduction in the rate at which the population increased, just as is generally assumed to have been the case for the country as a whole. This is most apparent in the annual growth rates in tables 3.3 and 3.4. Even after the 1840s, when grain prices began to subside, Daoyi's growth rate never reached the heights attained during the late eighteenth century. Thus while the crude growth rate of the male population ranged between 0 percent and 3 percent in the last quarter of the eighteenth century, it remained between -0.5 percent and 1 percent for most of the nineteenth century.[33] The net result was that while the male population increased by an average of 1.2 percent a year from 1774 to 1804, it increased by an average of only 0.2 percent a year in the period from 1805 to 1873.

Even though Huang (1990) and others have speculated that Chinese populations were distinguished from European populations by the elevated importance of mortality (Harrell 1995; Telford 1995), reductions in birth rates played a much more important role in slowing the increase of population in Daoyi than changes in the death rate.

---

[32] The pattern of internal migration also changed. Before 1810, 90 percent of internal migrations were by households, while 50 percent of the migrations after 1810 were by individuals.

[33] The calculation was restricted to males to remove the effects of the deterioration after the 1840s in the registration of female children.

According to table 3.3, the male crude birth rate decreased from 29.1 per 1,000 in the period before 1804, to 22.5 per 1,000 in the period after 1804. Although it was shown in table 3.6 that mortality responded to short-term fluctuations in conditions, death rates appear not to have been affected by the long-term increase in pressure: the male crude death rate actually declined, from 23.8 per 1,000 to 20.8 per 1,000. Preventive checks, in other words, may have played as important a role in the Chinese demographic system as in the European demographic system.[34]

While part of the decline in birth rates was due to the marital fertility reductions evident in figure 3.3, changes in male marriage patterns contributed as well. In contrast with the Western European demographic system, where age at marriage rose as economic pressure increased (Wrigley and Schofield 1981), in Daoyi it was the proportion of men ever marrying that responded to increased pressure. Table 3.5 shows that as the century progressed, men who were fortunate enough to marry did so at progressively younger ages, but steadily larger proportions of men never married at all. Thus while mean age at male marriage decreased from 22.3 *sui* before 1804 to 21.3 *sui* after 1804, the percentage of men aged 36–40 who had never married increased from 14 percent to 18.2. The net result was that the rate at which never married men aged 16–35 *sui* married decreased from an average of 88 per 1,000 before 1804, to 75 per 1,000 in the years after. The rate at which widowers remarried also decreased, from 39 per 1,000 before 1804, to 24 per 1,000 after 1804.

We know very little about the structure of the marriage market in which Daoyi participated. Thus, it is impossible to determine whether reductions in the proportion of men marrying were an immediate response to a deterioration in local conditions, a lagged response to worsening conditions two decades before, or some combination of the two. If Daoyi was integrated into a larger marriage market, reductions in the proportion of males marrying may have reflected the worsening of the district's economic position relative to neighboring districts, and a reduction in its ability to compete in the market for brides. If Daoyi's marriage market was internal, or if its marriage trends were representative of the region as a whole, reductions in the proportion of males marrying may also reflect a shortage of potential spouses induced by pressure-related increases in sex-selective infanticide approximately two decades before.

---

[34] See Lee 1994 and Wang, Lee, and Campbell 1995 for an extended discussion of the role of the preventive check in the Chinese demographic system.

Table 3.9. *Percentage of household types in each register*

Register year	Frag.	Sim.	Ext.	Ver.	Hor.	Diag.	Total (N)
1792	8.4	25.2	14.8	16.1	35.3	0.2	465
1795	10.4	24.5	14.5	17.4	33.2	0.0	482
1798	10.0	25.0	15.8	16.4	32.2	0.6	500
1801	13.9	23.3	14.2	18.2	30.4	0.0	527
1804	11.5	23.8	17.1	14.7	32.7	0.2	504
1810	12.4	24.6	17.4	15.7	28.0	1.9	483
1813	12.8	23.0	17.2	14.9	28.0	4.1	483
1816	14.2	22.4	16.7	14.6	25.8	6.3	492
1819	14.7	22.5	16.8	14.0	24.2	7.9	530
1822	12.1	23.5	17.1	15.0	24.1	8.2	473
1828	14.1	26.1	15.6	11.8	20.3	12.0	482
1831	16.2	25.6	13.7	11.3	21.4	11.8	468
1837	15.7	24.1	14.6	10.0	23.9	11.7	460
1840	17.3	22.7	14.4	10.2	23.8	11.7	480
1843	17.3	23.5	13.9	10.0	25.1	10.2	490
1846	15.6	23.9	15.0	9.7	24.5	11.3	486
1855	20.0	22.7	12.9	10.0	20.4	14.1	490
1858	20.5	20.3	14.4	8.8	19.6	16.5	479
1861	19.6	19.8	14.1	9.0	19.6	17.8	489
1864	17.1	21.5	11.8	9.2	18.9	21.5	433
1867	16.0	19.4	13.2	9.1	19.4	23.0	418
1873	16.7	17.2	12.9	10.9	17.0	25.2	412
Total	14.8	23.0	15.0	12.7	25.0	9.5	10,526

Households are only included in this calculation if the head of the household was alive at the time the register was compiled.

Increases in Malthusian pressure not only triggered a demographic response, but a social one as well: processes of household formation were permanently transformed, fundamentally changing the social context of daily life in Daoyi. As the district filled up, it not only became more difficult for families to migrate internally, but it also became more difficult for household members to depart and form new households. The rate at which households divided accordingly declined. Whereas the household division rate had been more than 12 per 1,000 household-years at risk until 1804, after that year the rate plummeted. The rate fluctuated around 4 divisions per 1,000 household-years for the remainder of the century under observation, peaking at 8 and reaching a nadir at 2. The only exception was after the end of the grain price crisis, when in the eight years between 1837 and 1846, some of the pent-up demand for household division was released. In those years, the rate temporarily jumped back to 10 divisions per 1,000 household-years.

Table 3.10. *Percentage of individuals in each register by household type*

Register year	Frag.	Sim.	Ext.	Ver.	Hor.	Diag.	Total (N)
1792	1.9	12.6	10.9	19.4	54.8	0.3	2,721
1795	2.1	12.4	10.8	21.7	53.0	0.0	2,836
1798	2.1	12.8	11.8	20.0	52.2	1.1	2,875
1801	2.9	12.3	10.4	22.3	52.0	0.0	2,938
1804	2.2	12.1	12.1	17.8	55.6	0.2	2,978
1810	2.6	12.4	12.5	20.9	47.4	4.2	2,839
1813	2.8	11.1	12.5	20.0	46.2	7.5	2,812
1816	3.2	11.1	12.6	18.5	43.2	11.5	2,776
1822	2.7	10.3	12.0	18.7	40.1	16.3	2,760
1828	3.0	11.5	10.5	14.3	36.5	24.3	2,956
1837	3.1	10.6	9.6	11.1	40.1	25.5	2,932
1840	3.7	10.5	9.7	12.5	41.2	22.5	2,864
1843	4.0	11.2	9.7	13.2	40.5	21.4	2,763
1846	3.5	10.8	10.3	12.4	38.0	25.0	2,792
1855	4.7	10.6	8.6	12.1	31.6	32.5	2,807
1858	4.6	9.2	9.1	10.5	30.0	36.6	2,869
1861	4.3	8.6	9.1	11.1	30.2	36.6	2,973
1864	3.4	9.0	7.4	10.4	27.6	42.2	2,803
1867	3.2	8.0	7.7	9.4	25.8	45.9	2,795
1873	3.1	6.8	7.5	9.9	23.5	49.2	2,867
Total	3.2	10.8	10.3	15.3	40.4	20.0	62,726

Individuals are only included in this calculation if they were alive at the time the register was compiled, and if the head of their household was also alive.

When households did divide, they did so at progressively later stages in the domestic cycle.[35] At the beginning of the century for which we have data, horizontal households, composed of heads and their married brothers, tended to divide fairly soon after the death of the head or one of his brothers, usually by the next triennial register or the one after that.[36] The rules changed after 1810, when the grain price crisis began. In horizontal households, the death of the head no longer precipitated a household division.[37] Instead, horizontal households turned into diagonal households, where heads were coresident not only with their brothers, but also with their cousins and their uncles. When such diagonal households did divide, they tended to do so between heads and cousins. Even after prices subsided, the new system remained, indicating that it was not just a short-term response to economic pressure, but a long-term adjustment to a changed environment. There were no more cases in which

[35] Processes of household division, including the events that normally precipitated division and the lines along which households divided, are investigated in more detail in Chapters 6 and 7.

[36] Between 1792 and 1798, 27 out of 33 household divisions were either between a household head's sons and his brothers, or between the head and his nephews.

[37] Between 1814 and 1828, only 6 divisions out of 49 were between a household head's sons and brothers.

horizontal households divided between sons and brothers, or heads and nephews, except between 1865 and 1867. Indeed, most divisions after the end of the crisis were not even in horizontal households, but in diagonal households.

As a result of these changes, households grew considerably at both extremes. Table 3.9 summarizes the distribution of households by type in each register during the century under observation. On the one hand, fragmentary households, households with no conjugal family ties, doubled from 10 to 20 percent of all households. On the other hand, an increasing number of people lived in more and more complex families. In 1792, the first register which provides detail on household structure, slightly more than one-third of the households were horizontal, consisting of a head, his brothers, and their families. Another one-quarter were simple, consisting only of a married couple, a married couple and their children, or a widowed parent and his or her children. The remaining households were divided between fragmented, extended, and vertical. By 1873, after several decades under the new rules of division, one-quarter of all households were diagonal, even though there had been almost no diagonal households at the beginning of the century. The proportion of households in all other categories, except for fragmented households, decreased.

Moreover, since complex households were considerably larger than simple households, the proportion of the population living in complex households increased even more quickly than the proportion of complex households. In table 3.10, almost half of the population in 1873 lived in the most complex household type, the diagonal household, even though less than 1 percent had in 1792. Half of the population, in other words, was living in a household where at least one member was a head's uncle, cousin, or cousin's son, or one of their spouses. The proportion of the population living in less complex household forms correspondingly declined. While more than one-half of all individuals lived in horizontal households in 1792, less than one-quarter did by 1873. The proportion of individuals living in other household forms fell from just under one-half of the population in 1801 to less than one-third in 1873.

As a result of the increase in household complexity, the proportion of individuals who were distant relatives of their household head increased, while the proportion of individuals who were immediate relatives decreased. Table 3.11 traces changes over time in the proportion of the population in different household relationships. In 1792, less than 1 percent of individuals were uncles, cousins, and cousins'

Table 3.11. *Percentage of individuals in each register by their relationship to household head*

Register year	Head	Head's mother	Head's wife	Head's children, etc.†	Brothers, brother's children/ etc.†	Uncles, cousins, cousins' children etc.†	Total (N)
1792	17.1	4.6	11.8	35.2	30.8	0.5	2,721
1795	17.0	4.2	11.7	37.5	29.2	0.4	2,836
1798	17.4	4.7	12.2	35.7	29.2	0.8	2,875
1801	17.9	4.5	11.8	35.9	29.5	0.4	2,938
1804	16.9	4.2	11.8	35.6	31.2	0.3	2,978
1810	17.0	3.8	11.1	38.0	27.5	2.6	2,839
1813	17.2	4.4	10.7	35.4	27.6	4.8	2,812
1816	17.7	4.5	10.7	33.2	26.8	7.0	2,776
1819	17.8	4.3	10.5	32.4	26.2	8.8	2,978
1822	17.1	3.8	11.0	32.1	26.2	9.8	2,760
1828	16.3	3.3	10.3	31.3	24.8	14.0	2,956
1831	16.8	3.6	10.9	29.7	24.9	14.3	2,792
1837	15.7	3.1	9.9	29.0	27.1	15.3	2,932
1840	16.8	3.3	10.0	28.8	27.6	13.5	2,864
1843	17.7	3.4	10.2	29.5	26.5	12.8	2,763
1846	17.4	3.6	10.5	27.3	26.0	15.2	2,792
1855	17.5	3.2	9.8	26.0	25.6	18.0	2,807
1858	16.7	2.9	9.1	24.5	23.9	22.9	2,869
1861	16.4	3.0	9.1	25.4	24.0	22.0	2,973
1864	15.4	3.1	8.6	25.2	22.5	25.2	2,803
1867	15.0	3.2	8.3	24.3	20.4	28.9	2,795
1873	14.4	3.0	8.0	23.8	19.7	31.1	2,867
Total	16.8	3.7	10.4	30.7	26.2	12.2	62,726

Individuals are only included in this calculation if they were alive at the time the register was compiled, and if the head of their household were also alive.

†Includes all spouses, descendants, and descendants' spouses.

sons, or their wives and daughters, but by 1873, 31 percent of individuals were. The proportion of individuals in other relationships correspondingly declined. The percentage of individuals who were descended from the household head, or married to one of his descendants, declined from 35 percent in 1792 to 24 percent in 1873. The percentage of individuals who were brothers, sisters, sisters-in-law, descendants of brothers, or the spouses of brothers' descendants declined from 31 percent to 20 percent.

By creating a subgroup of marginalized individuals who spent much of their existence at the bottom of the household hierarchy, the increase in the proportion of coresident distant kin changed Daoyi's social structure. Whatever inequalities between households already existed were augmented by inequalities within households. We will show in Chapter 7, that complex households, especially diagonal ones, were sharply stratified by relationship to the household head. The distribution of privilege followed traditional Confucian principles, so that discrimination increased in intensity as proximity to the head decreased. The uncles, cousins, and assorted other distant relatives who together accounted for nearly one-third of the population in 1873 were less likely to reproduce than the head's immediate relatives, not only because they had lower fertility within marriage, but also because if they were male, they were less likely to marry. The reduction in household division rates described earlier implied, moreover, that distant relatives had little or no hope of improving their lot by departing and forming their own household.

The rise of one prominent family, the Yangs, raises the possibility that the process of stratification within households was mirrored at a higher level by a process of stratification between households. From common beginnings,[38] the Yangs came to dominate Daoyi, by obtaining important banner positions, and by developing wealth and talent as measured by the purchase and award of examination degrees.[39] The first Yang to have a banner position was Yang Demei, who in 1792 was identified as a banner civilian subofficial (*zhishiren* in Han Chinese or *baitangga* in Manchu Chinese).[40] His son, Yang Fa, was appointed a non-commissioned officer (*niru lingcui* in Han Chinese) in 1810 and an overseer (*siku* in Han Chinese or *ulin niyalma* in Manchu Chinese) in 1837. These positions remained with the family at least until 1873. By 1828 another family member, Yang Changshan, age 32, was the first in Daoyi district to earn or purchase a studentship in the imperial academy (*jiansheng*).[41] In 1837, he was joined by his relatives Yang Wenxue and Yang Wende. Their ranks were joined by Yang Decheng in 1855 and Yang Deen in 1858. Two of Yang Changshan's

---

[38] While our records for the Yang family date back to 1774, there was no one of any distinction whatsoever until the emergence of Yang Demei.

[39] While our data are restricted to terse annotations of those individuals with banner occupations and/or examination degrees, the household registers suggest that the Yangs may have accumulated wealth through other means as well. First, the family was quite large, with households of 20 to 70 people—a reflection of labor and demographic power. Second, the family migrated from Daoyi to Dingjia fangshen—presumably a function of their ability to convert adjoining wastelands into private family farm land.

[40] By distinguishing Han Chinese from Manchu Chinese we are translating the terms *Hanyu* and *Manyu*. We are not referring to a language family, but to the fact that both these languages are spoken within the political confines of present-day China.

[41] Bannermen were assigned a fixed quota of such studentships. They could also purchase these degrees. While we do not know the price, we do know that *jiansheng* and *gongsheng* degrees were not cheap. Prices varied by province and even district. The best survey of the range of prices is still Tang 1931.

sons were named tribute students (*gongsheng*) in 1864. By 1873 the family accounted for all five such degrees in the district.[42]

Conclusion

Thus the long-term increase in pressure fundamentally altered demographic and social behavior in Daoyi at every level of social organization. Individual rates of immigration, fertility, and nuptiality, for instance, declined to the point where population growth stagnated. As pressure within the district increased, not only did internal migration cease, but rates and patterns of household division changed, leading to the appearance of diagonal households. These diagonal households, as we shall see, were characterized by severe differentials in fertility and nuptiality according to proximity to household head, reflecting the increasing stratification of society along lines of household relationship. At the same time, as we have just seen, disparities between households also increased, leading to the rise of elite families such as the Yangs, and the concentration of wealth and land in their hands.

This combination of institutional decay, increasing differentiation within and between households, and population concentration at the household and community level, reshaped the opportunity structure that defined individual fate and fortune in rural Liaoning. As we will discuss in Parts Three and Four, opportunities to marry and have children consequently declined in the household hierarchy, but persisted in the banner hierarchy. Liaoning peasants, in other words, changed their demographic behavior to fit their changing circumstances. And as we will discuss in Part Two, they could do so because of the multiple systems of population control available to them in the Liaoning demographic system.

---

[42] Stratification may have accelerated during the early twentieth century. By 1948, 10 percent of the population in Daoyi district owned 43 percent of the land (*Daoyi XZ* 1984, 10). Landlords, 4 percent of the population, owned 31 percent of the land. Rich peasants, 13 percent of the population, owned the other 13. While this appears largely to be the culmination of a process of land concentration during the Republican and Manchukuo periods, based on cases like the Yang family we can assume that the process dates back at least to the nineteenth century.

Part 2

The Liaoning demographic system

"May you live a hundred years and have many sons (changgming baisui; duozi duofu)"
(traditional Chinese proverb)

In late imperial China, mortality and fertility represented the warp and weft of individual fate and fortune. Chinese conceived of their life span as a function of individual fate; and the number and sexual composition of their children as a consequence of personal fortune. Moreover, they regarded both as largely out of their personal control. Demographers, until recently, agreed with these sentiments. The conventional demographic wisdom, dating as far back as Malthus, was that mortality and marital fertility were beyond human control. Marriage, which Malthus called the preventive check, was the only means to control fertility. Mortality, which Malthus termed the positive check, was the only sure means to control population size. Infanticide was rare, and had little effect on the overall rate of growth.[1] Fertility control within marriage was unknown.[2]

In this conception, there were no conscious positive or preventive checks to population growth in the late imperial Chinese demographic system. Marriage was early and universal. In the absence of any preventive check, Chinese population size alternated between periods of sustained growth when no checks operated at all, and periods of disastrous contraction when nature responded by imposing her own

---

[1] Indeed Malthus believed that where infanticide was common, it would reduce the preventive check, since such "vice" would remove the barriers to marriage for the poor, resulting ultimately in increased population growth. "This permission given to parents thus to expose their offspring tends undoubtedly to facilitate marriage and encourage population" (Malthus 1872, 104).

[2] Malthus himself was convinced that there could not have been much variation in coital frequency, let alone control over the "passions between the sexes." "The passions between the sexes has appeared in every age and every country to be so nearly the same that it may always be considered in algebraic language as a given quantity" (Mathus 1872, 259).

positive checks: epidemics, famines, and war (Chao 1986; Elvin 1973; Ho 1959; Huang 1990; Perkins 1969).

There is increasing evidence, however, that this was not true in late imperial China. Recently discovered population records, among the most complete and accurate demographic data for any historic population, have begun to illuminate the population history of China before this century (Lee, Campbell, and Wang 1993). Our analyses of elite Chinese population behavior based on such materials, most notably of the Qing imperial lineage, reveal the existence of a clear pattern of mortality control through infanticide, and marital fertility control through abstinence and restraint (Lee, Wang, and Campbell 1994; Wang, Lee, and Campbell 1995). In contrast with the European demographic system where there was only one form of voluntary control over population growth—marriage—the imperial Chinese demographic system was characterized by multiple forms of control. Chinese could vary their age at marriage, they could control their fertility within marriage, and they could regulate the survivorship of their births according to a wide variety of demographic, social, and economic circumstances. In consequence, Chinese demographic behavior during the late imperial period exhibits a form of rationality that was in many ways proto modern. While these results represent the behavior of an elite population, they provide a convincing picture of an alternative type of positive check and an alternative type of preventive check unidentified by Malthus, and most other demographers.

Chapters 4 and 5 represent the first detailed study of Chinese peasant population behavior before the twentieth century.[3] Chapter 4 reconstructs the structure of mortality by age and sex and analyzes among else how Liaoning peasants practiced infanticide on a wide scale to control the number and composition of their children. Chapter 5 reconstructs the patterns of nuptiality and fertility and demonstrates how Liaoning peasants controlled their fertility in response to such social conditions as household structure and family composition. Together, these two chapters delineate the dimensions of a rural Liaoning demographic system analogous to the elite Beijing system we have described elsewhere.

---

[3] There are, of course, numerous other studies of Chinese historical demography, most notably the pioneering work of Liu Ts'ui-jung (1992, 1995a and b), Steven Harrell (1985, 1995), and Ted Telford (1990, 1992, 1995). None of them, however, are of specifically peasant populations. While this is not true of the important studies of Taiwanese historical demography by Arthur Wolf (1980, 1985a and b) and Burton Pasternak (1983), none of these studies pre-date the twentieth century.

In rural Liaoning, in other words, commoners as well as elites frequently resorted to both sets of positive and preventive checks. As a result, Liaoning peasants, like their noble counterparts, were able to control their demographic behavior to a degree unparalleled elsewhere. The probability and timing of marriage, children, and even individual length of life were subject to a variety of different social strategies depending on household position and banner position, producing the distinctive social-demographic profiles we will see in Parts Three and Four. Demographic fate and fortune, in spite of traditional Chinese misconceptions, were often under human control.

4

Two types of positive check: infanticide and neglect[1]

> The woman's position is usually inferior in the Manchu family and she is subjugated . . . The inferior position of the woman is especially accentuated in the order of taking and serving meals. The woman before eating is obliged to feed every day and in the first place the men, even if they be ordinary paid workmen or slaves. However . . . If the family is not very numerous, all the family members eat together. (Shirokogoroff 1926, 126–127)[2]

We begin our discussion of the Liaoning demographic system with an analysis of mortality. The positive check does not fall equally on all

---

[1] This chapter has a long history, dating back to our initial foray into Chinese historical demography. We consequently have published several early versions based on partial data sets and alternate methodologies. Sections I and IV date back to work with Lawrence Anthony during the summer of 1984 (Lee, Anthony, and Suen 1988), and the spring of 1987 (Lee, Campbell, and Anthony 1995). Sections II and III date back to the summer of 1994 (Campbell 1995, Campbell and Lee forthcoming). Ronald Lee and Tom Pullum commented and assisted us in our calculations for earlier versions of this paper. We are grateful for their help as well as that of audiences at the Academia Sinica, Beijing University, the University of California, Berkeley, Liaoning University, and the University of Washington. See also Campbell and Lee 1996 for a more recent analysis of mortality in rural Liaoning using life event and time series analysis.

[2] Sergei Mikhailovich Shirokogoroff (1887–1939) was a Russian-born anthropologist who pioneered the ethnographic and linguistic study of Manchu and Han Chinese society during the early twentieth century. Originally a fellow of the Russian Imperial Academy of Sciences, Shirokogoroff began fieldwork in Siberia and northeast China in 1912. After October 1917, he resided in China permanently, eventually becoming a professor of sociology at Qinghua University where he trained many distinguished Chinese ethnologists, including Fei Hsiao-tung (Zhongguo Shehui Kexueyuan Jindai Shi Yanjiusuo Fanyishi 1981, 437–438; Fei 1939, xvii, Fei and Chang 1945). While much of Shirokogoroff's understanding of Manchu society came from more recent times and other places than late imperial Liaoning, his description of Manchu society and Manchu customs often seem relevant to our understanding of Daoyi. We therefore cite his work here and elsewhere when appropriate.

segments of a population. Death rates vary by age and sex as well as time.[3] Analysis of sex differentials in mortality rates reveals the effects of gender differentials on the allocation of resources, social roles, and the division of labor. Similarly, examination of age differentials in mortality rates may suggest the influence of age differentials in the allocation of resources, social roles, and the division of labor. The age and sex patterns of death, therefore, not only reconstruct the local mortality regime, something not yet done for late imperial China, but also provide insight into rural social organization.[4]

This was especially true in rural Liaoning, as families influenced the survivorship of children, adults, and the aged through the widespread practice of conscious infanticide and unconscious neglect. We divide this chapter into four sections. In section I, we establish the broad parameters of mortality by calculating life tables by sex for the registered population, and then compare age-specific death rates with those in model life table families. In section II, we extrapolate from the age pattern of mortality the proportion of population that did not register due to early death and late registration, and estimate how many infants and children died by infanticide and differential neglect. In section III, we compare the gender pattern of adolescent and adult mortality in Liaoning with the experience of other historical and contemporary populations in Europe and Asia. Finally in section IV, we contrast male and female age-specific death rates over time to reveal which age groups by sex were particularly vulnerable to mortality crises.

Gender patterns of mortality

Life table models of mortality provide a convenient summation of mortality experience by age, sex, cohort, and period (Chiang 1968).[5]

---

[3] In most human populations, the age pattern of mortality rates is J-shaped, with high but declining rates in infancy and childhood, relatively low rates in youth and young adulthood, and rapidly rising rates at later ages. Coale and Demeny 1966/1983 is one of the best-known efforts to model this age pattern of variation in human mortality.

[4] Genealogical populations which make up the majority of existing work on the historical demography of late imperial China record infants and children incompletely and hardly record females at all. As a result, these studies (Liu 1992; Harrell and Pullum 1995) have confined their study of mortality to adult males. The only notable exceptions are Lee, Campbell, and Wang 1993 and Lee, Wang, and Campbell 1994 on the mortality patterns of the Qing imperial lineage which draw on a system of continuous vital registration organized under the Office of the Imperial Lineage.

[5] For comparisons between populations, life table measures of mortality are preferable to more basic indices such as the crude death rate because they are unaffected by the age distribution of a population. They are derived directly from age-specific death

Comparison of age and sex patterns of mortality with those of model populations provides indirect evidence on cause of death. Mortality rates are themselves determined by patterns of both exposure and resistance. Mortality differentials, therefore, reflect variation in the factors that condition exposure and resistance.[6] These factors are not just genetic and biological, but social, economic, and cultural as well. By linking trends and patterns in mortality to the determinants of exposure and resistance, an analysis of the operation of the positive check can accordingly illuminate basic features of daily life in peasant societies such as in Daoyi.

Table 4.1 presents the male and female life tables for the intercensal periods for which we have complete data. According to these calculations (described in Appendix B), life expectancy at 6 months of age in Daoyi and surrounding communities was around 30. Males at 6 months of age, that is 2 *sui*, could expect to live 36 more years.[7] Females at 6 months of age could expect to live 29 more years. Life expectancy at birth was, therefore, in the high 20s for women and in the low 30s for men.[8] If these results are generalizable to other rural communities, life expectancy in late eighteenth- and early nineteenth-century Liaoning

rates ($_n m_x$ — deaths per 1,000 person-years at risk between ages x and x + n) or death probabilities ($_n q_x$ —the probability of dying before age x + n, conditional upon surviving to age x). In addition to being easier to compare, they are also somewhat easier for laypersons to interpret. In this chapter, the measures we most commonly refer to are e_x, the number of additional years an individual aged x can expect to live, and 1_x, the probability of surviving from birth to age x.

6   Johansson 1991, 1994, and Mosk and Johansson 1986 have emphasized the importance of patterns of both resistance and exposure to disease in explaining historical mortality patterns, levels, and trends. The view that changes in resistance brought about by improvements in nutritional intake were solely responsible for decreases in mortality before this century, usually associated with McKeown 1976, McKeown and Record 1962, has not held up under more detailed empirical scrutiny. See Lunn 1991 for a review of recent findings on the influence of nutritional status on specific infectious disease. More generally, see Schofield and Reher 1991 for a comprehensive review of recent findings on the determinants of mortality patterns and trends in historical Europe.

7   All ages in this chapter are in *sui*. By *sui* Chinese meant to indicate the number of calendar years in which a person had lived. People are accordingly 1 *sui* at birth, and their ages are incremented every new year. For example, individuals turn 2 *sui* at the first new year following their birth. *Sui* are therefore on average one and a half years higher than Western years of age. Thus the age intervals in our tables correspond roughly to standard Western age intervals in abridged life tables. For example, the age group 6 to 10 *sui* corresponds to Western ages 5 to 9.

8   We make these estimates by comparison with the regional model life tables calculated by Coale and Demeny. These life tables unfortunately do not distinguish the first year of life by month.

was comparable to life expectancy elsewhere in China,[9] and even abroad in France.[10]

The age- and sex-specific patterns of mortality reveal other similarities with historical population behavior elsewhere. Table 4.2 identifies the mortality levels implied by age-specific death probabilities in each of the four canonical "model" life table families that summarize the major age patterns of world mortality (Coale and Demeny 1966/1983).[11] While the "level" of mortality in Daoyi varies widely by sex and age group, most male and female age groups fall in the range between levels four through six.[12] If the relationship between mortality below age 5 and mortality above age 5 in Daoyi was similar to that in the model life tables, the implication would be a life expectancy at birth that was in the high 20s or low 30s.

As we might expect, given Daoyi's geography and climate, the age pattern of mortality in rural Liaoning was closest to that of the north European populations that make up Coale and Demeny's Model North. These were cold climate populations where airborne

[9] In Beijing, according to Lee, Campbell, and Wang 1993, male life expectancy among the imperial lineage, an elite urban population, during this same period was in the early to mid-30s at birth and mid-30s at ages 1 and 5, slightly higher than in Daoyi. By contrast, Harrell and Pullum's reconstruction of three genealogical populations from Shaoxing prefecture in Zhejiang Province, reveal a male life expectancy at birth during the period from 1800–1874 in the mid- to late 20s, slightly lower than in Daoyi, a result they explain by the downward bias in their method of calculation (1995, 148).

[10] In France, according to Blayo 1975, life expectancy in 1770 to 1779 was 28.2 for males and 29.6 for females at birth, 38.6 for males and 38.5 for females at age one, and 46.0 for males and 45.6 for females at age five. Life expectancy in 1780 to 1789 was 27.5 for males and 28.1 for females at birth, 37.6 for males and 37.1 for females at age one, and 45.5 for males and 44.3 for females at age five. By contrast in England, according to Wrigley and Schofield 1981, life expectancy at birth was higher for both sexes—36.3 in 1750 to 1775, 37 in 1775 to 1800, and 41.5 in 1800 to 1825.

[11] The Coale and Demeny 1966/1983 model populations and life tables were originally constructed to facilitate extrapolations from incomplete or partial demographic data. They found that the range of human mortality can be divided into four distinct age patterns of death rates which they labeled "West," "North," "East," and "South." Each of these four sets of regional model life tables are based on historical data from different regions of the world. The North model is derived from mortality data from Iceland 1911–1950, Norway 1856–80 and 1956–55, and Sweden 1851–1890. More recently, using data from contemporary developing countries, the United Nations' *Model Life Tables for Developing Countries* (1982) identified four more regional models, the Latin American, Chilean, South Asian, and Far Eastern, as well as a composite model, the General pattern.

[12] Coale and Demeny 1966/1983 divided each "Model" family into 24 mortality "levels" ranging from a life expectancy at birth of 18 to 75. Mortality levels are defined so that the higher the life expectancy, the greater the mortality "level," with life expectancy at birth increasing in increments in female life expectancy of approximately 2.5 years.

Table 4.1. *The female and male life tables in rural Liaoning*
(1792-1804, 1810-1822, 1828-1831, 1837-1846, 1855-1867)

Age group	Female						Male					
	N_x	N_{x+3}	m_x	q_x	Life expectancy	Standard deviation	N_x	N_{x+3}	m_x	q_x	Life expectancy	Standard deviation
1-5	583	474	75	316	29.0	0.5	1,784	1,518	61	266	35.9	0.33
6-10	1,012	958	23	109	37.2	0.4	2,738	2,617	20	96	43.8	0.24
11-15	969	922	18	85	36.5	0.3	2,929	2,859	8	39	43.2	0.21
16-20	1,248	1,163	24	112	34.6	0.3	2,766	2,704	9	42	39.8	0.20
21-25	2,012	1,909	18	85	33.6	0.2	2,625	2,559	8	39	36.4	0.20
26-30	2,043	1,945	17	81	31.5	0.2	2,500	2,445	8	38	32.8	0.20
31-35	1,978	1,890	15	75	29.1	0.2	2,367	2,296	9	44	29.0	0.20
36-40	1,852	1,742	19	93	26.2	0.2	2,362	2,266	13	65	25.2	0.20
41-45	1,673	1,569	21	100	23.6	0.2	2,050	1,940	17	81	21.8	0.20
46-50	1,449	1,375	19	90	21.0	0.2	1,711	1,589	24	114	18.5	0.20
51-55	1,255	1,158	24	112	17.8	0.2	1,404	1,273	31	144	15.5	0.10
56-60	1,160	1,057	29	136	14.7	0.1	1,281	1,088	48	214	12.6	0.10
61-65	1,007	879	43	194	11.6	0.1	1,021	855	60	262	10.4	0.10
66-70	770	609	67	289	8.7	0.1	702	542	77	324	8.1	0.10
71-75	450	332	102	405	6.2	0.9	369	249	123	467	5.8	0.10
75 +	500	323	137	505	3.7	0.1	368	230	150	538	3.7	0.10

n_x means the number of people in a closed population alive in a given age group in year x.

n_{x+3} means the number of people in a closed population alive in that age group three years after year x.

m_x means deaths per thousand person-years at risk by five year age-group.

q_x means the probability per thousand of dying within the next five years.

All ages in *sui*. By *sui* the Chinese meant to indicate the number of calendar years during which a person had lived. People are accordingly one *sui* at birth and two *sui* at the next New Year. *Sui* are, therefore, on average one and a half years higher than Western years of age.

Table 4.2. *Male and female age-specific mortality rates in rural Liaoning and corresponding Coale-Demeny model life tables levels*†

Age group	Males m_x	West	North	East	South	Females m_x	West	North	East	South
1–5	61	3	5	3	7	75	1	3	1	6
6–10	20	4	4	-6	-2	23	-6	3	-7	-2
11–15	8	3	6	-2	1	18	-7	4	-12	-9
16–20	9	6	6	2	4	24	-6	-8	-13	-9
21–25	8	1	12	8	10	18	2	-1	-2	1
26–30	8	2	12	8	10	17	4	2	1	2
31–35	9	12	12	8	9	15	6	5	4	3
36–40	13	10	9	7	6	19	4	4	1	1
41–45	17	10	8	6	5	21	4	4	1	1
46–50	24	7	6	4	2	19	7	6	4	2
51–55	31	7	5	3	2	24	7	5	4	3
56–60	48	4	3	1	-1	29	8	7	6	4
61–65	60	6	4	2	2	43	8	6	7	6
66–70	77	7	5	5	4	67	6	6	7	6
71–75	123	4	4	4	4	102	6	6	7	6
S. D.	-	4.0	3.1	3.9	3.7	-	5.2	4.2	6.5	4.8

†See Table 4.1 for years covered. To perform this approximation we assume that *sui* are one year rather than one and a half years less than Western age. Actual mortality levels should be slightly higher, especially in the early age-groups. The negative Coale-Demeny mortality levels calculated for some age groups were arrived at by extrapolation from tables in Coale and Demeny (1966/1983).

diseases, especially respiratory ones such as tuberculosis, dominated mortality. Diarrhea and other gastrointestinal diseases were much less important as causes of death than in populations in warmer, more southerly locations. Death rates were accordingly lower among infants and the aged, and higher during the middle adult years (Preston 1976, 116).[13]

Two striking anomalies, however, are apparent in table 4.2. Young adult men (21–45 *sui*) had *lower* death rates than would be predicted from male death rates at other ages, while adolescent and young-adult females (11–30 *sui*) had *higher* death rates than would be predicted from female death rates at other ages. Thus whereas male death rates below 21 *sui* and above 45 *sui* correspond to North levels three to six, male death rates between those ages corresponded to North levels eight to twelve. Conversely, whereas female death rates below 11 *sui* and above 30 *sui* correspond to North levels three to seven, death rates between these ages correspond to North levels two or lower.

[13] Model North, however, does not incorporate the full potential impact of tuberculosis mortality on the pattern of age-specific death rates. Data from countries where tuberculosis was highly prevalent, and distortions in the age pattern of mortality severe, were excluded. The most prominent distortions of the age pattern in the excluded data were in young adulthood and early middle age, where mortality was far higher than would be expected given mortality at younger and older ages.

Table 4.3. Gender differentials in age-specific mortality for rural Liaoning

Age	Prob. of dying in (age interval) (per 1000) [q(x)]		Female Prob. of dying in age interval (per 1000) [q(x)]		Male Prob. of dying in age interval per 1000 [q(x)]		Females alive at start of age interval [l(x)]	No. of Females who die in age interval [d(x)]		Males Alive at start of age interval [l(x)]	No. of Males who die in age interval [d(x)]	
	Male (1)	Female (2)	Natural (3)	Excess (4)	Natural (5)	Excess (6)	(7)	Natural (8)	Excess (9)	(10)	Natural (11)	Excess (12)
1	316.0	266.0	266.0	50.0	266.0	0.0	100.00	26.60	5.00	100.00	26.60	0.00
6	109.0	96.0	96.0	13.0	96.0	0.0	68.40	6.57	0.89	73.40	7.05	0.00
11	85.0	39.0	39.0	46.0	39.0	0.0	60.94	2.38	2.80	66.35	2.59	0.00
16	112.0	42.0	42.0	70.0	42.0	0.0	55.76	2.34	3.90	63.77	2.68	0.00
21	85.0	39.0	39.0	46.0	39.0	0.0	49.52	1.93	2.28	61.09	2.38	0.00
26	81.0	38.0	38.0	43.0	38.0	0.0	45.31	1.72	1.95	58.71	2.23	0.00
31	75.0	44.0	44.0	31.0	44.0	0.0	41.64	1.83	1.29	56.47	2.48	0.00
36	93.0	65.0	65.0	28.0	65.0	0.0	38.52	2.50	1.08	53.99	3.51	0.00
41	100.0	81.0	81.0	19.0	81.0	0.0	34.93	2.83	0.66	50.48	4.09	0.00
46	90.0	114.0	90.0	0.0	90.0	24.0	31.44	2.83	0.00	46.39	4.18	1.11
51	112.0	144.0	112.0	0.0	112.0	32.0	28.61	3.20	0.00	41.10	4.60	1.32
56	136.0	214.0	136.0	0.0	136.0	78.0	25.41	3.46	0.00	35.18	4.79	2.74
61	194.0	262.0	194.0	0.0	194.0	68.0	21.95	4.26	0.00	27.65	5.37	1.88
66	289.0	324.0	289.0	0.0	289.0	35.0	17.69	5.11	0.00	20.41	5.90	0.71
71	405.0	467.0	405.0	0.0	405.0	62.0	12.58	5.09	0.00	13.80	5.59	0.86
76	505.0	538.0	505.0	0.0	505.0	33.0	7.48	3.78	0.00	7.35	3.71	0.24

Notes on Columns: - (1) and (2) are q(x) for females and males from Tables 4.1.

- (3) and (4) divide female q(x) into a 'Natural' q(x) and an 'Excess' q(x) for females. 'Natural' q(x) is assumed to be the lower of the male and female values in (1) and (2). 'Excess' is the amount by which the female q(x) exceeds the male q(x).

- (5) and (6) divide male q(x) into a 'Natural' q(x) and an 'Excess' q(x) for males, following the procedures in columns (3) and (4).

- (7) is the number of females surviving to the beginning of each age interval, out of an original cohort of 100, implied by the q(x) values in (1). Calculated by multiplying value in previous row by survivorship probability implied by (1).

- (8) and (9) is the number of females in each age interval dying of 'natural' or 'excess' mortality. Calculated by multiplying number of females alive at beginning of interval in (7) by the probability of dying of 'natural' mortality in (3).

- (10), (11) and (12) repeat (7) (8) and (9) for males. Thus the percentage of female deaths which are excess is given by summing column (9). Similarly, the percentage of male deaths which are excess is given by summing column (12). Division is unnecessary since the original cohort size was 100. Columns (8), (9) and the last row of (7) sum to 100, as do (11), (12) and the last row of (10). These figures represent a conservative assumption. In most populations, for example the model populations in Coale and Demeny (1963), females actually have lower mortality than males at most ages. Applying such an assumption here would increase the percentage of female deaths considered excess, and decrease the proportion of male deaths considered excess.

The resulting age pattern of mortality sex differentials in Liaoning, with female excesses until late middle age and severe male excesses afterwards, is accordingly very different from the Coale–Demeny model life tables. Below age 46 *sui*, female death rates in rural Liaoning were higher than male death rates, even though in the model life table families, female death rates at a given level of mortality are always lower than male rates. Above age 45 *sui*, male mortality in Daoyi is not only higher than female mortality, but the male excess is larger than any of the Coale-Demeny model life table families would predict. The net result of this crossover pattern is that, whereas males at 2 *sui* could expect to live 7 years longer than females of the same age, females at 46 *sui* could expect to live 3 years longer than men of the same age.

Although discussions of excess female mortality in both historical and contemporary China usually focus on sex differentials during infancy and childhood, differences between recorded male and female mortality rates were often as large in adolescence and young adulthood (ages 11 to 45 *sui*) as in childhood, not just in relative terms, but sometimes even in absolute terms. According to table 4.3, which estimates the proportions of "natural" and "excess" deaths in a hypothetical cohort experiencing the mortality rates of Daoyi's registered males and females, most "excess" female deaths actually occurred in the later age groups: two-thirds, that is 14 percent of all registered female deaths, occurred during adolescence and early adulthood (11 to 45 *sui*), while one-third, that is 5 percent of all registered female deaths occurred during infancy and childhood (1 to 5 *sui*).[14]

Infanticide and neglect

The proportions of excess female mortality in infancy and childhood increase considerably, however, when we account for underregistration. Table 4.4 estimates the number of infants and children who died without ever being registered. We begin with an estimate of the

---

[14] In the absence of a universal standard as to what the natural relationship between male and female death rates is, the calculation in table 4.3 assumes that in each age group, the lower of the two sex-specific death rates is the "natural" level of mortality, and the portion by which the death rate of the other sex exceeds it is "excess" mortality. By the standards of the Coale and Demeny 1966/1983 model life tables, this is a conservative estimate of excess female mortality, since in the model life table families, at any given "level" of mortality, female age-specific rates are lower than male age-specific rates. Preston 1976, however, found that in high mortality populations, female death rates are often higher than male death rates, at least until young adulthood.

overall level of unregistered mortality, and then calculate how many of these missing children died before and after they were six months old. Our estimation procedure makes two plausible presumptions. First, that the overall pattern of mortality followed that of Coale and Demeny's Model North. Second, that unregistered children followed the same mortality pattern as registered children.[15]

Table 4.4 presents 6 estimates of male and female underregistration, neglect, and infanticide, one for each of the Model North levels from 4 to 9. We begin in column 3 by estimating the number of male births based on how many births were needed to produce the 1,404 males aged 16 *sui* in our population,[16] assuming that they spent the first fifteen years of life experiencing the death rates of the indicated North mortality level.[17] We then multiply the estimated male births by the natural sex ratio, 105 males to 100 females, to estimate the number of female births in column 4.

According to the estimates in columns five and six, roughly one-third of male births and two-thirds of female births were never registered;[18] presumably because they died before the mean age at registration, that is approximately 6 *sui*. In the model life tables, one-third to two-fifths of the children born in model levels 4, 5, and 6 died before reaching this age. The implication, summarized in columns 7 and 8, is that virtually all the missing males, and many missing females died a "natural" death.[19]

[15] We restrict these calculations to the eighteen intercensal periods, that is the fifty-four years, for which we have data before 1840 since the deterioration in completeness of recording after 1840, discussed in Appendix A, makes such calculations implausible.

[16] We exclude post-1774 immigrants and their descendants because their inclusion could distort the age structure. In our population, a total of 1,404 males reached 16 *sui* in the years 1772–1774, 1778–1780, 1784–1786, 1790–1804, 1808–1821, 1826–1831 and 1838–1840.

[17] The number surviving to age 15, that is l(15) in the life table, is not dependent on the mortality or age structure of the population above age 15. Thus our estimate is not dependent on the age structure of the population above age 15 or on the mortality of the population above age 15.

[18] To estimate the proportion of births which were unregistered, that is columns five and six, we subtract the 1,845 registered male births and 930 registered female births during the years under observation from the number of estimated births, and divide by the number of estimated births.

[19] We use q(x)'s and m(x) from the model life tables to estimate the proportion of children born who die "normally" before reaching the mean age at registration. The mean age of male registration is 5.7 *sui*, or 4.2 Western years, which we round to 4. To calculate the proportion of males dying by age four, we use q(0) directly from the regional model life table then calculate a $_3q_1$ from the m(1) using Grenville's method described in Shryock *et al.* (1971, 444). The mean age of female registration was 6 *sui*, or 4.5 Western years, which we round to 5, in order to use the l(5) (proportion of births still alive at age 5) directly from the model life table.

Table 4.4. *Estimated underregistration and female infanticide*

Model North life table	1(15)	Estimated Births		Estimated percent unregistered		Normal Deaths before mean age at registration		Estimated % girls born dying of neglect before registration	Estimated % girls born dying of infanticide
		Male	Female	Male	Female	Male	Female		
(1)	(2)	(3)	(4)	(5)	(6)	(7)	(8)	(9)	(10)
4	47,123	2,979	2,837	38.1	68.8	41.7	41.4	-	27.4
5	50,711	2,769	2,637	33.4	66.4	38.5	38.2	3.2	25.0
6	54,158	2,592	2,468	28.8	63.6	35.5	35.2	6.2	22.2
7	57,473	2,442	2,325	24.4	61.8	32.6	32.4	9.0	20.4
8	60,662	2,314	2,203	20.3	59.7	29.9	29.7	11.7	18.3
9	63,734	2,203	2,098	16.3	57.8	27.4	27.2	14.2	16.4

1. Regional model life tables for this calculation were selected based on the mortality rates of relevant age groups rather than life expectancies. Rates for males in the first four age groups, that is, in the first twenty years of life, ranged from Model North 4 to Model North 6. The higher levels (7 though 9) are included because they correspond to the mortality rates for adult males.

2. 1(15) is the number of males surviving to age 15-Western years out of an original birth cohort of 100000 who experienced the indicated mortality level. 1(15) is not dependent on the mortality or age structure of the population above age 15.

3. We estimate the number of births in the period under observation by calculating how many male births would have to occur to produce the observed number of 16 *sui* males in our population, assuming the males born had to spend the first fifteen years of life in the indicated mortality level. In our population, a total of 1404 males reached 16 *sui* in the years 1772-1774, 1778-1780, 1784-1786, 1789-1804, 1808-1822, 1826-1831, and 1835-1840 (Post-1774 immigrants and their descendants are excluded because their inclusion could distort the age structure). Thus to estimate the number of male births that had to occur to produce the 1404 males at 16 *sui*, we divide 1404 by 1(15) from the indicated model life table and multiply to 100,000. Thus our estimate is not dependent on the age structure of the population above age fifteen or on the mortality of the population above age fifteen.

Table 4.4. (*footnotes cont.*)

4. To estimate the number of female births, we multiply the estimated male births by the natural sex ratio at birth, 100/105.

5. To estimate the number of unregistered male births we subtract the number of male births registered in the above listed years from the number of predicted male births. To arrive at a percentage, we divide the result by the number of estimated births. There were 1845 registered male births in the years listed in (3) where the parents were neither immigrants nor the descendants of immigrants.

6. There were 930 female births registered.

7. and 8. We use $q(x)$'s and $m(x)$'s from the model life tables to estimate the proportion of children born who die "normally" before reaching the mean age at registration. To calculate the proportion of males dying by four Western years of age (mean age of registration of males is 5.7 *sui*, or 4.2 Western years, which we round to four) we use $_1q_0$ directly from the regional model life table then calculate a $_3q_1$ from the $_4m_1$, by using Grenville's method described on p. 444 of Shryock and Siegel. As for females, their mean age at registration was 6.0 *sui* (4.5 Western years) which we round to 5 Western years in order to use the 1(5) (proportion of births still alive at age five) directly from the model life table.

9. To estimate the percentage of girls dying before registration as a result of neglect, we compute the difference between the number of deaths predicted by the mortality levels selected based on male data (4 though 9) and the number predicted by the mortality level selected based on female data (4). We based this calculation on an assumption that the difference in observed mortality levels between the two sexes is produced by differential neglect, and that the mortality levels indicated for males in the population are the "natural" levels in the population. Note that this estimate is only for deaths before mean age at registration.

10. We assume that the remaining unregistered girls died in the first year of life, producing an extremely high mortality rate among girls at age one *sui* (zero Western years) that was not reflected in our data because almost no girls were registered at one *sui*. We assume that the deaths were due to infanticide or neglect that was indisguishable from infanticide.

"Excess" female child mortality (ages 2 to 5 *sui*) accounted for some of the remaining missing girls. Assuming that the mortality rates of never-registered children (2 to 5 *sui*) were the same as those of registered children, and that only the portion of the recorded female death rate that exceeded recorded male rates could be attributed to differential treatment, the estimates in column nine of table 4.4 suggest that 5 to 10 percent of the females born in Daoyi died of "excess" mortality at ages 2 to 5 *sui*, before they could be registered.[20] It is impossible to say whether such "excess" mortality reflected deliberate discrimination against girls with respect to the allocation of resources, or the unintended effects of other gender differentials in treatment. Studies of contemporary South Asia have attributed excess female mortality in childhood there to discrimination against daughters in the allocation of nutrition and health care.[21] While such factors may also have been involved in explaining results from Daoyi, it may also be the case that local conditions, for example, climate, raised the importance of other factors, for example, gender differentials in the allocation of clothing, or the proportion of time spent indoors.

If the mortality of registered and unregistered children was indeed the same, the remainder of the missing females must have died at age one *sui*, most likely as the victims of infanticide. According to column ten, these deaths accounted for between one-fifth and one-quarter of all girls born.[22] Direct evidence on infant mortality elsewhere in China at this time suggest that most of these deaths, if not all of them, were probably due to infanticide.[23] Calculations based on precise dates

[20] We make the assumption that higher female mortality in childhood reflects gender differentials in the treatment of children because accumulated evidence on the biological and genetic origins of mortality sex differentials in childhood suggests that when environmental factors are held equal, female children should if anything have a slight advantage with respect to most of the major causes of death (Waldron 1983, 1986, 1987).

[21] See, for example, Basu 1989, Bhatia 1983, Chen *et al.* 1981; D'Souza and Chen 1980; and Das Gupta 1987. Most of these studies claim roles for differentials in the allocation of both food and health care. Basu, however, argues that the role of differences in food allocation in explaining childhood mortality sex differences has been overstated, and that other gender differences in the treatment of children, in particular parents' greater willingness to seek modern medical care for boys, are more important. Das Gupta points out that discrimination was more severe for girls with older siblings.

[22] In our data, we have almost no one registered before two *sui* and cannot, therefore, directly calculate the level of infant mortality. Moreover, in Daoyi we do not have precise dates of death, so that even if we had individuals registered before two *sui*, we could not distinguish between differentials in neonatal mortality, presumably attributable to infanticide, and postneonatal mortality, presumably attributable to neglect.

of birth and death recorded in the genealogy of the Qing imperial lineage reveal mortality sex differentials in the first few weeks of life, attributable to infanticide, that accounted for all of the lineage's excess female infant mortality (Lee, Wang, and Campbell 1994).[24]

Thus infanticide in the first year of life and "excess" mortality at later ages together accounted for nearly one-third of all female deaths in rural Liaoning, and even 3 to 4 percent of male deaths.[25] Since infanticide alone accounted for more than one-half of "excess" female deaths, the majority of "excess" female deaths were likely to have been the direct result of deliberate discrimination. Liaoning peasants may not, of course, have thought of such behavior as murder. Traditionally, the Chinese did not consider children during the first year of life as fully "human" (Furth 1987; Hsiung 1995b). "Life" rather began some time after two *sui*, that is from around the sixth month of life onwards.[26] Liaoning peasants therefore probably conceptualized infanticide as a form of "post-natal abortion."[27]

---

[23] Indeed, where precise dates of death (year, month, and day, as opposed to just year and month) are available for the 33,000 children born between 1700 and 1840 to parents in the imperial lineage (15,249 sons, but only 5,949 daughters), death rates are *ten* times higher for females (72 per 1,000) than for males (7.5 per 1,000) during the first day of life, four times as high for females than for males during the first week of life, and twice as high for females than for males during the first month of life, a clear indication of infanticide. By the third month of life, death rates in the imperial lineage are higher for males than females (Lee, Wang, and Campbell 1994).

[24] Our estimates suggest that overall, as many as one-tenth of the females born into the lineage died as the result of infanticide.

[25] The figures for females assume that one-fifth of all female births were victims of infanticide and were never registered, two-thirds of the remaining girls survived to be registered, and one-fifth of these surviving girls were victims of excess mortality. The two-thirds figure comes from assuming that the proportion of "normal" deaths was somewhere between the figures for Model North levels 6 and 7 in table 4.4. The figure for males comes from assuming that one-third of males died before being registered, and that 9 percent of those who were registered (summing column 12 in table 4.3) died of "excess" male mortality.

[26] The *Collection of Important Documents of the Tang (618–907)* records in an imperial edict in 623 that "People when they are first born are just young animals (*huang*). At four *sui* they become minors *xiao*. At sixteen *sui* they become youths *zhong*. At twenty-one *sui* they become adults *ding*. At sixty *sui* they become old *lao*" (*Tang huiyao* 85.1555). According to a famous passage from the *Rites of Zhou*, a compendium of statements on early political institutions and policies probably completed in the second century BC, "People should be registered after they have grown their teeth." In a well-known commentary on this passage Qiu Jun, a fifteenth-century statesman, explained: "The human body is not fully developed until teeth are grown. Boys grow their first set of teeth in the eighth month and their second set in their eighth year. Girls grow their first set of teeth in their seventh month and their second set in their seventh year. They should then all be recorded in the population register" (*Daxue yanyi bu* 13.14). We would like to thank Liu Ts'ui-jung for bringing the passage from the *Tang huiyao* to our attention.

Adolescent and adult mortality

Nevertheless, a sizable proportion of "excess" female deaths in table 4.3 occurred at later ages when deliberate neglect was unlikely to have been a contributing factor. It is impossible from available data to identify specific reasons either for the excess mortality of females during adolescence and young adulthood, or for the excess mortality of males in later adulthood. Mortality patterns are affected by any number of factors, including genetic makeup, biological predisposition, housing conditions, work patterns, living standards, social behavior, previous disease experience, and personal hygiene. Gender differences in any of these factors have the potential therefore to create mortality sex differentials. Without more precise ethnographic data about Daoyi and surrounding communities, it is impossible to tell which factors were the most important. We can, however, advance tentative explanations by analogy to findings from historical European populations, as well as historical and contemporary Chinese populations.

Excess female mortality in adolescence and young adulthood was a common phenomenon in historical European populations, and high mortality populations in general. In a review of mortality sex differences in historical Europe, Henry (1989) noted that the pattern of sex imbalances in age-specific mortality rates was virtually universal throughout Western Europe during the nineteenth century. As in Daoyi, girls between the ages of 5 and 14, in some cases 19, had higher mortality than boys of the same age. Women between the ages of 25 and 44 had higher mortality than men of the same age.[28] More generally, through an international comparison of mortality patterns, Preston 1976 has shown that where mortality is high, female death

---

[27] Such attitudes were commonplace elsewhere in China and in East Asia in general. See the essays in Lee and Saito forthcoming on infanticide in Qing China and Tokugawa Japan and on abortion in contemporary Asia.

[28] In relative terms, female excesses in Daoyi were more pronounced than in Europe, but in absolute terms, they were similar. Whereas table 4.2 indicates that, in Daoyi, female death rates in the relevant age groups were often one-and-a-half times those of males, and sometimes even twice those of males, in the European populations presented in table 1 of Henry 1989, female rates were usually higher than male rates by only one-tenth, or even less. Absolute differentials in Daoyi and Europe are more comparable, however, and thus the apparent severity of relative differentials in Daoyi may simply be a byproduct of the low mortality of Daoyi males in the relevant age groups. In general, there is no consensus as to whether examining relative or absolute differentials is more useful—there are shortcomings associated with each technique. In one of the most influential analyses of mortality sex differentials, Preston 1976 applied a technique based on orthogonal regression to analyze variations in mortality sex differentials, but that technique cannot be made use of here since it is useful primarily for comparisons across populations.

rates in youth and young adulthood are usually higher than those of males.[29]

Analyses of historical mortality data have revealed the cause of death structure underlying this pattern. Relying primarily on French and Swedish data, Henry attributed the excess mortality of females between the ages of 5 and 19, sometimes even 24, to infectious diseases, especially tuberculosis, and the excess mortality of females between the ages of 24 and 39, sometimes even 44, to maternal mortality (Henry 1989, 106–109).[30] In an international comparison of cause of death structures and their associations with mortality sex differentials, Preston (1976) found that in high mortality populations, death rates from infectious diseases, especially tuberculosis, were higher for females than for males in youth and adolescence. Female mortality excesses in young adulthood, meanwhile, were attributable almost entirely to maternal mortality.[31]

Explanations of these cause-of-death patterns focus on the low value placed upon women by households in traditional rural populations.[32] The low valuation of women stemmed from the lack of economic opportunities for females in a pre-modern agrarian economy, and gave rise to cultural norms that favored discrimination against them in the allocation of sustenance. Low levels of sustenance

[29] Heligman 1983 showed that, at least until recently, female mortality excesses were also common in South Asian populations, in some cases across an even wider range of age groups.

[30] Maternal mortality here refers to adult female deaths that can in some way be ascribed directly to the process of childbearing, including deaths resulting from delivery complications, or infection during delivery.

[31] Maternal mortality is not universally accepted as an explanation for excess female mortality in young adulthood (Schofield 1986). Some investigations have suggested roles for other causes of death. For example, in an examination of Sri Lankan data from 1962–1964, when female death rates in that country were for the most part still higher than male rates, Arriaga and Way 1988 concluded that, causes of death associated with nutritional status were more important in explaining sex differentials than deaths associated with the childbearing process.

[32] Historical studies that claim to have found support for such hypotheses include Ginsburg and Swedlund 1986, Humphries 1991, and Kennedy 1973. Shorter 1982 presents an iconoclastic view that the physical and psychological burdens associated with women's roles in historical societies were directly responsible for patterns of excess female mortality, but as Henry 1989 has noted, there are some serious problems with his evidence. As for contemporary populations, Preston 1976, an international comparative study of sex differentials in contemporary populations using cause-of-death data, found in a regression analysis that indices of nutrition and education (thought to be a proxy for discrimination against women) and socio-economic development accounted for a large portion of the variation between countries in the mortality sex differential. Indices of social and psychological modernization had less explanatory power. See also Nathanson 1984 for a literature review on mortality sex differentials that focuses on contemporary populations.

compared with men are supposed to have increased women's mortality by reducing their resistance to infection.[33] Where fertility was high, the nutritional demands of pregnancy, and the dangers associated with giving birth, contributed to raising women's mortality risks even higher.[34] Modern ethnographic evidence for rural northeast China confirms that such explanations are relevant for Daoyi. According to Shirokogoroff, women were discriminated against when household resources were being allocated.[35]

Conversely when women were engaged in a highly-valued activity, such as taking care of newborn sons, their death rates were substantially lower.[36] In column 3 of table 4.5, coefficients estimated from a logistic regression of adult mortality on age, sex, marital status, and recent fertility experience show that for each son a woman gave birth to in the time between the previous and current registers, her odds of dying in the next three years were reduced by one-third.[37] Results from a model restricted to the years before the registration of female births deteriorated rule out a selection effect in which the childbearing process weeded out unhealthy women: daughters born between the previous register and the current register do not influence

---

[33] Nutritional status can affect mortality from some, but by no means all, infectious diseases (Lunn 1991). Mortality from tuberculosis, a major killer in the nineteenth and earlier twentieth century, is affected by nutritional status (Grigg 1958).

[34] Recent medical evidence, cited in Lunn 1991 and Schofield and Reher 1991, suggests that pregnancy may compromise immune function by suppressing corticosteroid production.

[35] As Johansson 1991 points out, gender differences in exposure to disease also played an important role in explaining sex differences in mortality in other historical populations. Thus men and women may have differed radically in terms of the disease environments they faced in their daily routines. Spending more time inside an unclean and poorly-ventilated household may not only have put young women at higher risk of being infected by insect-borne diseases such as typhus, but also at higher risk of contracting airborne diseases such as tuberculosis. However, without more detailed ethnographic evidence on gender roles in late imperial Chinese peasant society, it is difficult to do much more than speculate about a role for sex differences in exposure.

[36] The Chinese actually have a saying to express the fact that a woman's value within the household depends on whether or not she has produced a son: *mu yizi gui*.

[37] See Appendix B for an explanation of logistic regression. Another intriguing finding in table 4.5, that male mortality was affected much more by the death of a spouse than female mortality, resembles results from an international comparison of contemporary mortality differentials according to marital status (Hu and Goldman 1990). In almost every one of the sixteen developed countries covered by that study, the mortality risk associated with being widowed (relative to being married) was higher for males than for females. Relative differentials according to widowhood status were sharpest in Taiwan, where widowers had almost three times the mortality rates of married men, and widows had twice the mortality rates of married women.

Fate and fortune in rural China

Table 4.5. *Estimated coefficients (β) from logistic regressions of adult (21-60 sui) odds of dying in the next three years on age, sex, marital status, and recent fertility behavior*

	(1)		1792-1867 (2)		(3)		1792-1840 (4)	
	β	S.E.	β	S.E.	β	S.E.	β	S.E.
Male Age (Reference Category: Males Aged 21-25)								
26-30	-0.11	0.19	-0.09	0.19	-0.09	0.19	-0.23	0.23
31-35	0.18	0.18	0.20	0.18	0.21	0.18	-0.02	0.22
36-40	0.50	0.16	0.52	0.17	0.52	0.17	0.24	0.21
41-45	0.79	0.16	0.81	0.16	0.81	0.16	0.74	0.20
46-50	1.10	0.16	1.12	0.16	1.11	0.16	0.82	0.20
51-55	1.37	0.16	1.37	0.16	1.36	0.16	1.16	0.20
56-60	1.95	0.15	1.94	0.15	1.93	0.15	1.63	0.20
Female Age (Reference Category: Males in Same Age Group)								
21-25	0.49	0.19	0.55	0.20	0.60	0.21	0.45	0.26
26-30	0.74	0.18	0.79	0.18	0.85	0.18	0.66	0.24
31-35	0.40	0.17	0.45	0.17	0.51	0.17	0.40	0.23
36-40	0.42	0.14	0.47	0.15	0.52	0.15	0.53	0.20
41-45	0.17	0.14	0.22	0.14	0.25	0.15	-0.09	0.19
46-50	-0.35	0.15	-0.30	0.16	-0.28	0.16	-0.23	0.20
51-55	-0.18	0.14	-0.12	0.15	-0.11	0.15	-0.30	0.20
56-60	-0.62	0.13	-0.55	0.14	-0.55	0.14	-0.57	0.19
Female Marital Status (Reference Category: Currently Married Females)								
Never Married			0.10	0.28	0.04	0.28	-0.03	0.35
Widowed			0.06	0.12	0.04	0.12	-0.02	0.15
Male Marital Status (Reference Category: Currently Married Males)								
Never Married			0.15	0.10	0.14	0.10	0.02	0.14
Widowed			0.27	0.10	0.26	0.10	0.23	0.14
Mothers' Births Since Previous Register								
Male					-0.29	0.11	-0.37	0.15
Female							0.02	0.18
Fathers' Births Since Previous Register								
Male					-0.07	0.11	-0.20	0.14
Female							-0.30	0.22
Constant	-3.68		-3.76		-3.74		-3.49	
- 2 * Log Likelihood	11493		11485		11476		6650	
Degrees of Freedom	28592		28588		28586		17252	

1. All ages are in *sui*. Models 1, 2, and 3 (1792-1867) include all registers where the immediately following register is also available: 1792, 1795, 1798, 1801, 1810, 1813, 1816, 1819, 1828, 1837, 1840, 1843, 1855, 1858, 1864. Model 4 (1792-1840) excludes 1840 and following registers because of deterioration in the completeness of female registration.

2. To obtain percent change in odds of dying associated with a unit change in one of the independent variables, exponentiate the estimated coefficient, subtract one, and multiply by 100.

mother's subsequent mortality.[38] Caring for a young son must either have allowed wives to lay claim to a larger share of household resources, and/or exempted them from household duties that exposed them to infection.

Whereas Daoyi's pattern of female excesses was observed in many if not most high mortality populations, and was likely to have been rooted in social pathologies common to most rural societies, Daoyi's pattern of male excesses at later ages was a largely Chinese phenomenon. Goldman (1980) has observed that in Hong Kong, Singapore, and Korea during the middle of this century, adult male mortality rose more quickly with age than in any of the Coale and Demeny model life table families, creating severe excesses in male mortality in late middle age, a pattern she named "Far East." Campbell (1995) has shown that this "Far East" pattern was not only apparent among males in Daoyi, but also in a variety of other late imperial Chinese populations, including lineage populations from Anhui, Beijing, and Jiangnan, as well as in at least one Republican Chinese population, that of Beijing's Inner Left District in the late 1920s.[39]

While the precise reasons for the Far Eastern pattern remain unclear,[40] given Daoyi's location and climate, tuberculosis may be a plausible explanation for the excess mortality of older males. The extended periods that the peasants of Daoyi spent inside their tightly-sealed, poorly-ventilated homes during the winter would have facilitated the transmission of tuberculosis.[41] Poor living standards would have

---

[38] The absence of an association between male births and father's subsequent mortality rules out the possibility that this pattern reflects a lower likelihood of a son being registered if his parent died within a few years of his birth.

[39] See Campbell 1995 for an in-depth analysis of the mortality pattern from 1640 to 1990 in Beijing. Among other things, Campbell compares the age-specific death rates for historical Chinese populations published in Liu 1985, Telford 1990 and Lee, Campbell and Wang 1993 with a variety of model life table families and found that, for males, the best fit was consistently with the UN Far East family.

[40] Some tentative explanations have been advanced. Goldman 1980 suggests that tuberculosis may explain at least some of the pattern of excess male mortality, since male death rates from respiratory tuberculosis in middle age in Hong Kong and Singapore during the 1950s and 1960s were three times those of females, and these differentials actually widened at later ages. As Goldman notes, however, male death rates in a variety of major cause groups, including cardiovascular, would have to be set equal to female rates before male excesses at later ages disappeared. Elo and Preston 1992, meanwhile, hypothesize that the "Far Eastern" pattern of mortality may be related to the high prevalence of hepatitis B in many ethnic Chinese populations.

[41] Mason and Smith 1990 provide a succinct review of the accumulated evidence on tuberculosis morbidity and mortality. The probability of being infected by tuberculosis is affected not only by one's chances of coming into contact with an infectious case, but also by the infectiousness of the case, and the duration of exposure to the case. After infection, the progress of the disease is conditioned by the

contributed to the progress of the disease once infection had occurred. Moreover, morbidity data in the earlier Daoyi registers, summarized in table 4.6, confirm that a chronic respiratory disease that the Chinese called *laozheng*, most likely tuberculosis, was highly prevalent among males.[42] Almost 9 percent of the adult male population and more than 25 percent of the disabled male population were specifically annotated as suffering from *laozheng*, presumably in its highly visible, more advanced stages.

Age and gender patterns of crisis mortality

The age and gender patterns of mortality crises were quite different in Daoyi from peasant populations elsewhere. Female children, especially female infants, bore the brunt of any mortality spike. Most of these deaths, however, were unregistered and are not therefore included in any direct estimation of age-specific death rates by sex. As a result, the correlations between vital rates and average annual grain prices in table 3.6 were stronger with birth rates than death rates and with female birth rates, rather than male birth rates. When prices were high, female birth rates substantially declined, driven in part by increased female infanticide.

Nevertheless, an examination of registered deaths reveals that other age groups suffered as well. Just as mortality was not constant with respect to age, it was far from constant over time. We turn in section IV to the temporal patterns of registered mortality during the century under observation. Figures 4.1 and 4.2 summarize life expectancy by age for both sexes for the sixteen intercensal periods for which we have consecutive registers. The differences across time are considerable. During the period from 1817 to 1819, life expectancy

---

new host's ability to resist the bacilli. Among the factors that can weaken resistance are malnutrition, overwork, and pregnancy.

42 It is possible, of course, that other chronic respiratory diseases were highly prevalent. Recent findings from China suggest that the domestic environment in which the northeast Chinese peasants lived was highly conducive to the development of chronic respiratory diseases, and even lung cancer. In studies carried out in Shenyang, sleeping on a coal-heated *kang* has been identified as a risk factor for lung cancer (Wu-Williams *et al.* 1990; Xu *et al.* 1989). Other studies carried out in China have identified time spent cooking with low-quality coal, and the use of low-quality coal as a fuel for domestic heating as risk factors for chronic respiratory disease (Chen *et al.* 1990; Gold 1992; Xu and Wang 1993), lung cancer (He *et al.* 1991; Mumford *et al.* 1987), and even stroke (Zhang *et al.* 1988). See Chen *et al.* 1990, 133 and Gold 1992 for recent reviews of findings on the health effects of domestic pollution in developing countries.

Table 4.6. *Major illnesses of adult males in Daoyi 1774-1786*

Illnesses	1774 N	1774 %	1780 N	1780 %	1786 N	1786 %
Blindness	27	4.7	37	3.5	39	4.5
Deaf	1	0.2	5	0.5	5	0.6
Dumb	1	0.2	1	0.1	2	0.2
Leg Injury	16	2.8	24	2.3	35	4.1
Arm Injury	13	2.3	22	2.1	32	3.7
Tuberculosis	47	8.1	82	7.9	79	9.2
Mental Illness	13	2.3	24	2.3	38	4.4
Other Illness	11	1.9	34	3.3	58	6.8
Other Severe Illness	1	0.2	7	0.7	22	2.6
Total Illness	130	22.5	236	22.6	310	36.0
Total Adult Males	577		1044		857	

N = Number of adult males reporting specified illness.
% = Percentage of adult males reporting specified illness.

Table 4.7. *Correlation of age-specific death rates and total crude death rates*

Age Group		Females		Males
1–5	xxx	0.61*	xxx	-
6–10		-		0.62*
11–15		-		-
16–20		-		0.72**
21–25		-		-
26–30		-		-
31–35		-		-
36–40		-		0.74
41–45		-		-
46–50		-		0.65*
51–55		0.59*		0.89*
56–60		-		0.83*
61–65		-		0.67*
66–70		-		0.65*
71–75		-		0.58*
75 and up		0.71*		0.57*

Correlations with a significance of 0.01 are indicated by *. Correlations with a significance of 0.001 are indicated by **. All correlations not significant at the 0.01 level have been omitted.

All ages in *sui*. By *sui* the Chinese meant to indicate the number of calendar years during which a person had lived. People are accordingly one *sui* at the next New Year. *Sui* are, therefore, on average one and a half years higher than Western years of age.

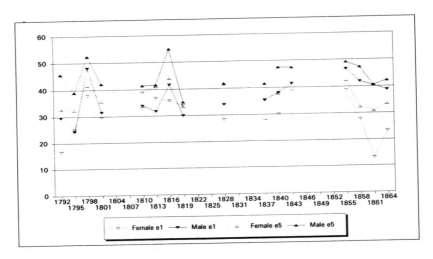

Figure 4.1. *Male and female life expectancies at ages 1 and 5 sui,*
by intercensal period

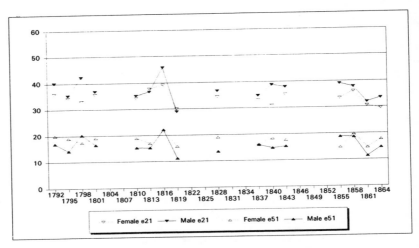

Figure 4.2. *Male and female life expectancies at ages 21 and 51 sui,*
by intercensal period

Table 4.8. *Life expectancy during good periods versus bad periods*†

Age	Female				Male			
	Good period e_x	Bad period e_x	Difference	Standard deviation	Good period e_x	Bad period e_x	Difference	Standard deviation
1	35.0	25.5	9.5	2.2	45.0	31.4	13.6	0.2
6	40.6	34.0	6.6	1.5	50.5	39.0	11.5	1.0
11	40.0	32.0	8.0	1.3	49.0	39.0	10.0	0.9
16	39.0	31.1	7.9	1.1	45.0	36.0	9.0	0.8
21	37.0	31.0	6.0	0.9	41.0	33.0	8.0	0.8
26	35.0	28.1	6.9	0.9	37.4	29.1	8.3	0.7
31	32.2	26.0	6.2	0.8	34.0	26.0	8.0	0.7
36	29.0	23.2	5.8	0.8	29.5	22.0	7.5	0.7
41	25.4	21.0	4.4	0.7	26.0	19.0	7.0	0.6
46	23.0	19.0	4.0	0.7	23.0	15.3	7.7	0.6
51	19.4	16.1	3.3	0.6	20.0	12.4	7.6	0.6
56	16.0	13.4	2.6	0.6	16.2	10.4	5.8	0.5
61	13.0	11.0	2.0	0.5	13.1	9.0	4.1	0.5
66	10.0	8.3	1.7	0.4	10.4	7.0	3.4	0.4
71	7.1	6.0	1.0	0.4	7.3	5.0	2.3	0.4
75	4.0	3.5	0.6	0.2	4.2	3.3	0.9	0.2

†Male bad periods:1789-01, 1816-19, 1843-46, 1855-58. Male good periods: 1795-98, 1861-64, 1864-67. Female bad periods: 1819-22, 1828-31, 1861-64, 1864-67. Female good periods: 1816-19, 1843-46, 1855-58.

All ages in *sui*. By *sui* the Chinese meant to indicate the number of calendar years during which a person had lived. People are accordingly one *sui* at birth and two *sui* at the next New Year. *Sui* are, therefore, on average one and a half years higher than Western years of age.

at age five (e_5) was in the low forties and fifties. During the period immediately following, from 1820 to 1822, e_5 was in the middle thirties, the result apparently of unusually poor harvests in 1822.[43]

Ironically, the other Daoyi subgroup most affected by crisis occupied the opposite end of the social spectrum from infant females: elderly males. As Daoyi's male mortality excesses at later ages would suggest, being a patriarch in a patriarchal society was a mixed blessing: not only did men lose their mortality advantage as they aged, they seem to have borne the brunt of any mortality crises.[44] The difference between elderly males and infant females, of course, is that whereas the deaths of elderly males were unplanned, those of infant females were not.

Mortality fluctuations appear to have been driven largely by changes in the mortality of older men. Table 4.7 correlates age-specific death rates by sex to total death rates. The correlations are particularly strong for males ages 46 *sui* and older. They were considerably less strong for females with the exception of the very young and the very old, below 5 *sui* and above 76 *sui*. There were virtually no other significant correlations between total death rates and female age-specific death rates. The high female mortality between 11 and 30 *sui* that we identified in tables 4.3, in other words, was independent of short-term variations in overall mortality. The high male mortality above 46 *sui* that we also identified in table 4.3, however, was a product of short-term variations.

43 1822 was apparently the only bad harvest year during the period under consideration. According to the local gazetteer, "in 1822 there was inadequate spring rain. Moreover, violent winds during the fourth and fifth months devastated the fields. The harvests were extremely poor—approximately half the normal yield" (*Fengtian TZ*, 1934/1982, 36.723). The result was a considerable decline in life expectancy at six months of age to 30 for females (with a standard deviation of 2.8) and 32 for males (with a standard deviation of 1.9).

44 The finding that male death rates, especially at later ages, rose the most when mortality increased is actually quite common. In an analysis of excess mortality in contemporary China during the Great Leap Forward famine 1958-19-61, Ashton *et al.* found that the death rates of males above age 40 increased the most during the crisis (1984, 617-9). Similarly, Dyson (1991) found a pattern of increased vulnerability among older males in earlier South Asian famines, while others have found the same pattern in Europe. In Finland, although proportional increases in mortality during the Great Famine of 1866-1868 did not differ by sex in 1866 and 1867, they were much higher for males in the worst year, 1868 (Pitakenen and Mielke 1993). In Holland during the Hunger Winter of 1944–1945 and in Greece during World War II, food scarcity led to much larger increases in male mortality than in female mortality (Watkins and Menken 1985, 656). After a review of evidence on age and sex differentials in mortality crises, Watkins and Menken 1985 concluded, "In most situations where reasonable data are available, the sex and age differentials in excess mortality appear to favor women and young adults" (656).

Male life expectancy, in other words, fluctuated far more than female life expectancy. The contrast in mortality by age and sex between good and bad periods can tell us much about the differential gender pattern of mortality in Daoyi. In table 4.8 we contrast life expectancy by sex during the three best three-year periods with the three worst three-year periods.[45] In spite of the high standard deviations, male life expectancy varied far more than female life expectancy, especially at later ages. Older men were apparently more exposed to risk than older women, either as the price of the preferential treatment they had received at earlier ages, or as the result of their greater responsibilities in old age.

Conclusion

The results shown in this chapter, of course, are not generalizable for China as a whole.[46] In Daoyi, the banner population was tied to the land and had no recourse to emigration and emancipation. The population, as we saw in Chapter 2, was accordingly under far greater demographic pressure than most late imperial Chinese communities. Moreover, the range of possible responses to this pressure was tightly circumscribed.

Nevertheless, results from the analysis of this seemingly unusual village inform our understanding not only of the behavior of historical populations, but of contemporary Chinese ones as well. We have shown that historical European patterns of excess female mortality were present in late imperial China, most likely with the same root causes. We have also shown that the "Far Eastern" mortality pattern described in Goldman (1980) was present as early as the eighteenth century and as far away as the rural Liaoning frontier.

Most important, by adding an indirect estimate of female infanticide for one of the lowest social strata, hereditary state peasants, to the

[45] We defined a good year as a year where the life expectancy at age five is more than one standard deviation about the average life expectancy at age five for that sex. Similarly, we defined a bad year as one where the life expectancy at age five was one standard deviation below the average life expectancy for that year. Good years for females were 1816–1819 and 1828–1831, while bad years were 1795–1798, 1861–1864, and 1864–1867. Good years for males were 1798–1801 and 1816–1819, while bad years were 1795–1798, 1819–1822, 1861–1864.

[46] In a population that might be expected to have been much more homogeneous than late imperial China's, that of historical England's, mortality differences between communities were often greater than differences between states, and between centuries (Wall 1981). As Clifford Geertz has said, there is no such thing as a "representative" community (Geertz 1959). We would like to thank John Shepherd for bringing this article to our attention.

precise calculations already made for one of the highest social strata, the imperial lineage itself, we have shown that female infanticide was commonplace at both ends of the late imperial social spectrum (Lee, Wang, and Campbell 1994). The combination of these findings suggests that there is no longer any reason to think that infanticide was restricted to a particular segment of society, or only practiced during times of economic stress.[47] Our study, here and elsewhere, belies such assertions. In rural Liaoning, peasants regarded infanticide as a routine form of post-natal abortion by which they could choose the number and sex of their children in response to a variety of short-term and long-term circumstances.

The patterns of mortality and fertility in rural Liaoning were, therefore, the product of deliberate decision making. In Chapter 2, we already demonstrated that parents in Daoyi and surrounding communities practiced infanticide as a response to such economic conditions, as food prices. In Chapter 4, we will show that these parents also used infanticide and other techniques of fertility control regularly to achieve goals for family composition, and that the frequency with which they resorted to infanticide was affected by social organization, such as household structure and family composition.

In conclusion, mortality in the Liaoning demographic system was not always beyond human control. It was a parental choice exercised over one-tenth to one-quarter of all female births and even over some male births. In rural Liaoning, as in imperial Beijing, there were two types of positive check.

---

[47] Previously, a common misperception was that infanticide in China was a response to poverty and famine and limited to daughters Arthur Wolf and Susan Hanley, for example, claim that "although female infanticide was common in some parts of China in difficult times, there is no evidence that the Chinese ever tried to limit the number of sons. In Japan in sharp contrast, infanticide and abortion were commonplace not only as a response to natural and social catastrophes, but as a kind of family planning with long range objectives" (Wolf and Hanley 1985, 5).

5

Two types of preventive check: nuptiality and fertility[1]

Until recently it was widely accepted that fertility in late imperial China was neither constrained by nuptiality nor controlled by couples. On the one hand, the availability of resources from the extended family meant that young people could marry without regard to current economic conditions. Thus in contrast with Europe, fertility was not constrained by changes in the proportion married. On the other hand, under normal conditions, Chinese couples never attempted to control the number of their children, especially their sons, and practiced infanticide only in response to famine and extreme poverty. There have accordingly been very few detailed analyses of the specific circumstances under which Chinese parents may have deliberately controlled their fertility.[2] As a result, a number of misperceptions have arisen regarding reproductive behavior in China before this century.

This chapter provides yet another set of evidence showing that the historical reality was much more complex than commonly assumed. Specifically we demonstrate that just as there were two types of

[1] We composed this chapter initially with Guofu Tan during the fall of 1987 for the JCCS Conference on Chinese History in Economic Perspective, but revised it substantially during winter 1989, summer 1990, and spring 1994 for seminars at the Academia Sinica, Keio University, the Institut national d'etudes démographiques, Indiana University, the University of California at Los Angeles, the University of Michigan, and the University of Virginia, as well as for two panels of the Association of Asian Studies and the Western branch of the Association of Asian Studies organized by William Lavely and Charlotte Furth respectively. We would like to thank George Alter, Francesca Bray, Susan Naquin, Jean-Laurent Rosenthal, and Susan Watkins in particular for their comments and assistance. See Lee, Campbell, and Tan 1988, 1989, and 1992 for some of these earlier drafts.
[2] The exceptions, in addition to the earlier renditions on which this chapter is based, are Lee, Wang, and Campbell 1994; and Wang, Lee, and Campbell 1995, which analyze the Qing imperial lineage.

positive check, there were also two types of preventive check, both before and after marriage. In section I, we analyze nuptiality to establish that, in Liaoning, opportunities for males to marry and father children were constrained by a shortage of single women, the result of both female infanticide and customary strictures against widow remarriage. In section II, we show that, within marriage, fertility was low by historical European standards, and that low rates were as much the result of restraint within marriage as they were of female infanticide and neglect. Finally, in section III, we also demonstrate that Liaoning peasants controlled their fertility in response to such social conditions as household structure, household position, and social status. We conclude that in rural Liaoning infanticide was only one of several methods by which peasants determined the number, timing, and circumstances of their children according to both economic and social conditions.

Nuptiality

In Liaoning, as in Europe, variations in the timing and probability of marriage were a key component of the preventive check, but the mechanisms that linked population pressure to marriage differed. In Western Europe, where young men and women delayed marriage until they had the means to support a family, the lower real incomes and reduced economic opportunities that accompanied excess population had a direct, negative effect on the marriage rate.[3] The marriages that were delayed or foregone reduced the birth rate, helping to bring population into line with resources. In Liaoning, a deterioration in economic conditions may have lowered marriage rates, not only in the short term by making it more difficult for households to come up with the brideprice needed to obtain wives for their sons, but in the long term as well, by reducing the future supply of marriageable women. In Chapter 3, we showed that female infanticide increased in prevalence when prices were high. Such increases would eventually result in a shortage of potential brides, imposing an absolute limit on the proportion of men who could marry.[4]

---

[3] See Wrigley and Schofield 1981 for evidence on England, Weir 1984 for an analysis of France.

[4] Based on his analysis of lineage genealogies from Tongcheng, Anhui, Telford 1992 makes a similar argument for the importance of constraints on the proportion of men ever marrying in that area during the late Ming and early Qing.

Table 5.1. *Marital status of the population by age and sex, 1774-1873*

Age (*sui*)	Men					Women				
	Never married %	Married %	Widowed %	Re-married %	N	Never married %	Married (first wife) %	Married (later wife) %	Widowed %	N
16	87.2	12.6	0.1	0.0	728	92.0	7.7	0.3	0.0	313
17	82.1	17.5	0.3	0.1	865	63.7	35.6	0.7	0.0	416
18	75.5	24.0	0.3	0.2	893	44.6	53.9	1.5	0.0	527
19	67.6	31.6	0.7	0.1	759	34.0	64.0	1.7	0.2	520
20	60.4	38.3	1.2	0.1	932	23.5	72.9	3.4	0.2	612
21	56.2	42.1	1.1	0.7	856	18.3	78.2	3.3	0.2	611
22	49.1	48.5	1.2	1.2	748	12.7	82.1	4.9	0.3	592
23	43.1	54.0	1.9	1.0	829	9.6	84.1	5.7	0.6	654
24	42.0	53.8	1.8	2.4	838	7.1	87.5	4.9	0.6	678
25	33.9	62.4	1.8	1.8	711	5.8	86.3	7.0	0.9	672
26-30	29.0	64.7	3.6	2.7	3,833	2.5	89.0	6.7	1.9	3,175
31-35	20.4	69.3	6.0	4.3	3,547	1.0	86.5	8.7	3.8	3,014
36-40	17.8	68.1	8.2	5.9	3,514	0.6	83.7	9.0	6.7	2,817
41-45	16.0	65.7	10.7	7.6	3,222	0.5	80.0	8.6	10.9	2,590
46-50	13.2	63.9	14.1	8.8	2,773	0.2	72.5	7.9	19.4	2,261
51-55	12.6	59.7	19.0	8.7	2,269	0.4	64.9	6.4	28.3	2,010
56-60	11.2	56.1	24.3	8.4	1,934	0.3	58.1	4.6	36.9	1,766
61-65	12.2	51.2	29.0	7.6	1,523	0.1	44.6	3.1	52.2	1,506
66-70	10.3	44.8	37.4	7.5	1,060	0.0	34.0	2.6	63.4	1,189
71 +	11.0	40.0	43.2	5.7	1,219	0.0	23.7	1.8	74.5	1,525

†Almost all of these women were the wives of remarried widowers. There is only one instance of polygyny in the registers. In that case, the husband died within three years of taking his second wife.

Comparison of the proportions of men and women ever-married provides ample evidence of the constraints on male marriage imposed by female infanticide and excess mortality. According to table 5.1, a summary of the marital status of our population by age and sex, marriage in Daoyi was universal for females but not for males. Whereas only one-twentieth of females were still single at age 25 *sui*, one-third of men were. Imbalances continued at later ages, so that while almost all women married by age 30 *sui*, one-tenth of men aged 71 and above had never married.[5] The men who failed to marry by age 25, in other words, were not delaying marriage so much as foregoing it: a separate calculation shows that four-fifths of them would eventually die single.

The shortage of women was attributable not only to the female infanticide and excess mortality described in Chapter 4, but also to peasants' adherence to traditional norms that discouraged widows but not widowers from remarrying. According to the age-specific probabilities of marriage and remarriage in table 5.2, whereas 28 percent of widowed men between the ages of 26 and 30 *sui* remarried within three years, only 12 percent of widowed women of the same age did.[6] As a result, one-third of the 1,276 widowers in our population, 417, eventually remarried, but only one-tenth of 1,210 widows, 110, ever remarried. Had widows been able to remarry in larger numbers, these widowers would have been removed from the market, and a substantially larger number of young bachelors would have been able to marry.

Men and women in Daoyi nevertheless married much earlier than their counterparts in Western Europe, where the mean age at marriage tended to be in the late 20s or even early 30s (Hajnal 1965). Table 5.3 presents the distributions of age at marriage for cohorts of men and women born between 1774 and 1840 who married before 1873. Mean age at marriage, 19.8 *sui* or women and 22.3 *sui* for men, was close to the values reported for most other Chinese populations.[7] The bulk

---

[5] Sex imbalances in the proportion marrying were by no means restricted to Daoyi. Telford 1992 estimates that one-fifth of the sons in the Tongcheng, Anhui lineages he studied never married. Analyzing data from the 1988 Two-Per-Thousand Survey of 800,000 married women, Wang and Tuma 1993 estimated that in Chinese cohorts born between 1900 and 1925, 94 percent of women but only 69 percent of men were married by age 25. By age 35, 99 percent of women had married, but only 93 percent of men had done so. That imbalances at later ages were less severe for twentieth-century cohorts most likely indicates that female mortality excesses in infancy, childhood, and young adulthood were less severe than in Daoyi.

[6] Most second wives, by definition, had to be marrying for the first time and were therefore younger than their husbands. Remarried husbands were almost ten years older than their spouses (36 *sui* compared with 28 *sui*).

[7] Telford 1992 estimated that in Tongcheng, Anhui, mean age at male marriage was

Table 5.2. *Percentages of men and women marrying within the next
three years, 1792-1867*†

Age (in *sui*)	Men				Women			
	Never married		Widowed		Never married		Widowed	
	%	N	%	N	%	N	%	N
11–15	18.0	2835	0.0	2	12.3	1095	-	-
16–20	30.2	2067	26.7	15	44.7	789	0.0	1
21–25	26.7	1199	27.1	48	51.0	241	21.4	14
26–30	19.7	717	27.8	97	42.6	54	12.2	41
31–35	11.1	485	17.9	140	20.0	15	2.6	78
36–40	6.3	431	9.7	195	14.3	14	4.5	132
41–45	3.1	327	7.9	215	0.0	8	1.5	202
46–50	0.5	206	1.2	247	0.0	2	1.0	304
51–55	0.0	161	2.1	289	0.0	6	0.8	369
56–60	2.0	149	0.9	321	0.0	4	0.7	434
61–65	0.0	139	1.0	312	0.0	1	0.2	527

†This calculation was restricted to registers where the immediately succeeding register is also
available: 1792, 1795, 1798, 1801, 1810, 1813, 1816, 1819, 1828, 1837, 1840, 1843, 1855, 1858, 1861, 1864.

of marriages occurred in late adolescence and early adulthood: over
90 percent of the women who married had done so by age 25 *sui*, as
had almost 75 percent of men. Many marriages, however, occurred in
early adolesence. By age 16 *sui*, 19 percent of the women who would
marry had already done so, as had 17 percent of the men.[8]

Analysis of the age differences between spouses reveals that the
preference for a bride in her late teens or early 20s overrode concern
with how her age compared with that of her husband. As a result, the
major constraint faced by bachelors and widowers seeking to marry
was not the number of never-married women of their own age, but
rather the number of never-married women in early adulthood. According to table 5.4, even though husbands were on average 1.8 years
older than their wives, the emphasis on obtaining a bride who was
just entering her peak reproductive years led to a pattern in which

between 21 and 22 Western years. In the Qing imperial lineage for most of the
eighteenth and nineteenth centuries, the average age at which daughters married
was between 20 and 21 (Lee and Wang 1996). According to the Two-Per-Thousand
Survey, for Chinese born between 1900 and 1925 who married by age 35, mean
Western age at marriage was 19.0 for females and 22.2 for males (Wang and Tuma
1993).

8   The range of ages over which marriages occurred, however, suggests that families
did not have fixed goals for an age at which to obtain a bride for their son or
marry off their daughter, raising the possibility that there was room in the Chinese
demographic system for a short-term impact of economic fluctuations on marriage
rates. The common assumption that the extended family system made economic
conditions irrelevant to decisions to marry needs to be reexamined.

Table 5.3. *Ages at first marriage for men and women born 1774-1840*†

Age at Marriage (Sui)	Women		Men	
	%	Cumulative %	%	Cumulative %
10 or Below	1.85	1.85	0.64	0.64
11	0.66	2.50	0.68	1 .33
12	1.11	3.61	1.30	2.63
13	1.72	5.34	2.04	4.67
14	2.55	7.88	2.95	7.62
15	4.31	12.19	4.18	11.80
16	6.73	18.92	5.55	17.35
17	9.56	28.49	6.39	23.75
18	10.92	39.41	7.42	31.17
19	11.66	51.08	7.72	38.89
20	10.51	61.58	7.96	46.85
21	9.11	70.69	7.20	54.05
22	7.31	78.00	6.40	60.45
23	5.75	83.74	5.41	65.86
24	4.27	88.01	4.64	70.50
25	3.08	91.09	4.00	74.50
26	2.55	93.64	3.75	78.25
27	2.01	95.65	3.33	81.58
28	1.52	97.17	2.95	84.53
29	0.86	98.03	2.37	86.90
30	0.57	98.60	2.10	88.99
31-35	0.82	99.42	6.14	95.13
36-40	0.45	99.88	2.32	97.45
41-45	0.12	100.00	1.13	98.59
46-50	0.00	100.00	1.22	99.80
51 +	0.00	100.00	0.20	100.00
Mean Age in *Sui*	19.78		22.31	
N	812		1790	

†To carry out this calculation, we first tabulated the ages at which men and women born between 1774 and 1840 were first listed in a register as being married. We then redistributed these counts under the assumption that women had equal chances of having married in the three years up to and including the current register year, but that men had equal chances of having married in the years after the preceding existing register up to and including the current register year. Women are treated differently because in our data there is no annotation of their out-marriage if it occurred in one of the three-year period not covered by an available register. They are counted among the disappeared. Men's marriage, by contrast, can always be inferred by comparison of their marital statuses before and after a missing register.

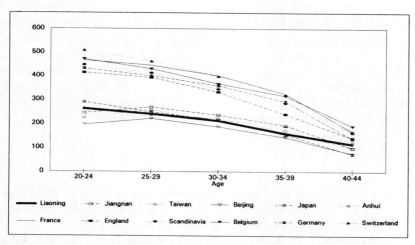

Figure 5.1. *Age specific marital fertility rates in China and Europe*
(births per 1,000 married person-years at risk)

All rates are for monogamous females with one exception. Rates for Beijing are for monogamous males, but should closely approximate those for females. Rates for Anhui, Jiangnan, and Liaoning were produced by first multiplying rates based on male births by 1.97, then multiplying by an adjustment factor to compensate for possible under-registration of male births. For Liaoning, this factor was 1.5. For Anhui and Jiangnan, it was 1.1. Sources: Europe: M. Flinn 1981, Anhui: Telford 1992, Beijing: Wang, Lee, and Campbell 1995, Japan: Kito 1991, Jiangnan: Liu 1992, Liaoning: Authors calculations, Taiwan: Wolf 1985.

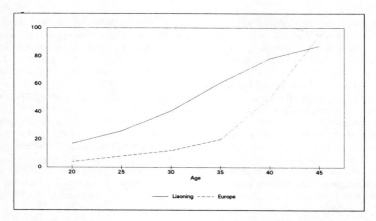

Figure 5.2. *Percentage of women subsequently infertile by age,*
Liaoning and Europe

The European data are from Henry, L. 1961. "Some data on natural fertility," *Eugenics Quarterly* 8.2:81-91.

the age difference between spouses depended on the husband's age at marriage. Marriages in which the newlyweds were both children or adolescents were almost non-existent, so that all except for one of the 77 males who married by age 15 *sui* had wives who were older than they were. Three-quarters had wives who were 4 or more years older. Men marrying in their late teens and early 20s tended to have wives who were the same age or younger, although the proportion of older wives was still considerable. Men marrying later tended to have substantially younger wives.

Fertility

Population growth in Liaoning was checked not only by limited opportunities for male marriage, but also by low fertility within marriage. Figure 5.1 summarizes marital age-specific fertility rates for Liaoning and compares them with those of other historical populations, both Chinese and European.[9] According to the rates in figure 5.1, the total marital fertility rate (TMFR) in Daoyi was 4.2, 6.3 once we adjust for missing children due to underregistration.[10] This rate is slightly lower than the ones calculated for other Chinese populations, but like them it is far lower than any of the rates calculated for European populations. Indeed, it is no more than two-thirds the fertility rate characteristic of European populations, especially below age 35.[11] Chinese fertility rates are so low that they are almost inconceivable

---

[9]   In a very recent study (1992), Liu Ts'ui-jung calculated the fertility and marital patterns of over 40,000 couples derived from 50 genealogies covering 12 provinces. The total marital fertility rate ranged from 4.1 to 6.1 and averaged slightly less than 5.2. Since her calculations do not include childless couples and therefore overestimate fertility by some 10 percent, these marital fertility rates are very close to our own and may in fact be slightly lower.

[10] These figures, based on our calculations in table 4.5, generously assume 33 percent male underregistration as well as a sex ratio at birth of 105 boys to 100 girls. Assumptions about underregistration necessarily derive educated guesses about the level of infant and child mortality, and are accordingly open to quibbling. However, the similarity of the resulting rates to other historial Asian populations including the best recorded population in late imperial China, the Qing imperial lineage, confirms that our assumptions are reasonable (Wang, Lee, and Campbell 1995).

[11] According to Chris Wilson's exhaustive survey of historical data, natural fertility in Western Europe in fact ranged from 7 to 11 children with an average of 8.5 births (Wilson 1984).

Table 5.4. *Difference between ages of spouses by husband's age at marriage in first marriages of men born 1774-1840 (row percentages in parentheses)*

Husband's Age (sui)		Husband's age minus wife's age												
	5-10	-9 to -5	-4	-3	-2	-1	0	1	2	3	4	5-9	≤10	N
≤10	1 (50.0)	1 (50.0%)	0 (0.0%)	0 (0.0%)	0 (0.0%)	0 (0.0%)	0 (0.0%)	0 (0.0%)	0 (0.0%)	0 (0.0%)	0 (0.0%)	0 (0.0%)	0 (0.0%)	2 (100.0%)
11-15	3 (4.0%)	36 (48.0%)	16 (21.3%)	9 (12.0%)	7 (9.3%)	3 (4.0%)	0 (0.0%)	1 (1.3%)	0 (0.0%)	0 (0.0%)	0 (0.0%)	0 (0.0%)	0 (0.0%)	75 (100.0%)
16-20	2 (0.4%)	56 (11.0%)	58 (11.4%)	57 (11.2%)	99 (19.4%)	93 (18.2%)	81 (15.9%)	41 (8.0%)	15 (2.9%)	6 (1.2%)	1 (0.2%)	2 (0.4%)	0 (0.0%)	511 (100.0%)
21-25	2 (0.3%)	20 (3.4%)	13 (2.2%)	29 (5.0%)	51 (8.8%)	58 (10.0%)	108 (18.6%)	71 (12.2%)	57 (9.8%)	51 (8.8%)	50 (8.6%)	71 (12.2%)	1 (0.2%)	582 (100.0%)
26-30	1 (0.3%)	1 (0.3%)	5 (1.5%)	4 (1.2%)	4 (1.2%)	8 (2.4%)	28 (8.4%)	19 (5.7%)	30 (9.0%)	31 (9.3%)	30 (9.0%)	139 (41.6%)	34 (10.2%)	334 (100.0%)
31-35	0 (0.0%)	1 (0.7%)	0 (0.0%)	1 (0.7%)	3 (2.0%)	0 (0.0%)	5 (3.3%)	6 (4.0%)	3 (2.0%)	6 (4.0%)	5 (3.3%)	53 (35.1%)	68 (45.0%)	151 (100.0%)
36-40	0 (0.0%)	0 (0.0%)	0 (0.0%)	0 (0.0%)	0 (0.0%)	0 (0.0%)	2 (3.3%)	1 (1.7%)	1 (1.7%)	1 (1.7%)	3 (5.0%)	20 (33.3%)	32 (53.3%)	60 (100.0%)
41-45	0 (0.0%)	0 (0.0%)	1 (5.3%)	0 (0.0%)	1 (5.3%)	0 (0.0%)	0 (0.0%)	1 (5.3%)	0 (0.0%)	2 (10.5%)	1 (5.3%)	5 (26.3%)	8 (42.1%)	19 (100.0%)
46-50	0 (0.0%)	0 (0.0%)	0 (0.0%)	0 (0.0%)	0 (0.0%)	0 (0.0%)	1 (5.6%)	0 (0.0%)	1 (5.6%)	0 (0.0%)	0 (0.0%)	4 (22.2%)	12 (66.7%)	18 (100.0%)
51+	0 (0.0%)	0 (0.0%)	0 (0.0%)	0 (0.0%)	0 (0.0%)	0 (0.0%)	1 (12.5%)	0 (0.0%)	1 (5.6%)	0 (0.0)	0 (0.0%)	2 (25.0%)	5 (62.5%)	8 (100.0%)
Total	9	115	93	100	165	162	226	140	107	97	90	296	160	1760‡

†Husband's age in register where he is first listed as married.

‡Smaller than total for males in Table 5.2 because ages were not available for some wives.

without assuming widespread sexual restraint and/or the technology for family limitation.[12]

Low fertility in Liaoning was the product of early stopping, late starting, and wide spacing. The peasants of Daoyi, in other words, behaved just like members of the Qing imperial lineage (Wang, Lee, and Campbell 1995). First, most couples stopped having children while the wife was still young. Whereas most studies of historical European populations have found a female mean age at last birth within one year of age 40 (Coale 1986, 11), according to table 5.5 the mean age at last birth in Daoyi was 35 *sui*, that is only 33.5 Western years of age. In consequence, the pattern of subsequent female infertility in Liaoning, depicted in figure 5.2, was radically different from any known historical European population, with far more "infertile" couples at virtually every age.[13] The gap between China and Europe was quite wide, a factor of four, and did not begin to narrow until well after age 35. By age 40 over four-fifths of all Liaoning couples had stopped giving birth, compared with only one-half of the European couples. It was not until age 45 that both populations reached similar proportions of subsequent infertility.

Second, in Daoyi many young couples started childbearing late, delaying their first birth until well after their marriage. Table 5.6 summarizes intervals between marriage and first birth by age of mother in Daoyi.[14] Whereas in most European populations the mean interval to first birth was less than 2 years, in Daoyi it was almost 4.[15]

---

[12] Leridon (1977, 147) concludes after a lengthy theoretical analysis, "First, that the biological maximum for women who remain fecund and exposed to risk from their fifteenth to their forty-fifth birthdays, and who do not breast-feed their children, would be 17 to 18 children. Second, taking into account a minimum level of sterility, and more realistic assumptions on nuptiality, the mean number would be around 13 children. Third, since in practice it is very rare for women not to breast-feed their children at all, the observed average would not exceed 11 children. Four, at the opposite extreme, under conditions of irregular ovulation, early sterility, prolonged breast-feeding, and late marriage (i.e. around age twenty-five), the average number of children, even in a natural fertility situation might be only 4 children." Since virtually all Chinese females apparently married between 15 and 20, the extreme lower bound of fertility, in the absence of control, should therefore have been between 5 and 6 children.

[13] Leridon 1977, 101—102.

[14] As we do not have the precise date of marriage, only the year of the register in which the marriage first appeared, these calculations of first birth intervals are prone to considerable error. In our calculations, we compensate for not having the precise date by assuming that marriages take place halfway between the register in which they appear and the previous register.

[15] In Europe, the average interval from marriage to first birth before 1750 was 16 months for France and 14 months for England (Flinn 1981, 33).

Table 5.5. *Ages at last birth in completed marriages, 1774-1873*†

Age group	First marriage				Later marriage			
	Men		Women		Men		Women	
(*sui*)	N	%	N	%	N	%	N	%
Childless	94	9	94	9	20	19	20	19
11–15	7	1	2	0	-	-	-	-
16–20	25	2	34	3	-	-	1	1
21–25	69	6	89	8	1	1	1	1
26–30	153	14	152	14	3	3	11	10
31–35	204	19	206	19	10	9	26	22
36–40	199	19	220	21	15	13	29	25
41–45	164	15	179	17	20	17	24	21
46–50	106	10	71	6	26	22	4	3
51–up	54	5	27	2	21	18	-	-
Total	1,075	100	1,075	100	116	100	116	100
Mean Age at Marriage	24		23		35		27	
Mean Age at Last Birth	36		35		45		37	

†We define completed marriages as those where the marriage is under observation from the time the wife marries in and both spouses live at least until the wife is 46 *sui*.

As a result, more than 10 percent of the intervals between marriage and first birth were over 10 years in length. Thus in spite of an age at marriage around 20, many couples did not have children until the wife was past 30. Such results are hardly unexpected: long intervals between marriage and first birth were until recently common throughout China and much of Asia, and are usually attributed to the relatively low coital frequencies assumed to characterize arranged marriages.[16]

Third, birth intervals in Daoyi were long, a partial function of long breast-feeding (Hsiung 1995a).[17] Table 5.7 presents birth intervals in Daoyi by birth order and completed family size. According to table 5.7, the mean interval between first and second births was 8.4 years for families with two children, 6.4 for families with three, and 4.1 years

[16] Long intervals between marriage and first birth were the norm, not the exception, in the historical and contemporary Chinese populations for which data are available. In the subset of the imperial lineage for which appropriate data on date of marriage are available, intervals between marriage and first birth were also relatively long by the standards of historical European populations (Wang, Lee, and Campbell 1995). Wang and Yang 1996 find from their analysis of the 1988 Two-Per-Thousand Survey, that intervals between marriage and first birth for rural couples in the 1950s and early 60s were quite long by the standards of developing countries. See Rindfuss and Morgan 1983 for a more general discussion of long intervals to first birth in Asia, and the possible association between arranged marriage and low coital frequency.

[17] Evidently long breast-feeding was the norm. According to Shirokogoroff 1926, 120 "The period of suckling can be prolonged up to the age of 5–6 . . . Usually the [Han] Chinese (*nikan*) woman suckles for a very long period."

Table 5.6. *Interval between marriage and first birth by age of mother*
(row percentages in parentheses)

Mother's age (*sui*)	Interval (in years)†					
	0 or less	1-3	4-6	7-9	10 or more	Total
20 Or Below	78	110	17	-	-	205
	(38.0%)	(53.7%)	(8.3%)		-	(100%)
21–25	100	171	130	32	3	436
	(22.9%)	(39.2%)	(29.8%)	(7.3%)	(0.7%)	(100%)
26–30	12	20	61	34	35	162
	(7.4%)	(12.3%)	(37.7%)	(21.0%)	(21.6%)	(100%)
31–35	6	11	5	10	28	60
	(10.0%)	(18.3%)	(8.3%)	(10.0%)	(46.7%)	(100%)
36–40	1	5	0	5	21	32
	(3.1%)	(15.6%)	(0.0%)	(15.6%)	(65.7%)	(100%)
41–45	1	0	0	1	5	7
	(14.3%)	(0.0%)	(0.0%)	(14.3%)	(71.4%)	(100%)
Total	198	317	213	82	92	902
	(21.9%)	(35.1%)	(23.6%)	(9.1%)	(10.2%)	(100%)

†Intervals were calculated by subtracting lunar year of marriage from lunar year of birth. Year of marriage was defined as the register year in which the marriage first appeared. Marriage may actually have taken place earlier, thus true intervals may have been somewhat longer. Children were included in this calculation only if they were born before 1840 in a first marriage occurring after 1792 in which the wife is under observation from the time of marriage.

for families with four or more. While patterns of longer intervals for later births and shorter intervals in larger families were also apparent in Europe,[18] Daoyi's intervals were as a whole far longer than in Europe. In England and France, the mean interval between the first and second births was approximately 2 years, that is, only one-half as long.[19] While the intervals calculated for Daoyi are undoubtedly exaggerated by the omission of unregistered births, even the most liberal assumptions from table 4.7 about the proportion unregistered would not close the gap with Europe.[20]

Peasants used female infanticide not only to respond to short-term changes in economic conditions, but also to achieve long-term goals

[18] Birth intervals tend to lengthen slightly as birth order increases because of age-related reductions in fecundity. Tautologically, larger families tend to have shorter intervals because they could not have become so large unless the intervals between births were narrow.

[19] In Europe, it was between 28 and 31 months, while in France, it was between 23 and 26 months (Flinn 1981, 33.)

[20] Evidence from other late imperial Chinese sources confirms that Daoyi's long intervals were not an artifact of underregistration: birth intervals in the much better-recorded Qing imperial lineage are also much longer than intervals in Europe. In the lineage, for example, the mean interval from the first to the second birth ranged from 69.6 months (for families with a completed family size of two) to 36.1 months (for families with a completed family size of six). See Wang, Lee, and Campbell 1995.

Table 5.7. *Preceding birth intervals (in years) by birth order, completed family size, and sex of child†*

Completed Family size	Mean birth interval			Mean Difference‡ between male female births		
	2	3	4+	2	3	4+
Birth order						
2	8.4	6.4	4.1	0.8	1.3*	0.3
3	-	6.7	4.5	-	2.2*	0.7
4	-	-	4.5	-	-	0.8*
Last birth	-	-	5.7	-	-	1.0*
Mean	8.4	6.6	4.5	0.8	1.8*	0.6*
N	154	282	805	-	-	-

†This calculation only includes children born between 1792 and 1840 to the 883 completed first marriages that begin before 1840.

‡All the differences between male and female births (male interval minus female interval) that are starred are significant at the $\alpha = 0.05$ two-tailed probability level.

for family size and sex composition. In table 5.8, which presents sex ratios of registered births by birth order and completed family size for approximately 1,000 completed marriages, the ratio of male to female births increased with the number of children already born, but decreased with completed family size. Thus, in single child families there were 576 boys for every 100 girls. For families with two children ever born there were 211 boys per 100 girls at the first birth and 450 boys to 100 girls at the second birth. For families with three children ever born the ratio was 156 boys to 100 girls at first birth, 194 boys to 100 girls at second birth, and 324 boys for every 100 girls at the last birth. This highly unnatural pattern continues through all other completed family sizes. Such behavior suggests that parents were relatively unconcerned about the sex of their first few children, but after several births, they only allowed additional children to survive if they were male. The closer a girl's parity was to a couple's completed family size, the less likely her parents were to allow her to survive to registration.[21]

[21] Similar parity-specific patterns of gender discrimination have been reported in many contemporary Asian societies, suggesting that such behavior is common to societies with strong son preferences. Das Gupta 1987 suggested that, in India, sex discrimination against girls is more pronounced for later births. Muhuri and Preston 1991 found that in Bangladesh, a newborn girl's changes of surviving were reduced if she had older siblings. In the East and Southeast Asian societies in which sex ratios at birth have been rising as the result of sex-selective abortion, including Korea, Taiwan, Hong Kong, and Singapore, sex imbalances have been most pronounced at later parities (Park and Cho 1995, and Zeng *et al.* 1993).

Table 5.8. *Sex ratios by birth order and completed family size (male births per 100 female births)†*

Birth order	Completed family size					Total
	1	2	3	4	5 or more	
1	576	211	156	158	88	188
2	-	450	294	229	139	265
3	-	-	324	278	149	240
4	-	-	-	422	138	223
5 or more	-	-	-	-	162	162
Total	576	290	240	246	138	214
N	115	328	428	401	599	1871

†This calculation only includes children born between 1792 and 1840 to the 883 completed first marriages which begin before 1840. Births past 1840 are included in the completed family size, but are not included in the computations of sex ratios because of the decline in female registration after 1840. Inclusion would show even more lopsided sex ratios in later parities.

Fertility and family composition

Fertility preferences and behaviors, however, were hardly monolithic. Rather, they were as complex as Daoyi village itself, with 12,000 individuals distributed across a variety of household types, relationships, and family sizes. Not only did individuals have different long-term goals regarding the number and sex of their children, they varied in their response to short-term changes in conditions. Fluctuations in the fertility of the most sensitive individuals contributed disproportionately to variations in Daoyi's birth rate. In this section, we identify these individuals, and show that their sensitivity depended on immediate circumstances. While long-term goals for family size and sex composition varied with socioeconomic standing,[22] fertility decisions were conditioned in the short term by such factors as how many children had already been born, the couple's current household context, and the sex of the child.

[22] Empirical work has already confirmed that in late imperial China, couples adjusted their fertility according to the level of their social and economic privilege. Wealthy couples, for example, had more children than poorer couples (Harrell 1985; Wang, Lee, and Campbell 1995). According to the analysis of three lineages in Xiaoshan Xian, Zhejiang from 1550 to 1850 in Harrell 1985, members of the richer branches of the lineages had more children than members of the poorer branches. This behavior can be attributed to a long natalist tradition in Chinese society that enjoined parents to translate wealth into reproduction. See Chapters 7, 9, and 10 for similar analyses of population behavior in rural Liaoning.

Table 5.9. *Birth rates by household type and birth order during periods of high and low fertility*†

	Birth rates‡			
	Jiaqing high	Jiaqing low	Daoguang low	Remaining years
Simple households				
First Born Boys	0.14	0.12	0.14	0.21
Later Boys	0.13	0.03	0.06	0.11
Only Boys	0.29	0.19	0.02	0.25
All Boys	0.15	0.06	0.07	0.15
First Born Girls	0.10	0.07	0.01	0.12
Later Born Girls	0.06	0.02	0.02	0.04
Only Girls	0.03	0.02	0.02	0.04
All Girls	0.07	0.03	0.02	0.06
Multiple-family households				
First Born Boys	0.18	0.11	0.11	0.14
Later Born Boys	0.11	0.09	0.09	0.10
Only Boys	0.17	0.10	0.07	0.11
All Boys	0.13	0.10	0.09	0.11
First Born Girls	0.15	0.07	0.04	0.09
Later Born Girls	0.07	0 04	0.03	0.05
Only Girls	0.07	0.00	0.00	0.03
All Girls	0.09	0.04	0.03	0.06
Total				
First Born Boys	0.17	0.12	0.11	0.15
Later Born Boys	0.11	0.08	0.09	0.10
Only Boys	0.21	0.10	0.06	0.13
All Boys	0.13	0.09	0.09	0.11
First Born Girls	0.14	0.07	0.04	0.10
Later Born Girls	0.07	0.04	0.03	0.05
Only Girls	0.06	0.01	0.00	0.03
All Girls	0.09	0.04	0.03	0.06

†Periods of extreme fertility were defined by examination of variations in the female birth rate. The Jiaqing High consists of the years 1792, 1793, 1794, 1796, 1797, 1798. The Jiaqing Low consists of the years 1807, 1808, 1809, 1810, 1811, 1812, 1813, 1814, 1815, 1816, 1817, 1818. The Daoguang Low consists of the years 1828, 1830, 1831, 1832, 1833, 1834, 1835, 1836, 1837, 1839, 1840, 1842, 1843.

‡The calculation of only-child rates uses a numerator consisting of only births, and a denominator consisting of married women between 16-35 *sui* who have not yet had a child and will only have one child. For the calculation of rates for first-born children we use a numerator consisting of first births and a denominator consisting of married women between 16-35 *sui* who have not yet had a child and will have at least two children in their lifetime. For the calculation of rates of later-born children we use a numerator consisting of non-first births, and a denominator consisting of married women between 16-35 *sui* who have already had one child and will have at least two children in their lifetime.

Table 5.10. *Proportional change in birth rates during periods of high and low fertility, by household type and birth order*†

	Jiaqing High			Jiaqing Low			Daoguang Low		
	Change	10 % Confidence interval		Change	10 % Confidence interval		Change	10 % Confidence interval	
Simple Households									
First Born Boys	-0.35	-0.68	-0.08	-0.44	-0.76	-0.02	-0.35	-0.67	0.09
Later Born Boys	0.11	-0.24	0.56	-0.73	-0.89	-0.54	-0.43	-0.64	-0.19
Only Boys	0.16	-0.44	1.03	-0.59	-0.88	-0.20	-0.93	-1.00	-0.80
All Boys	0.00	-0.26	0.30	-0.60	-0.75	-0.43	-0.51	-0.66	-0.35
First Born Girls	-0.14	-0.63	0.62	-0.36	-0.81	0.29	-0.89	-1.06	-0.69
Later Born Girls	0.42	-0.23	1.33	-0.50	-0.86	-0.05	-0.62	-0.87	-0.31
Only Girls	-0.27	-1.20	1.84	-0.48	-1.20	-0.01	-0.56	-1.20	-0.12
All Girls	0.21	-0.23	0.79	-0.42	-0.71	-0.08	-0.71	-0.88	-0.51
Multiple-Family Households									
First Born Boys	0.28	0.00	0.62	-0.17	-0.35	0.04	-0.23	-0.38	-0.10
Later Born Boys	0.08	-0.10	0.28	-0.07	-0.22	0.09	-0.10	-0.23	0.04
Only Boys	0.57	0.00	1.23	-0.11	-0.38	0.21	-0.40	-0.56	-0.20
All Boys	0.18	0.20	0.34	-0.10	-0.20	0.02	-0.19	-0.28	-0.10
First Born Girls	0.62	0.22	1.10	-0.31	-0.50	-0.09	-0.57	-0.70	-0.42
Later Born Girls	0.39	0.12	0.57	-0.23	-0.41	-0.03	-0.41	-0.54	-0.26
Only Girls	1.56	0.16	3.64	-0.70	-0.97	-0.36	-0.71	-0.90	-0.45
All Girls	0.56	0.31	0.84	-0.28	-0.41	-0.14	-0.51	-0.60	-0.42
Total									
First Born Boys	0.13	-0.11	0.40	-0.22	-0.37	-0.04	-0.26	-0.40	-0.11
Later Born Boys	0.10	-0.07	0.28	-0.16	-0.28	-0.02	-0.15	-0.27	-0.03
Only Boys	0.61	0.13	1.17	-0.24	-0.45	0.01	-0.51	-0.63	-0.36
All Boys	0.15	0.01	0.29	-0.18	-0.27	-0.08	-0.25	-0.32	-0.17
First Born Girls	0.45	0.11	0.84	-0.31	-0.49	-0.11	-0.60	-0.72	-0.47
Later Born Girls	0.39	0.12	0.57	-0.24	-0.41	-0.06	-0.46	-0.56	-0.30
Only Girls	1.16	0.03	2.77	-0.59	-0.88	-0.20	-0.63	-0.88	-0.46
All Girls	0.49	0.27	0.73	-0.28	-0.40	-0.15	-0.54	-0.61	-0.45

This was particularly true of the price of food. The comparison of annual birth rates with annual average grain prices yields a number of truly significant results. As we saw in table 3.7, correlations between grain prices and birth rates are not only quite strong, they are stronger for females than for males, especially in complex households. Indeed, strong negative correlations exist for virtually all grain prices regardless of the type of price (monthly low or monthly high) or the variety of grain. When food prices were high, people had fewer children, especially fewer girls.

Fetal wastage and standard methods of family planning would have produced dramatically different results. Spontaneous abortions would have affected males more than females.[23] Restraint would have produced stronger correlations with lagged prices than current prices. In fact, though, correlations between prices and fertility are not only stronger for females than for males, according to a calculation not presented here, they are marginally stronger for current prices than for lagged prices.[24] Some parents, in other words, made their fertility decisions in response to conditions at time of birth rather than conditions at time of conception. The unnatural response of birth rates by sex to immediate economic conditions, therefore, can only mean that in Liaoning many peasants limited their fertility through sex-selective infanticide as well as abstinence.

To identify the individuals whose fertility varied the most when birth rates fluctuated, we define three periods of extremely high and low overall birth rates, then differentiate changes in rates by sex, parity, and household type.[25] The three periods are a period of high fertility in the 1790s that we call the Jiaqing High and two periods of extremely low fertility, one in the 1810s that we call the Jiaqing Low and another between the 1830s and 1840s that we call the Daoguang Low. Table 5.9 summarizes birth rates during these three periods by

---

23 According to Leridon (1977, 15), the natural sex ratio for stillbirths is 120—130 dead boys per 100 dead girls.

24 If the peasants were limiting their fertility solely through sexual restraint rather than infanticide we would expect even more pronounced correlations between births and prices with a lag of one year or more. In fact we discovered that while the relationship indeed remains strong, the values for both sexes weaken rather than increase. Therefore, while some couples may have practiced restraint, other couples preferred to rely on infanticide as a means of fertility countrol in time of economic pressure.

25 We take this approach, rather than use correlation or regression, because of the likelihood that the relationship of the fertility of population subgroups to overall fertility may be asymmetric. For example, the population subgroups whose fertility increases the most when overall rates rise may not reduce their fertility by a similar amount when overall rates decline.

birth order, sex, and household structure.[26] Table 5.10 measures the differential sensitivity of these rates by contrasting them with rates in the remaining years of "normal" fertility. The indices presented are proportional changes in rates during the specified periods from the rates during "normal" periods.

During periods of extreme fertility, most couples adjusted their fertility in the same direction, but the precise calculus varied according to whether or not they already had children. The birth rates of couples who were about to begin their fertility careers changed more than the rates of couples who had already begun having children. According to table 5.10,[27] during periods of high prices and low fertility, first-birth rates declined more than later-birth rates. During the Jiaqing Low, the male first birth rate declined by 22 percent for all household types combined, while the rate for later male births declined by only 16 percent. Similarly, during the Daoguang Low, the male first-birth rate declined by 26 percent, but the rate for later male births declined by only 15 percent. When prices were low and fertility was high, meanwhile, the rate for male first births increased by 13 percent, but the rate for male later births increased by only 10 percent. The cumulative effect of such sensitivity on the part of the first birth rate was that when times were bad, the proportion of late starters increased dramatically.

As we might expect, female fertility was especially sensitive. The availability of female infanticide made girls especially vulnerable to changes in conditions. In table 5.10, when fertility was low, birth rates dropped by as much as two-thirds for only girls, slightly less for first-born girls, and by only one-third for later-born girls. By contrast, when fertility was high, birth rates doubled for only girls and increased by over one-third for first- and later-born girls. Such patterns imply that when the peasants of Daoyi were reducing their fertility, "poorer" or "lower" parents, represented by the peasants who would only ever have one daughter, were especially likely to postpone births. When rates were on the increase, however, the same parents were disproportionately likely to hurry their next birth.

---

[26] Parity-specific rates were calculated by dividing the number of births of the specified parity, n, by the number of married female person-years at risk. Females were considered at risk if they already had exactly $n-1$ registered births. For the category of only births, births were only included if they were a couple's only birth, and mothers were only considered at risk if they would have only one birth during their entire lifetime, but were currently childless.

[27] See table 5.9 for specification of years of high and low fertility.

Household type, a proxy for wealth and an important determinant of a couple's social context,[28] also played a key role in fertility decisionmaking, especially when a daughter was involved. In table 5.10, during the two periods of low fertility, parents in complex households reduced their female birth rate by 28 percent and 51 percent respectively, but parents in simple households reduced their female birth rates even more, by 42 percent and 71 percent. In contrast, when fertility was high, parents in complex households increased their female birth rate by more than one-half while parents in simple households raised theirs by only one-fifth. Simple households were so impoverished compared with complex households that they not only killed far more girls than normal when times were bad, they allowed no extra ones to live when times were good.

Within the multiple-family household hierarchy, past reproductive success, a proxy for a couple's access to household resources, was also an important determinant of a couple's current fertility behavior. According to table 5.10, in all three periods of extreme fertility, the pattern described earlier, in which only-child birth rates were the most sensitive, first-birth rates the next most sensitive, and later-birth rates the least sensitive, was far more apparent in multiple-family households than in single-family households. In multiple-family households, childless couples were on average younger than couples with children, or as will be shown in Chapter 7, lower in the household hierarchy. Couples who were so poor that they would only ever have one child, meanwhile, also tended to be at the bottom of the household hierarchy. When times were tight and multiple family households cut back on expenditures, it was these marginalized couples who were affected the most.

Conclusion

In conclusion, this chapter provides a variety of insights into the complexity of household decision making in eighteenth- and nineteenth-century Liaoning and perhaps, by extension, in China as a whole. Not all Chinese peasants necessarily practiced family limitation on the scale of these Liaoning peasants. But based on the evidence in this chapter, those who did were likely to have based their decisions

---

[28] Social surveys carried out in China during the early part of this century repeatedly claimed that on a per capita basis, larger households tended to be wealthier than smaller households. For example, see Fei 1939; Gamble 1921, 1933, 1954; Lang 1946; Levy 1949; and Yang 1965. Since none of these studies directly measured household complexity (that is the number and relationship of conugal units), size (that is the number of individuals), has to be taken as a proxy for it.

on a complex combination of interrelated factors, including economic conditions (Lee, Campbell, and Tan 1992), household type, access to household resources, number and sex of previous children, sex of child, and perhaps even long-term goals for family size and composition. Later chapters will show, moreover, that position within the hereditary household hierarchy and the ability-based banner hierarchy were also important. Thus while fertility decisions may have been reactive, they were nonetheless sophisticated and deliberate. A couple's completed fertility represented the combined effects of long-term goals for completed family size and a series of conscious short-term adjustments.

At the same time, this chapter in conjunction with Chapter 4 further illuminates how China's demographic system differed from that of the West. Whereas in the West, the most important preventive checks to population growth were increases in the ages at which males and females married, in China, reductions in the proportion of males ever marrying and deliberate, parity-specific adjustments to marital fertility combined to limit population growth. The ironic result of such widespread and wide-ranging methods of fertility control is that, while late imperial China had the largest population of any country in the world, it seems also to have had the lowest known marital fertility rates. The possibility must accordingly be considered that China's rapid increase in population between the seventeenth and nineteenth centuries did not result from the relaxation of the positive check, mortality, but rather from a conscious decision by married couples to increase their family sizes (Lee 1994).

In any case, just as there were two types of positive check in rural Liaoning, there were also two types of preventive check. In the second half of this book, we will see how these checks with their multiple forms of deliberate population control enabled couples to develop different demographic priorities and strategies; according to their household organization and household position in Part Three, and according to their banner organization and banner position in Part Four.

Part 3

Household organization and population behavior

A large family is a happy family (quanjia fu bu yile hu)
common Chinese proverb

The banner household, called *hu* in Han Chinese or *boigon* in Manchu Chinese, was defined by common residence and common consumption.[1] Household members lived together, ate together, and farmed together. Moreover, like most Chinese families, they did so largely free from government interference. While the banner administration could influence household behavior through the approval of household division, households were otherwise free to order their domestic affairs as they preferred. The household was therefore fundamentally a private, if regulated, form of organization.

It was also a universal institution. Everyone lived in a household no matter if it was a solitary hut or a large compound of many courtyards and families. Many Chinese scholars and scholars of China accordingly described the household as the paramount social institution in Chinese society (Baker 1979). Confucius went so far as to describe the ideal Chinese state as analogous to the Chinese family, and the ideal head of state as analogous to the head of a household.[2]

This was equally true in rural banner communities such as Daoyi and surrounding villages. The Qing state preferred large families to ensure an adequate supply of family labor to work the family farm

---

[1] The banner administration distinguished between *zhenghu* and *linghu*. *Zhenghu* are the original households defined when the banners first incorporated. *Linghu* are the new households created as the original households divided and merged. See Fu 1983 for a detailed discussion of the banner household registration system. We would like to thank Pamela Crossley for bringing this article to our attention.

[2] His most famous statement in this regard is from *The Great Learning*: "Their families being regulated, their states were rightly governed. Their states being rightly governed, the whole kingdom was made tranquil and happy" (Legge 1971, 1.359). See too his pronouncements on filial piety in *The Analects*, 1.2, 6, 11; 2.5, 7; 4.18, 19, 21.

and to pay the family taxes. The banner administration accordingly encouraged the formation of such large households and bolstered household hierachy by recognizing a primogenitary system of household headship. In consequence, the household domestic cycle and the individual life cycle were inextricably bound together. Individual position within the household depended largely on parental position.

So did individual demographic performance. Demography provides a precise set of measures to analyze household organization as well as population behavior. In Part Three, we demonstrate how demographic analysis can elucidate social structure, and how analysis of social structure can also illuminate how demographic decisions are made. We divide our presentation into two chapters. We begin in Chapter 6 with an analysis of the domestic cycle and household formation. We then show in Chapter 7 how the hierarchical nature of such households defined the structure of opportunities to marry and bear children. We use, in other words, demographic behavior to reveal how different type of multiple-family households decided demographic behavior, and identify the shifting lines of cleavage and solidarity within the rural household that could lead to household division. Our results indicate that many families followed the Liaoning demographic system and allocated marriage, children, and other vital resources in accordance with household position. The individual demographic fate of many men was, therefore, often sealed at birth.

6

Domestic cycle and household formation[1]

Big brother, though born of the same mother and living in the same house [as his brothers], his position was entirely different from theirs. In the large Gao household, he was the eldest son of an eldest son, and for that reason his destiny was fixed from the moment he came into the world. (Ba Jin, *Family*, 35)

In rural Liaoning, household structure, household position, and the rules of household formation combined to determine individual fate. Demographic decisions were decided by family strategy more than by personal preference. The family as a whole allocated labor and redistributed wealth; nurtured the young and cared for the aged. Family members who wanted to marry or bear children accordingly vied for a finite cache of rights and resources, distributed unequally by gender, by family relationship, and by seniority. The Liaoning peasant household was therefore not only a locus of affect and socialization, but also an arena of negotiation and conflict.

Household organization is a product of such negotiation. But just as these decisions can change household structure, so the arrangement of relationships within the household, in turn, influences individual opportunities and expectations to marry, to bear children, to retire, and to depart. Thus, each step along the household progression is the product of two reflexive forces: group strategy and individual will.

The domestic cycle reflects the common resolution of tensions within the domestic group. Rules of household formation show how people normatively resolved their competing claims. From them we can deduce the relationships between household members, and

[1] The ideas for this chapter date back to collaborative work with Jon Gjerde on comparative family history and household morphology (Gjerde, Tien, and Lee 1987; Lee and Gjerde 1986). We gratefully acknowledge his assistance. The text, however, is entirely new. We completed the analysis during the summer of 1988 and the winter of 1989, but did not write up results until the spring of 1991.

understand how authority was transmitted and transmuted within the household.

Any study of rural social organization in the eighteenth and nineteenth centuries should, therefore, start with the ideal models of household formation and the domestic cycle in late imperial China. The ideal household is married sons living with their parents. Inheritance in theory was partible. In consequence, while married sons are supposed to remain together during the lifetimes of their parents, they are assumed to divide the household upon the death of their parents (Shiga 1978; Wakefield 1992). Given such rules of household formation and the moderate fertility and high mortality thought to be characteristic of many Chinese populations, the average, actual, resulting household is hypothesized to have been relatively small and simple (Lang 1946; Levy 1949).[2] Many people have gone so far as to dismiss the large ideal household as a "myth" (Hsu 1943).[3] However, there have been virtually no empirical longitudinal studies of Chinese household formation before the late twentieth century.[4] And what work has been done, has been restricted largely to the island province of Taiwan (Wolf 1985b).

In this chapter, we describe the domestic cycle and household formation in Daoyi and surrounding communities based on some 10,000 linked household observations beginning in 1792.[5] We first introduce in section I, a standard system of formal household classification and contrast three idealized systems of household progression. We then apply this system in section II to analyze household structure and the domestic cycle in rural Liaoning, and demonstrate in section III

---

[2] Zhao 1994 provides a good review of such literature. His analysis is also a good example of such thinking. Using simulation programs developed by the Cambridge Group for the History of Population and Social Structure, he concludes that "the constraints of high mortality meant that a considerable number of people could not have lived in such [multi-generational] households" (425).

[3] Ever since Francis Hsu's 1943 article on "The Myth of the Chinese Family Size," it has been customary to begin discussions of the Chinese family system with a denunciation of the view that the "large" or "joint" family was the typical family in China. The simulation studies by Zhao 1994 are only the most recent example. Empirical studies by Arthur Wolf, however, have demonstrated that in Taiwan, as in Liaoning, the vast majority of the population in fact lived in multiple-family households (Wolf 1984, 1985b). We await similar studies from other provinces.

[4] While Liu 1995b is entitled as an analysis of "family structure in traditional Chinese lineages, ca 1200—1900," her data in fact provide no information on residence. Her article, therefore, is not an analysis of family structure, which requires coresidence, but rather of kin relations.

[5] The registers before 1789 are organized by lineage units called *mukūn* in Manchu Chinese or *zu* in Han Chinese. We discuss this social organization and contrast it with the residential household in Chapters 8, 9, and 10.

how the domestic cycle in turn dictated and dominated many facets of the individual life cycle. Finally, we conclude in section IV with a detailed discussion of household division, as division was the only way individuals could actively change their hereditary familial fate.

Classification of household morphology and household progression

Comparative sociologists commonly distinguish between three idealized systems of household progression: nuclear, stem, and joint.[6] In all three systems the nucleus is the conjugal family unit, that is, parents and their children.[7] The principal differences are that in the nuclear system, children leave home when they marry; in the stem system, a single married child remains; and in the joint system, all married children usually of one or the other gender remain.

Each household system is defined by different practices of coresidence, inheritance, and retirement. Ideally all stem households share three characteristics: formal retirement of the head upon old age, unigeniture inheritance, and expulsion of non-heirs upon marriage. Similarly all joint households share two characteristics: partible inheritance and virilocal residence of the married heirs.

Household headship, in other words, varies dramatically by household system. The stem system is characterized by exclusivity. The heir is set apart from his siblings as he matures and remains within the household after marriage. The joint household system, in contrast, is inclusive. Multiple heirs are each provided with part of the estate and all remain within the household after their marriage. Decisions of production and consumption are often corporate. Whereas the household head is the most powerful individual in the joint household, his authority is constrained relative to his stem household counterpart.

In all three systems household structures overlap, however, as the systems follow overlapping cycles of simplicity and complexity. Figure 6.1 reproduces in ideographs the sequences of all three systems. Nuclear households proceed along a system of five stages beginning with an unmarried individual, then a married couple, then a married

---

[6] See Lee and Gjerde 1986 for a discussion of comparative household morphology. Hajnal 1982 and Todd 1982 are two highly influential attempts to contrast stem and joint household systems and assess their larger implications for social formation.

[7] The conjugal unit is central to all these models because it is the smallest unit of household construction above the individual. That is not to say that households cannot exist if they do not contain conjugal units. Indeed conjugal units are absent in both "solitary" and "no family" households.

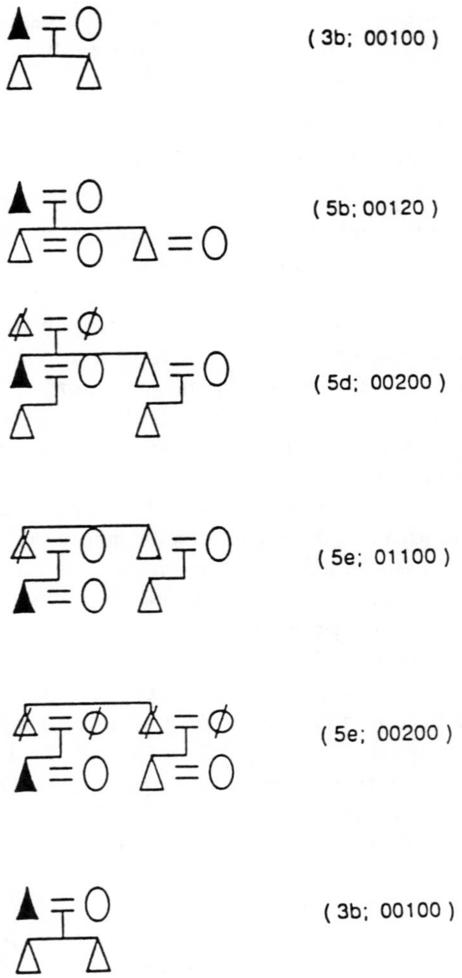

Figure 6.1. *Ideographs of domestic cycle transitions*

couple with coresident children, then a married couple with departed children, and finally, with the death of one of the spouses, a widowed individual. Stem households proceed in four stages beginning with a married couple with children, then a married couple with a married heir, then a retired couple, with a married child, and finally, with the death of the original parents a married couple with children again. Joint households proceed in five stages beginning with a married couple with married children, a household of married brothers upon the death of the parents, a household of uncles and nephews with the death of the new heir, a household of coresident cousins with the death of the uncle, and finally a married couple with children as the coresident cousins divide the household. In all three cycles, of course, a number of half-stages proliferate as household members marry, bear children, and die.

The purpose of any system of household classification is to recognize variation among household types and to distinguish patterns of authority among them as households move up and down the domestic cycle.[8] The most popular method of classification, developed by the Cambridge Group for the Study of Population and Social Structure, is based upon the number of kin-related conjugal family units (Hammel and Laslett 1974; Laslett and Wall 1972). The Cambridge system distinguishes between four major categories of households: the fragmentary household, that is, a household that lacks even a single conjugal unit; the simple family household, that is, a household with just one conjugal unit; the extended family household, that is, a conjugal family unit with coresident kin who do not constitute a separate conjugal family unit; and the multiple-family household, that is, a household with two or more coresident conjugal family units.

Domestic cycle and household structure

Classification of household structure in Daoyi and surrounding communities according to this system shows that in rural Liaoning, contrary to common assumptions, most people lived in multiple-family households.[9] Table 6.1 tabulates individuals and households by household structure according to a slightly modified version of the canonical

---

[8] Such methodological issues have generated considerable interest in the field of family history. See the pioneering articles by Lutz Berkner (1972, 1975, 1978) as well as the broader essays in Hareven 1978 and Hareven and Plakans 1987.

[9] Wolf 1985b found similar household complexity in nine districts in northern Taiwan during the early twentieth century. Over three-quarters of the population lived in multiple-family households which he termed stem, grand, and frereche.

Table 6.1. *Population by household type, 1792-1873*†

	Population		Households	
	N	%	N	%
Fragmentary				
Single	494	0.8	494	4.7
Widows Alone	726	1.2	726	6.9
Coresident Siblings	489	0.8	222	2.1
Coresident Relatives	278	0.4	117	1.1
Simple Family Households				
Married Couples	1,292	2.1	642	6.1
Married Couples with Child(ren)	3,868	6.2	1,102	10.4
Widowers with Child(ren)	643	1.0	280	2.7
Widows with Child(ren)	949	1.5	397	3.8
Extended Family Households				
Extended Upwards	3,726	5.9	923	8.7
Extended Downwards	299	0.5	77	0.7
Extended Laterally	2,152	3.4	518	4.9
Extended Combination	287	0.5	57	0.5
Multiple Family Households‡				
Vertical	9,616	15.3	1,335	12.7
Horizontal	25,348	40.4	2,637	25.0
Diagonal	12,553	20.0	1,001	9.5
Total	62,720	100.0	10,528	100.0

†For the purposes of this calculation we exclude all households when the head is annotated as having recently died or emigrated and no new head has yet been appointed.

‡Vertical households are multiple family households where no brothers, brother's sons, cousins, cousin's sons or uncles are present. Horizontal households are multiple family households which have brothers or brother's sons present but no uncles, cousins, or cousin's sons. Diagonal households are multiple family households which have uncles or cousins present.

Earlier registers, before 1792, do not identify people by residential household.

Cambridge system and indicates that 75 percent of the population lived in households with two or more conjugal units. Vertical households, consisting of a married head with his married son(s), account for less than one-quarter of these multiple-family households. Horizontal households, that is married brothers living together, account for more than one-half of these households. Diagonal households with coresident cousins and/or uncles account for almost one-fifth of these households. While 30 to 40 percent of the population at any given time lived in "ideal" multi-generational households, 70 to 80 percent lived in multiple-family households. Household complexity, in other words, was a function of the number of familial conjugal units not the number of familial generations.[10] Low fertility and high mortality do not preclude household complexity.

A comparison of household structures over three year intervals explains how this complexity evolved. Table 6.2 summarizes 8,500 before-and-after observations of household structure in adjacent registers. The vertical axis presents original household structure arranged in order of increasing complexity and the horizontal axis identifies household structure three years later. The diagonal accordingly corresponds to households where structure remained unchanged. Entries below the diagonal are transitions to simpler forms of household structure, while entries above the diagonal are transitions to more complex forms of household structure.

Households change structure rarely—over four-fifths retain the same structure after three years—and the ones most likely to change were the smallest and account for the fewest people. Simpler households are more volatile than complex households, a function of their small size and heightened vulnerability to death and marriage. Thus, in table 6.2 fragmentary households change structure most frequently, diagonal and horizontal households least frequently. The household setting for most individuals in Daoyi was therefore extremely stable.

When households change, they follow the predicted progression, moving up or down in the classic household cycle. The direction in which they move varies: households are as likely to increase in complexity as decrease. Thus of the simple households that change, 37 percent become fragmentary while 35 percent move up the stem cycle and grow into vertical or horizontal households. Similarly most vertical households either remain in the stem cycle and deteriorate into an extended household (40 percent) or move into a joint cycle and expand into a horizontal household (40 percent).[11]

---

[10]　This distinction between multi-generation as opposed to multi-family households is largely lost in such literature as Liu 1995a and Zhao 1994.

[11]　Most of the so-called extended households in fact were extended vertically.

Table 6.2. Three-year household structure transitions, 1792-1867†

Previous household type	Present household type (if a transition has taken place)								Total transitions		Total No transitions	
	Frag. %	Sim. %	Ext. %	Ver. %	Hor. %	Diag. %	Departure %	Extinction %	N	%	N	%
Fragmentary	-	20	8	-	-	-	2	69	255	19	1,077	81
Simple	37	-	18	29	6	-	-	11	345	18	1,583	82
Extended	14	40	-	15	19	3	5	5	341	27	942	73
Vertical	-	13	40	-	40	2	2	3	233	21	852	79
Horizontal	1	3	24	3	-	33	33	3	320	15	1,846	85
Diagonal	2	1	18	1	18	-	60	-	105	15	598	85
N	182	228	273	159	195	120	197	245	1,599	18	6,898	82

†We restrict our calculations to registers for which the immediately preceding register is also available: 1795, 1798, 1801, 1804, 1813, 1816, 1819, 1822, 1831, 1840, 1843, 1846, 1858, 1861, 1864, 1867.

Table 6.3. *Household structures produced by division†*

Previous household Type	Number dividing	Present household type					
		Frag.	Sim.	Ext.	Ver.	Hor.	Diag.
		N	N	N	N	N	N
Fragmentary	4	8	-	-	-	-	-
Simple	1	1	1	-	-	-	-
Extended	18	20	13	7	-	-	-
Vertical	4	3	2	2	-	1	-
Horizontal	107	25	52	29	51	57	13
Diagonal	63	13	15	26	10	40	29

†See Table 6.2 for list of registers included in this calculation.

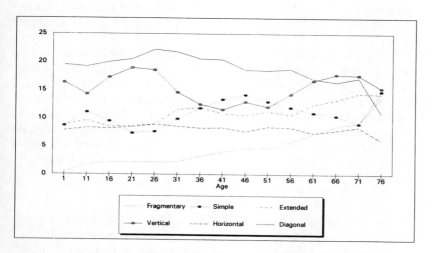

Figure 6.2. *Percentage of individuals in each household type, by age*

Between the least and most complex households, we can distinguish opposing centrifugal tendencies. On the one hand, the simplest households are more likely to deteriorate and eventually disappear. Fragmentary households accordingly account for two-thirds of the 245 household extinctions under observation; while simple households account for half the remaining disappearances. On the other hand, the most complex households are likely to become even more intricate and eventually divide. Thus, diagonal households account for two thirds of the 197 household divisions; while horizontal households account for almost all of the remainder. The two processes, extinction and division, appear almost symmetrical.

Moreover when households divided they did not necessarily return to simpler household forms of stage one or two. Even after a division, most multiple-family household members continued to live in a multiple-family environment. Table 6.3 summarizes the 197 cases of household division.[12] Of these, 174 involved multiple-family household divisions which produced 369 households: 41 fragmentary, 69 simple, 57 extended, and 202 multiple-family households. Surprisingly almost half (29) of the diagonal multiple-family households to divide (63) remained diagonal after household division. As a result, while household division inevitably caused major changes in household structure, these were minor fluctuations within the overall framework of the multiple-family household progression. In rural Liaoning multiple-family households were perennial households. As these households multiplied through division, multiple-family household structure became increasingly universal throughout northeast China.[13]

In Daoyi and surrounding communities, the joint household cycle was the dominant cycle with all its implications for power and hierarchy. But, in contrast with peasant households elsewhere in China,[14] many households progressed beyond the horizontal stage of married brothers living together to the diagonal stage of married uncles and nephews. They did so because of the greater power of the household head and the greater impediments to household division under the banner system which we will discuss in section IV of this chapter.

Household formation and life cycle

The predominance of multiple-family households and the tendency of such households to remain complex meant that most people lived their entire life in a domestic setting surrounded by distant relatives.[15] Figure 6.2 plots the proportion of people by age group and household type to demonstrate the degree to which the domestic cycle dominated the individual life cycle, by determining individuals' household

---

[12] This calculation was restricted to registers where the immediately succeeding register was also available.

[13] Zhao 1994 assumes that when households divide they do so into their single conjugal unit components. As a result his simulation suggests that multiple-family households were less common than they in fact were in rural Liaoning.

[14] According to Wolf 1985b, most multiple-family household divisions were what he calls frereches, composed most commonly of married brothers living together (34, 39—42).

[15] Such large and complex households appear to have been typical elsewhere in Manchuria as well. According to Shirokogoroff in northern Heilongjiang, "The incorporated Chinese *nikan* live in great families, just like the Manchus. But the [recent] Chinese emigrants from China Proper usually form small families composed only of a married couple and children" (1926, 97).

context. Throughout the life span, the proportion of individuals in different household types changed very little, and multiple-family households predominated. The only clear age patterns are that more children lived in multiple-family households and more aged lived alone.

The only exception to this apparent stasis was a cycle in which certain individuals alternate between vertical and simple households. We can distinguish three stages in this progression. First, when children in simple households reach their twenties and begin to marry, their households become vertical, causing the proportion of people in such households to increase sharply. Second, as these same children enter middle age and their parents begin to pass away, the proportion of the population in vertical households declines and the proportion in simple families increases. The cycle completes itself when these individuals enter old age and their own children begin to marry. The proportion of people in vertical households rises once again and the proportions of people in simple families correspondingly decrease.

The domestic cycle also shaped the individual life cycle by dictating location within the household hierarchy. Table 6.4 summarizes 23,000 before-and-after observations of individual male family relationship in adjacent registers. Once again the vertical axis depicts original family relationship, in order of increasing distance from the household head, while the horizontal axis represents the new relationship three years later. The diagonal means no change. For the most part, entries below the diagonal represent an increase in proximity to the head, while entries above represent a decrease. The results show that while most people maintained the same household relationship from one register to the next, when people did change they did so according to a classic household progression in which headship was transmitted from father to son and all other relationships were determined accordingly.

The patrilineal domestic cycle in conjunction with male primogeniture, in other words, determined social mobility within the household. The higher one's parentage, that is the closer one's parents were to the head, the greater the chances of becoming head. Most head's sons who changed relationship over a three-year period either succeeded to the headship or became a head's brother. While some brothers achieved headship, most either became uncles or died without ever changing their relationship again. Nephews, that is brothers' sons, moved even further away, in most cases becoming cousins and cousins' sons.

Table 6.4. *Family relationship transitions by previous relationship, males 1792-1867*†

Previous relationship	Present relationship (if a transition has taken place)							Exit	Total changes		No changes	
	Head	Sons, grandson	Brother	Brother's son, grandson	Uncle	Cousin	Cousin's son, grandson					
	%	%	%	%	%	%	%	%	N	%	N	%
Head	-	-	-	-	-	-	-	100	485	11	3,715	89
Son, Grandson	35	-	25	12	-	2	-	23	1,651	17	7,763	83
Brother	16	-	-	-	37	2	-	44	355	13	2,279	87
Brother's Son, Grandson	10	20	5	-	3	35	11	18	955	24	2,978	76
Uncle	11	-	7	-	-	6	-	75	121	17	605	83
Cousin	21	5	17	5	28	-	4	20	316	18	1,426	82
Cousin's Son, Grandson	7	24	6	13	3	34	-	13	224	30	533	70
Total N	813	263	539	246	293	459	121	1,373	4,107		19,299	

†See Table 6.2 for list of registers included in this calculation.

Table 6.5. *Family relationship transitions by birth order and relationship at birth, 1792-1873*†

Relationship at Birth	N	Head	Son, grandson	Brother	Brother's son, brother's grandson	Uncle	Cousin, cousin's son	No change‡
		%	%	%	%	%	%	%
Son								
First Born	151	60	-	1	1	1	-	36
Later Born	194	16	-	51	1	21	1	37
Grandson								
First Born	203	35	40	-	23	3	10	35
Later Born	107	11	57	37	17	22	7	27
Brother's Son								
First Born	114	47	11	2	3	4	36	31
Later Born	111	9	29	43	2	23	35	28
Brother's Grandson								
First Born	47	30	45	-	17	-	23	38
Later Born	20	20	80	20	20	5	45	25
Cousin's Son, Cousin's Grandson								
First Born	15	27	33	-	-	13	40	40
Later Born	13	-	31	15	31	8	31	61
Total	975							

†This calculation is restricted to males born in or after 1792 who remained under observation until their death. Results accordingly represent percentage of men of each birth order and relationship at birth ever attaining specified household relationship.

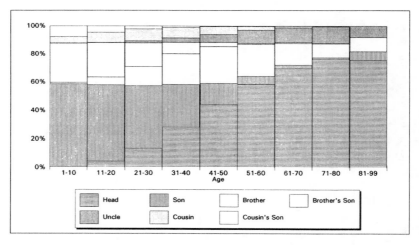

Figure 6.3. *Male household relationships, by age*
(percentage of males at each age in specified relationship)

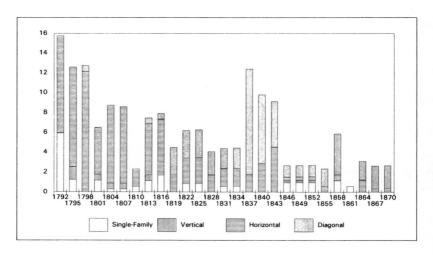

Figure 6.4. *Type-specific annual household division rates*
(divisions per 1,000 household-years at risk)

Among male siblings, birth order dictated the order of precedence. Table 6.5 summarizes the percentage ever attaining each family relationship for the 975 men whom we have under observation from birth to death and who had at least one brother. Regardless of parentage, first-born children had a much greater probability of eventually becoming a household head than later-born children. For example, 58 percent of heads' first-born sons eventually headed a household of their own, in contrast with only 16 percent of heads' later-born sons. Similarly, 47 percent of brothers' first-born sons eventually became a head, in contrast with only 9 percent of their later-born sons. In rural Liaoning, household succession apparently followed rules of primogeniture precedence.

Some men not fated to become heads by the circumstances of their birth were still fortunate enough to acquire it by luck. Figure 6.3 summarizes the distribution of family relationships by ten-year age group. One means of acquiring headship, apparently, was to outlive all the other heirs. The proportion of individuals who were head rose steadily with age, even relative to members of the same generation. As a result, between two-thirds and three-quarters of all men over age sixty were household heads in their own right, a much higher proportion than in any of the other age groups.

Familial cleavage and household division

With social mobility determined by parentage, birth order, and luck, one of the few ways individuals could change their domestic fate was to depart from the household, either legally or illegally. Legal departure meant household division and was usually a group decision.[16] Illegal departure meant departure not just from the household, but from government control altogether and was usually an individual act.[17] In both cases, as a new head or the relative of one, departed individuals enjoyed increased entitlement to and perhaps increased control over the resources in their new households.

While inheritance was partible in Daoyi, it was not equal. The eldest son not only received considerably larger shares than his younger brothers, so did his eldest child.[18] The rationale for such favoritism

---

[16] Shirokogoroff 1926, 140—141, has a very detailed discussion of household division among "Manchus."

[17] Such individuals are annotated on the household registers as "escaped" (*taoding*).

[18] This is true for much of late imperial society as well. There is increasing evidence that in much of late imperial society while inheritance was partible, it was not in equal shares (Dennerline 1986; Wakefield 1992).

was that the household head and his heir not only bore the burden of parental support, but also the responsibility for ancestral sacrifices and ancestral traditions (Chikusa 1978). The sole family division document we have been able to locate from Daoyi, which we translate in Appendix C, reflects such inequities. Although it is from a far more contemporaneous and egalitarian period—1956—the elder brother, Lang Zhongqing, still receives almost twice as much land as his younger brother, Lang Wenlin.

In any case, opportunities to depart during the century under observation became scarcer as time went on. During the nineteenth century, the Malthusian trend of rising resource pressure discussed in Chapter 3 reduced the frequency of household division, and changed the conditions under which it could occur. According to figure 6.4, which summarizes annual household division rates, before 1819, almost all the households that divided did so at the horizontal stage of the joint household cycle. After 1820, however, division became rare. Of the households that did divide, an increasing proportion did so at the diagonal stage.

This tightening was reflected in time trends of individual rates of legal and illegal departure summarized in figure 6.5. Initially, between 1792 and 1802, departure was relatively common, with as many as 15 of every 1,000 people leaving their households each year, that is more than double the rate for the century as a whole. With the exception of a peak between 1837 and 1845, subsequent rates were lower. On average, no more than 5 individuals per 1,000 at risk left their households in a given year. In fact, legal departures were so uncommon between 1861 and 1864 that only 4 individuals in all left their households.

Reductions in the frequency of division and departure transformed inheritance. In the early years, when it was still practical for brothers to divide a household between them, each could expect to acquire control over a share of the inheritance. Later the rules changed, so that even when a head died, his children, siblings, and even his distant relatives remained together rather than divide the household. It was no longer possible for anyone but the head's eldest son to hope for control over the inheritance. Unigeniture inheritance became the rule. Partible inheritance became the exception. [19]

---

[19]   In an unpublished paper, based on the analysis of over 200 wills from eighteenth- and nineteenth-century Taiwan and Fujian, Michael Finegan (1988) identified a pattern where richer families delayed household division, presumably because of their desire to preserve the ideal Confucian multi-generational family.

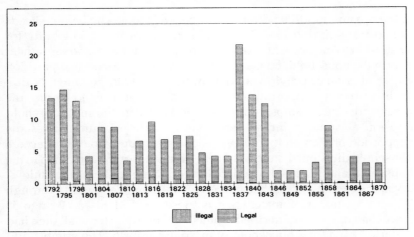

Figure 6.5. *Annual illegal and legal departure rates*
(departures per 1,000 person-years at risk

The shift in division rules affected the distribution of household types. Over time, increasingly elaborate multiple-family households accounted for a larger and larger proportion of the population. Before 1810, while horizontal households could still divide upon the death of the head, there had been almost no diagonal households. [20] After 1810, when horizontal households ceased dividing, the number of diagonal households began to climb steadily.

As a result, individual household context changed dramatically, with progressively larger proportions of the population living in the most complex household types. Table 3.10 presented the proportion of individuals living in different household types in each register. According to table 3.10, the proportion of the population living in diagonal households grew mainly at the expense of the proportion living in horizontal households. Thus while more than one half of all individuals lived in horizontal households in 1792, less than one-quarter lived in horizontal households by 1873. By the late nineteenth century, the "myth" of the Chinese multiple-family household had become a reality.

Legal departure was nevertheless almost the only way in which men of low parentage could hope to head a household of their own. Table 6.6 identifies the proportion of relationship transitions attributable to participation in a household division. The contrast is stark. While only 9 percent of sons and 11 percent of brothers who became head did so through household division, 74 percent of the nephews, 86 percent

[20] The single exception was in 1801, when there was one diagonal household recorded.

of the cousins, and 100 percent of the cousin's sons who became heads did so through division. Thus while rules governing eligibility for succession to the headship constrained opportunities for advancement within the household, household division and the associated partition of the inheritance provided opportunities for advancement without.

Even though opportunities became more constrained during the nineteenth century, most individuals still participated in a household division at some point in their lives. Table 6.7 summarizes the proportion of men and women in each age group who experienced a household division, distinguishing between those who remained in the household and those who departed. According to these calculations, divisions were particularly common for young males aged 11 through 30, and for mature females, that is those aged 31 to 40. By age 50 more than one-fifth of married women and one quarter of all men had departed from their household of marriage or birth. The number and age structure of the people left behind were roughly similar. By age 50 more than one-half of all men and two-fifths of all married women had been involved in a division.

The probability that a household would divide was strongly correlated with its household size and structure. Table 6.8 presents rates of division in multiple-family households by the number of conjugal units as well as by household type. As we might expect, the rate of division increases steadily with both household size and complexity. The overall rate of division almost quadruples in moving from households with two conjugal units to households with five or six, going from 6 per 1,000 to 22 per 1,000. Similarly, the rate of division increases steadily in going from vertical to horizontal and from horizontal to diagonal households. Only vertical households remained stable whatever their size, reflecting the authority of the heads over their married sons in traditional China.

The calculation of annual rates of departure by household type in table 6.9 reinforces the correlation between complex structure and departure. While only 1 of every 1,000 vertical households divided in an average year, 14 of every 1,000 horizontal households and 24 of every 1,000 diagonal households did. Whereas in vertical households, the head's authority over the rest of the household was reinforced by his power as everyone's father or father-in-law, in more complex households he had to contend with ambitious men of his own generation, or even the one above. Clearly the more complex the household, the more likely the division.

Table 6.6. *Percentage of each type of household relationship transition due to departure, males 1792–1867*

Previous relationship	Head		Son, grandson		Brother		Present relationship — Brother's son, grandson		Uncle		Cousin		Cousin's son, grandson		Total	
	%	N	%	N	%	N	%	N	%	N	%	N	%	N	%	N
Head	-	-	-	-	-	-	-	-	-	-	-	-	-	-	-	-
Son, Grandson	9	573	-	-	11	414	10	196	17	45	20	36	-	-	9	1,264
Brother	11	55	-	-	-	-	-	-	6	130	86	7	-	-	6	192
Brother's Son, Grandson	74	91	50	190	56	49	-	-	17	24	7	332	9	100	25	786
Uncle	62	13	-	-	44	9	31	16	-	-	-	-	-	-	16	22
Cousin	86	66	50	16	74	53	-	-	24	88	-	-	-	-	43	239
Cousin's Son, Grandson	100	16	89	54	100	13	62	29	33	6	22	77	-	-	54	195
All Relationships	25	814	57	260	24	538	16	241	14	293	6	452	8	100	21	2,698

See Table 6.2 for a list of the registers included in this calculation. Males were only included if they were alive in the current register.

Table 6.7. *Percentage ever experiencing a household division, by age and sex*

Age group (sui)	Men					Women				
	Never experienced a division	Departed	Remained after a division	Age specific departure rate†	N	Never experienced division	Departed	Remained after a division	Age specific departure rate	N
1-10	97	2	-	5.3	6,480	100	-	-	-	1,203
11-20	86	7	7	8.4	7,080	93	4	3	4.1	5,334
21-30	73	14	13	7.1	5,487	82	8	9	4.4	4,607
31-40	62	19	20	4.9	4,245	72	14	15	7.6	3,438
41-50	55	22	24	5.6	3,122	61	18	21	5.6	2,214
51-60	47	25	29	0.0	1,920	55	22	23	6.8	1,434
61-70	45	25	31	4.5	1,043	55	23	23	1.8	815
71 +	40	26	35	-	469	-	-	-	-	

†To calculate this probability we first compute a ten year rate D_{10} = (percent departed in next age group - percent departed in current age group) / (percent never departed in current age group). We convert D_{10} by subtracting the tenth root of $1 - D_{10}$ from 1.

Table 6.8 *Division rates according to household type and size (divisions per 1000 household years at risk)*

Conjugal units	All households†		Vertical		Horizontal		Diagonal without brother		Diagonal with brother	
	Rate	N	Rate	N	Rate	N	Rate	N	Rate	N
0	0.6	9,444	-	-	-	-	-	-	-	-
1	1.7	16,251	-	-	-	-	-	-	-	-
2	5.6	9,510	0.3	3,444	6.8	4,974	17.2	696	22.7	264
3-4	15.3	7,326	3.2	1,584	17.7	4,113	23.3	687	19.3	933
5-6	21.9	2,325	0.0	264	25.9	1,236	30.1	366	17.4	459

†Includes simple households.

Fate and fortune in rural China

Table 6.9. *Annual departure rates 1792-1873†(per thousand household or person years)*

Household type	Legal departures		Illegal departures		HH years at risk	Person years at risk	Legal rate		Illegal rate	
	hh	person	hh	person			hh	person	hh	person
Fragmentary	7	10	11	11	6756	8583	1.0	1.2	1.6	3.8
Simple	1	3	15	18	9795	27015	0.1	0.1	1.5	0.7
Extended	26	52	12	12	6534	26589	4.0	2.0	1.8	0.5
Vertical	7	29	9	13	5319	38910	1.3	0.7	1.7	0.3
Horizontal	153	907	38	51	10782	104286	14.2	8.7	3.5	0.5
Diagonal										
No Brothers	41	208	4	4	1881	19995	21.8	14.4	2.1	0.2
Brothers	51	410	3	3	2001	28149	25.5	14.6	1.5	0.1
Total	286	1699	92	112	45816	253746	6.0	6.7	2.4	0.4

†We include all three-year, six-year, and nine-year intercensal periods in this calculation.

Table 6.10. *Percent of household dividing in next three years according to mortality status of specified relations, 1792–1867*†

Mortality events (in both preceding and succeeding three-year intervals)	Vertical households			Horizontal households			Diagonal households		
	at risk	number dividing‡	% dividing	at risk	number dividing	% dividing	at risk	number dividing	% dividing
Death of the head	173	5	2.89	264	43	16.29	64	6	9.38
No such death	578	0	0.00	1,221	36	2.95	426	30	7.04
Death of a son	66	2	3.03	108	6	5.56	26	6	23.08
No such death	685	3	0.44	1,377	73	5.30	464	30	6.47
Death of a brother				191	29	15.18	22	0	0.0
No such death				1,294	50	3.86	468	36	7.69
Death of a brother's widowed wife				50	11	22.00	2	0	0.0
No such death				1,435	68	4.74	488	36	7.38
Death of an uncle							122	16	13.11
No such death							368	20	5.43
Death of an uncle's wife							45	10	22.22
No such death							445	26	5.84
No deaths	366	0	0.00	661	11	1.66	156	3	1.92
Deaths, but not of above relations	161	0	0.00	334	5	1.50	124	7	5.64
Deaths, including one of above relations	224	5	2.23	490	63	12.86	210	26	12.38
Total	751	5	0.67	1,485	79	5.32	490	36	7.35

* Only the registers where the immediately preceding and succeeding registers are both available are included in this calculation.

† 'At risk' is defined as the number of households in the current register where a death (or no death) of the specified type occurred in either the preceding three years or the following three years.

‡ 'Divisions' are the number of these households that divide within the next three years.

Table 6.11. *Lines of cleavage in multiple-family household departures*

Line of cleavage†	Fragmentary	Simple	Extended	Vertical	Horizontal	Diagonal	Total
Head - Nephew etc.	2	1	5	-	58	2	68
Head - Brother	-	-	1	-	12	-	13
Head - Son etc.	-	-	3	3	5	1	11
Son etc. - Son etc.	-	-	2	5	3	-	10
Son etc. - Brother	1	-	5	-	59	1	66
Son etc. - Nephew etc.	-	-	4	1	32	1	38
Brother - Brother	-	-	-	-	5	-	5
Brother - Nephew etc.	-	-	1	-	8	2	11
Nephew etc. - Nephew etc.	-	-	3	-	10	-	13
Head - Cousin or Cousin's Son	1	-	4	-	-	66	71
Head - Uncle	1	-	-	-	-	3	3
Son etc. - Cousin etc.	-	-	2	-	-	16	18
Cousin etc. - Cousin etc.	-	-	-	-	-	6	6
Other	2	-	3	-	1	17	23
Total	7	1	33	9	193	114	357

†By line of cleavage we refer to the line along which households divide, that is, the relationships before division of the heads of the resulting households.

Table 6.12. *Percentage of males departing by household division before next available register, by household type and relationship, 1792-1873*

Relationship	Extended %	Extended N	Vertical %	Vertical N	Horizontal %	Horizontal N	Diagonal %	Diagonal N
Head	0.0	15	0.0	5	0.1	119	0.0	74
Son								
Eldest	15.3	13	28.6	7	1.6	128	0.0	62
Non-Eldest	0.0	6	33.3	9	4.2	95	0.0	38
Grandson								
Eldest	66.7	30	60.0	15	3.5	114	0.0	20
Non-Eldest	-	-	75.0	8	0.0	52	0.0	9
Brother								
Eldest	100.0	4	-	-	77.8	18	16.7	6
Non-Eldest	25.0	4	-	-	82.5	120	2.7	75
Brothers' Son, Grandson								
Eldest	85.7	14	-	-	90.3	269	12.8	47
Non-Eldest	80.0	5	-	-	91.3	138	19.2	26
Uncle								
Eldest	100.0	1	-	-	-	-	67.0	49
Non-Eldest	-	-	-	-	-	-	77.8	18
Cousin								
Eldest	60.0	5	-	-	-	-	87.4	119
Non-Eldest	100.0	2	-	-	-	-	88.6	88
Cousin's Son, Grandson								
Eldest	100.0	1	-	-	-	-	90.8	109
Non-Eldest	-	-	-	-	-	-	94.2	52
Total	43.8	73	45.5	44	46.8	1,053	49.4	792

Household members hoping to depart and form a new household could not do so at will. They had to wait for somebody important to pass away. According to table 6.10, a summary of household division frequencies and probabilities by recent mortality events, households tended to divide only upon the death of a senior member. In each of the five instances where vertical households divided, the head died. In 79.7 percent (63 of 79) of the cases of horizontal household division, a head, a son, a brother, or a brother's widowed wife had just died, even though such deaths occurred in only 33 percent of the observations of horizontal households. Similarly, 72.2 percent (26 of 36) of diagonal household divisions were associated with the death of one of six types of members, even though such deaths occurred in only 42.8 percent (210 of 490) of observations of diagonal households.[21]

Which type of death could precipitate a departure depended very much on household type, a reflection of how the roles of household members depended on the structure of the household in which they lived. Each household type had pivotal relations whose authority bound members together while alive, and whose deaths led to division. Horizontal households only divided upon the death of a head, a brother or a brother's widowed wife. Diagonal households, meanwhile, only divided upon the death of the head, an uncle or an aunt. Each household type, in other words, had its own characteristic set of precipitating events.

A household's structure accordingly determined not only when it would divide, but how. Each household type had characteristic lines of cleavage along which it could divide. Table 6.11 summarizes the prior family relationships of some 700 household heads who participated in a household division. Vertical households were so tightly bound by parental authority that on the rare occasion when they divided it was only between brothers and only upon the death of their father. Similarly, the strength of fraternal ties among brothers meant that while horizontal households divided more frequently, they largely did so along uncle—nephew lines of cleavage upon the death of the eldest brother. While some horizontal households did divide along brother—brother lines, they were ten times more likely to divide along either head—nephew or son—brother lines.

---

[21] Because the lag between the death of a key member and the division of the household could be longer than one or two intercensal periods, these calculations actually underestimate the importance of deaths as precipitating events. According to a manual inspection of the circumstances surrounding divisions, over 90 percent of departures could be explained as being the result of a death.

As household complexity increased even more, the lines of cleavage moved even farther away from the head. Diagonal households were ten times more likely to divide along head-cousin lines than along head-nephew or son-brother lines. The addition of increasingly distant relations to a household, in other words, forced previously antagonistic household members to merge their interests and ally together. Tensions between brothers were overshadowed by the conflict between the head and his cousins.

Solidarity between household members also depended on household structure. Table 6.12 summarizes the percentage of individuals by relationship and household type according to whether they remain or depart after a division. In horizontal households, the predominance of head-nephew and son-brother lines of cleavage meant that the head and his descendants usually broke cleanly from brothers and their descendants. During division, only 3 percent of the head's sons and grandsons departed, while only one-sixth of brothers and their descendants remained. Reflecting the strength of the bonds between heads and their brothers in diagonal households, when diagonal households divided, brothers and their descendants almost always remained behind with the head. Only 5 percent ever departed, while only 15 percent of uncles and cousins ever remained.

Conclusion

The household was the most basic and the most important social organization in rural Liaoning. This chapter demonstrates that household structure and individual position within the household were beyond individual control. People were unable to change their domestic environment at will, having to wait instead for certain precipitating events. When households did divide, they did so according to preset patterns. As a result, when an individual departed, their new household relationship was as much a function of their parentage as their old household relationship. Moreover, the decision to depart was the product of group strategy rather than individual will.[22]

The breakdown of the domestic cycle during the nineteenth century further sealed the fate of many men. Shortcomings aside, individual mobility through departure was the only compensation for the rigid

---

[22] "Division of the household and independence of the young, as very frequently seen among the peasants, are definitely disintegrative forces and will weaken group solidarity" (Fei 1946, 131). Fei's essay has many insights into the dynamics of household structure and household formation in China before the second half of the twentieth century.

hierarchy characteristic of the ideal Chinese multiple-family household. While position within the household at any given point in time was fixed by relationship to the household head, the potential for relationships to change made it possible to hope for different levels of privilege and responsibility over the life course. The rules of household formation in rural Liaoning came increasingly to encourage the preservation of elaborate multiple-family households, reinforcing the authority of the household head.

In Daoyi and surrounding villages, the patterns of household formation consequently present a picture of slow, delicate change. Individual position in the household largely depended on fate: gender, birth order, age, and existing household structure. And as we will see in Chapter 7, many important individual demographic events were in turn linked intimately to household structure and household position. The probability of marriage, children, their number, their gender composition, and even their death, were related not only to the household context, but also to the individual's position within such organizations. As a result, the demographic fate of many men was predetermined.

7

Domestic hierarchy and demographic privilege[1]

> All relations between the family members are regulated in detail by custom. The seniors occupy honorable places and exercise great influence until they fall into senility or complete physical debility. They are always honored by the expression of general attention. They are served at the tables with the best pieces of food, sometimes even separate tables are put up for them and special dishes are prepared. (Shirokogoroff 1926:98)

In Liaoning the myth of the large peasant household was a reality. The vast majority of the rural population lived in complex households with more than one conjugal family unit.

The hierarchical nature of such households defined the social and economic context of their daily life. Household structure determined the composition of the family work force. Household position determined access to family rights and resources. Household parentage determined the probability of rising to headship in their own right. All decisions from the commonplace—when they could eat, what they could wear—to the extraordinary—who they could marry, when they could have children—had to be negotiated within the household.

And yet with the exception of Arthur Wolf's pioneering analysis of nuptiality and fertility in Taiwan there has been little attempt to differentiate demographic patterns by specific family relationships.[2]

---

[1] We outlined this chapter and did the majority of the initial analysis during the first half of 1988. Lee completed an initial draft in the summer of 1988, and revised it during the summer of 1989 in light of new results on mortality. We presented preliminary versions of sections I and II to seminars at the Academia Sinica, Cambridge University, the Ecole des hautes etudes en sciences sociales, the University of Michigan, and the University of Washington, as well as to a panel on Chinese historical demography at the 1990 annual meeting of the Association of Asian Studies.

[2] Wolf's well-known thesis in Wolf and Huang 1980 is that different forms of marriage (major, minor, and uxorilocal) had different levels of fertility as well as different levels of divorce.

In this chapter we reconstruct such patterns for the 2,000 unique peasant households (10,000 household observations) in our population. The chapter is divided into three sections. In section I, we summarize the formal structure and hierarchy of family relationships and outline the theoretical lines of authority within these multiple-family households. In section II, we calculate vital rates by family relationship in order to demonstrate that the privileges and responsibilities inherent to such hierarchy had many fundamental demographic consequences. Finally in section III, we use demographic measures to demonstrate how each of the three most common forms of multiple-family households—vertical, horizontal, and diagonal—had different patterns of sodality and consequently different patterns of entitlement.

The canonical household hierarchy

In theory, all households, regardless of the configuration of relationships, were highly authoritarian patriarchies ruled by a household head. The head had supreme authority over all members of the household including his wife, his children, his junior relatives (brothers, sisters, cousins, and nephews) and their families. He controlled the family economy both as a unit of production and as a unit of consumption. He served as the family priest and as the family judge. The fundamental organizing principle repeatedly cited in numerous Ming and especially Qing books of family instructions simply states, "All junior and inferior relatives must consult the head of the family about every event, large or small. Before they do anything, they should ask his permission even when he is not their parent. The family can only be in order when the orders come from one person."[3]

The late imperial state, as we have seen, reinforced household hierarchy through a legal code that upheld such Confucian ideals.[4] The three general principles are well known: Generation, that is, parents over children; Age, that is, senior relatives over junior relatives; and

---

[3] The original statement is from Ouyang Xiu quoted in Chu T'ung-tsu 1961, 30.

[4] See Chapter 2. The organizing principles came from Confucian ideology and were summarized by what was called the Five Human Relationships (*wulun*): ruler—minister, father—son, elder brother—younger brother, husband—wife, and friend—friend. Three of these five human relationships deal specifically with the family: father—son, elder brother—younger brother, and husband—wife. Each of these may be taken as representative of a larger group. Thus the father—son relationship includes all parent—children relationships and by extension the relationship between senior and junior relatives. Elder brother—younger brother not only includes all relationships between siblings, but may be extended to cover the relationship between older and younger relatives of the same generation. Similarly the husband—wife relationship represents the ideal hierarchy between the sexes.

Gender, that is, men over women, and especially husbands over wives. Parents, for example, had the legal right to punish physically and even kill their children when they were disobedient.[5] Only parents who killed their children without any cause were punished, but by at most 100 blows of a bamboo rod or, under the revised "reformist" code of 1910, by a fine of 15 ounces of silver. On the other hand, the minimum punishment for unfilial behavior was also 100 blows. Disobedience or impoliteness could be punished by banishment. Cursing or physically resisting a parental beating could be punished by death. Parents, at least in theory, had absolute power over their children.

This was especially true of banner households.[6] The organization of labor under the banner system reinforced familial hierarchy. In Liaoning, as in many provinces, the household was the customary unit of production. Tenancy and hired farm hands were largely uncommon in these provinces. Instead, most households absorbed distant relatives as laborers, or vice-versa. Social relations within many rural Liaoning households resemble class relations outside.[7]

In rural Liaoning, the household head can, therefore, be virtually equated to landlords elsewhere. This tradition was so strong in Daoyi that elderly villagers can still recall the short purse strings that bound them to the household head during the late Republican and early Communist eras. Even the ex-village head during the late 1940s and early 1950s, for example, had to turn over his official salary to his elder brother who was household head. He was only able to gain control over his own income by forcing a household division.[8]

In theory, all three organizing principles are hierarchical. Generation takes precedence over Age; and Age takes precedence over Gender. The wife of the eldest son owes obedience first to her father-inlaw, then to her mother-in-law, and only third to her husband because of the supremacy of Generation and Age over Gender.

[5]   The role of familial principles in the Qing legal code is discussed in a number of texts such as Zhu 1987. See Baker 1979 for a more general discussion.

[6]   According to Shirokogoroff 1926, 98; "The general management of the economic activities of the family members belongs to the family chief, but in regard to the family law the direction and control are reserved to the eldest, if he is not such a tottering old man that he can no longer direct family affairs. If any one refuses to obey the orders or persuasions of the family chief the offense can be punished with beatings by the order of the senior. The Manchus do this especially if the individual includes in himself the quality of the senior and also that of the family chief. However this separation of the family chief is often practiced among the Chinese (*nikan*)."

[7]   Chikusa 1978 is still the best ethnography of the traditional family system in Liaoning.

[8]   Personal communication July 17, 1987.

Competing claims of precedence, however, created numerous internal tensions within the late imperial household. Thus a younger son might recognize that he was subordinate to his elder brothers, but might also believe that he was superior to his sisters-in-laws because of his gender. Similarly while parents might clearly recognize their own inferiority to their own parents and elder brothers, they might not agree that their children were inferior to their younger brothers. The heavy emphasis on male superiority and patrilineal descent in Chinese society easily made for conflict in social values.

In rural Liaoning these tensions were also exacerbated by the extreme complexity of many multiple-family households. Many Liaoning peasants lived in a complex household environment surrounded by relatives who were not from their immediate family. In many cases even the head could be outnumbered by distant relatives: uncles, cousins, nephews, and their families. Table 7.1 measures the average number of family members by household type and by family relationship. In vertical households the head ruled over just 6 people on average, his wife and 5 children or grandchildren. In horizontal households the household head ruled over 8 people, 3 from his own family and 5 from his brother's family; while in diagonal households the head ruled over 10 people, just 2 from his own family, 2 from his brother's family, and as many as 6 from his uncle's family. In each type of household the configuration of relationships was fundamentally different.

As the household progressed from a horizontal to a diagonal structure, moreover, the nature of the household head's authority changed. In vertical households, the head also ruled as a parent and husband. In horizontal households, he also ruled as an elder brother and senior relative. In diagonal households, however, the head had no additional leverage over his uncle and cousins. Indeed his authority over his uncle was highly ambiguous since his uncle by definition was also his senior relative. As household complexity increased, in other words, the head faced more and more people over whom he had less and less authority.

We are confronted, in other words, with three sets of questions. First, to what degree did these changing relationships influence the vital events of peoples' lives: the probability and duration of their marriages, the frequency and composition of their children, and finally their length of life itself?

Table 7.1. *Family members by relationship to household head,*
1792-1873†

Relationship	Extended	Vertical	Diagonal	Horizontal	Overall‡
			Household type		
Head	1.00	1.00	1.00	1.00	1.00
Spouse	0.60	0.80	0.69	0.78	0.62
Son	0.66	2.10	0.87	1.28	0.93
Son's Family	0.29	2.97	0.40	1.12	0.74
Daughter	0.17	0.17	0.12	0.25	0.16
Father Mother	0.42	0.11	0.42	0.27	0.22
Brother	0.42	-	0.79	1.44	0.54
Brother's Family	0.33	-	1.07	3.42	1.01
Sister	0.02	-	0.04	0.02	0.02
Uncle and Aunt	0.08	-	1.88	-	0.20
Cousin	0.04	-	2.17	-	0.21
Cousin's Family	0.02	-	2.33	-	0.22
Other Kin	0.05	-	0.80	-	0.09
Total	4.10	7.2	12.54	9.61	5.95
Households	1,575	1,335	1,001	2,637	10,550

†Mean number of individuals per household by relationship.

‡This also includes includes fragmentary and simple households.

Second, how did the Chinese resolve the competing claims of proximity to the household head, on the one hand, and generation, age, and gender, on the other? Did the head's children really fare better than those of his brothers? Could the head's nephews actually fare better than his wives?

Finally, how did Liaoning peasants cope with the paradox of a household head who was younger than his coresident uncles and cousins?

To answer these questions we turn in sections II and III to quantitative demographic analysis of differential vital rates (nuptiality, fertility, and mortality) in our population.[9]

Household position and demographic privilege

Our methodology is extremely straightforward. To calculate nuptiality, we simply measure the proportions of married men by age group and family relationship. To compute fertility and mortality, we count the number of children born by the family relationship of the father, and the number of deaths by the family relationship of the deceased. We then divide these counts by the total number of person-years we

[9] In these calculations, our units of analysis are not the 12,000 individuals (6,326 men and 6,140 women) surveyed in our registers, but rather the 85,000 observations we have of them. We accordingly use five-year age groups to avoid duplication, though some undoubtedly occurs.

have under observation in each relationship to produce age-specific vital rates.

Such comparisons can nevertheless be complicated. This is especially true when comparing household members of different generations. It is important to remember that although these rates control for age in order to take into account individual mobility within the household, they do not take into account the different possible household circumstances of people of the same age and different generation. Since uncles and nephews in the same household are rarely in the same age group, for example, simple comparisons of their age-specific rates are highly problematic. We also ignore simple households as they by definition have little hierarchy to differentiate.

Nuptiality: We begin with nuptiality. In rural Liaoning marriage was neither universal nor automatic. Indeed although virtually all women who lived to 30 *sui* married, almost 20 percent of men who lived to that age remained bachelors. Table 7.2 calculates the proportion of married men by family relationship.

As we might expect, household position clearly influenced both the timing and the probability of marriage. Among senior relatives, household heads married earlier and in higher proportions than anyone except uncles, who were of course even more senior in their own right. Similarly among junior relatives, sons generally married earlier and in larger numbers than brothers' and cousins' sons. In each case, although the differences narrow considerably with age, they never disappear all together. In rural Liaoning, in other words, the higher the position, the earlier and more likely the marriage.

Differences between relations, however, narrow considerably with age. Thus while there are more unmarried relatives in their teens and twenties, by the last age group the proportions married are basically uniform for non-heads. Even oppressed members of the household could marry once they were past middle age and out of their prime child-bearing years. Apparently the household restricted the marriages of family members as a first step toward controlling their fertility.

Fertility: Fertility provides an even more sensitive measure of the effects of household hierarchy on demographic decisions. First, unlike marriage, the birth of children was an experience that people often repeated several times at different ages and in different household circumstances and family relationships. Second, the multiple methods of fertility and mortality control characteristic of the Liaoning demographic system enabled parents to adjust the number and sex of their

Table 7.2. *Percentages of men ever married by family relationship, 1792-1873*

Relationship	Age (in *sui*)							
	16-20		26-30		36-40		46-50	
	%	N	%	N	%	N	%	N
	Multiple-family households							
Head	52	54	86	196	93	394	97	613
Brother	27	183	76	427	89	595	92	507
Cousin	37	257	73	286	86	210	93	94
Uncle	-	-	88	52	90	81	93	132
Son	34	957	81	995	87	612	90	186
Brother's Son	26	634	75	395	79	151	87	23
Cousin's Son	38	115	72	54	81	16	-	-
Total Multiple-Family Households	31	2,874	78	2,772	88	2,287	94	1,680
Total Non-Multiple Family Households	10	1,282	50	1,063	70	1,232	76	1,112
Total All Households	25	4,156	71	3,835	82	3,519	87	2,792

†The following calculations for specific relationships only include households where the head is alive.

‡This total includes miscellaneous relationships not listed above, for example, grandson. Households where the head is dead are also included.

children according to a number of social and economic conditions including, for example, family relationship. Table 7.3 summarizes the number of boys already born by household relationship for married men age 16 through 50 *sui*.

The results indicate that children, like wives, were distributed according to the household hierarchy. Among senior relatives, household heads have by far the highest marital fertility. Similarly among junior relatives, the marital fertility of heads' sons is considerably higher than brothers' or cousins' sons. This was especially true in the early age groups where the gap between the largest and smallest number of boys was almost a factor of two. Moreover, were we to remove the control for marriage these contrasts would only increase.

Nevertheless, while household heads and heads' sons may have had more children than other relatives, they had proportionally fewer daughters. Table 7.4 contrasts the number of girls and boys born to each family relation, restricted to the years before female registration deteriorated. Figure 7.1 depicts these results. The closer people were

Table 7.3. *Boys already born by family relationship, married men 1792-1873*

				Age (*sui*)				
	16-20		26-30		36-40		46-50	
Relationship	Boys	N	Boys	N	Boys	N	Boys	N
	Multiple-family households							
Head	0.20	35	0.82	182	1.49	385	1.94	601
Brother	0.25	51	0.60	325	1.30	520	1.69	461
Cousin	0.09	96	0.48	211	1.00	172	1.60	85
Uncle	0.11	9	0.64	45	1.36	85	1.83	127
Son	0.21	332	0.73	797	1.31	521	1.72	160
Brother's Son	0.17	179	0.64	285	1.12	121	1.50	18
Cousin's Son	0.17	46	0.42	38	0.73	15	-	-
Total Multiple-Family Households	0.18	936	0.66	2,158	1.29	2,013	1.80	1,562
Total Non-Multiple Family Households	0.15	62	0.60	330	1.00	607	1.23	593
Total All Households	0.18	998	0.65	2,488	1.22	2,620	1.64	2,155

†The following calculations for specific relationships only include households where the head is alive.
‡This total includes miscellaneous relationships not listed above, for example, grandson. Households where the head is dead are also included.

Table 7.4. *Children already born by family relationship (married men 1792-1840)*

	16-20			26-30			36-40			46-50		
				Age (sui)								
Relation	M	F	N	M	F	N	M	F	N	M	F	N
				Multiple-family households								
Head	0.22	0.14	22	0.97	0.50	124	1.49	0.77	243	1.94	1.03	410
Brother	0.18	0.06	33	0.64	0.41	227	1.36	0.82	351	1.60	0.95	299
Cousin	0.15	0.10	40	0.54	0.23	78	0.94	0.56	54	1.84	0.84	19
Uncle	-	-	-	0.90	0.22	18	1.50	0.79	24	2.03	1.00	40
Son	0.23	0.12	218	0.79	0.42	566	1.38	0.79	342	1.78	1.05	87
Brother's Son	0.19	0.13	119	0.68	0.51	182	1.21	0.98	80	1.33	1.67	9
Cousin's Son	0.23	0.08	13	1.00	0.44	9	-	-	-	-	-	-
Total multiple-family Households	0.20	0.15	40	0.63	0.39	240	1.10	0.51	437	1.31	0.75	409
Total non-multiple family Households	0.20	0.12	562	0.75	0.43	1,338	1.36	0.78	1,200	1.81	1.00	913
Total All Households	0.20	0.12	602	0.73	0.43	1,578	1.29	0.71	1,637	1.65	0.92	1,322

†The following calculations for specific relationships only include households where the head is alive.

‡This total includes miscellaneous relationships not listed above, for example, grandson. Households where the head is dead are also included.

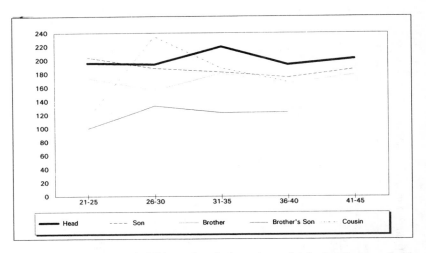

Figure 7.1. *Sex ratios of children already born in multiple-family households, by relationship* (values are presented only for age group-relationship combinations with more than 50 cases available)

to the line of succession, the larger the proportion of sons. The further away from the head, the larger the proportion of daughters. Brother's son is a particularly conspicuous example with slightly more girls even in absolute terms than the household head. Although the absolute values of these ratios may be exaggerated due to the underregistration of females, it is the unusual pattern of their relative values that is important. Presumably in expectation of their need to transmit headship, household heads and their sons were under far greater pressure to produce male heirs than other married men. By contrast, nephews who were unlikely ever to achieve headship found it more advantageous to have daughters.

In Daoyi, in other words, female infanticide was particularly acute among elite household members. Sexual differentials in infant and child mortality created numerous opportunities for hypergamous marriages. Lower household members in rural Liaoning, as a result, preferred daughters to sons, producing a sex ratio almost as unnatural as their elite counterpart.

Mortality: Death, of course, was the last demographic event; and in contrast with marriage and birth, embraced the entire population rather than simply the married couples of childbearing age. It is here that we can measure the differential treatment of the young and the aged with some precision. It is here too that we can analyze men and women separately rather than as married couples. We accordingly present our results in tables 7.5[10] and 7.6 by sex, by age group, by marital status and by family relationship.

The analysis of female mortality yields results very similar to the hierarchy of nuptiality and fertility. In most age groups women who were closely connected to the household head enjoyed lower mortality than those women who were not. This was true both for daughters (in the 1—10 and 21—30 *sui* age groups) and for widows (in the 51—60 *sui* age group). It was especially true for head's wives (in the 21—40 *sui* age group) who were in their prime childbearing years. Figure 7.2 contrasts the mortality rates of all wives. The head's wife was at the top of the hierarchy with the lowest mortality. Brother's wife was at the bottom with the highest mortality. Moreover, the gap between head's wife and brother's wife was almost a factor of two. Clearly the hierarchies of seniority and proximity were as important for women as for men.

Surprisingly, however, male mortality did not follow the canonical household hierarchy. Figure 7.3 depicts mortality rates for heads, brothers, cousins, sons, and brother's sons. According to these results, while young heads (below 40 *sui*) initially had relatively lower mortality rates, older heads (over 40 *sui*) suffered considerably higher mortality. Indeed, heads did the worst of any relationship within their generation, with a gap of almost a factor of two between them and their cousins. The pattern of male mortality, in other words, turned the standard hierarchy topsy-turvy, that is, upside down.

These results, moreover, suggest that for men, the relationship between nuptiality and fertility on the one hand, and mortality on the other, was roughly inverse. Men who fathered more children were more likely to die at an earlier age than those who did not. In Table 7.7 we accordingly contrast the mortality rates by age group and by number of children already born for the married male population at large. In virtually every age group men with more children suffered from higher mortality. The pattern is almost monotonic with a difference between those men with fewer children, that is less than

---

[10] This calculation is restricted to registers 1792, 1795, 1798, 1801, 1810, 1813, 1816, 1819, 1828, 1837, 1840, 1843, 1855, 1858, 1861, 1864. Totals include women in miscellaneous relationships, for example, granddaughter and grandson's wife, as well as women in households where the head is dead. Calculations for detailed relationships are restrictcd to households where head is alive, and presented only if there were more than 50 person-years at risk.

Table 7.5. *Female mortality by family relationship, 1792-1867 (deaths per thousand person-years)*†

Household Relationship	1-10 Rate	1-10 N	11-20 Rate	11-20 N	21-30 Rate	21-30 N	31-40 Rate	31-40 N	41-50 Rate	41-50 N	51-60 Rate	51-60 N	61-70 Rate	61-70 N
					Multiple-family household									
Married Women														
Head's Wife	-	-	-	-	12	650	13	1,423	20	2,049	21	2,145	41	1,316
Brother's Wife	-	-	0	98	11	1,321	18	1,975	14	1,738	24	918	34	295
Cousin's Wife	-	-	0	68	20	796	24	715	30	329	22	106	-	-
Uncle's Wife	-	-	-	-	24	126	13	299	21	381	39	381	49	229
Son's Wife	-	-	21	340	15	3,302	16	2,615	18	1,028	40	201	-	-
Brother's Son's Wife	-	-	36	138	19	1,403	12	688	35	198	-	-	-	-
Cousin's Son's Wife	-	-	-	-	31	162	0	86	-	-	-	-	-	-
Total‡	-	-	20	870	16	9,125	16	8,584	19	6,242	26	4,081	44	2,104
Unmarried Women														
Daughter	35	520	18	1,128	13	312	-	-	-	-	-	-	-	-
Brother's Daughter	46	548	18	1,135	24	248	-	-	-	-	-	-	-	-
Cousin's Daughter	36	97	20	152	-	-	-	-	-	-	-	-	-	-
Total‡	40	2,790	18	4,351	20	869	-	-	-	-	-	-	-	-
Widowed Women														
Head's Wife	-	-	-	-	-	-	-	-	-	-	14	588	49	894
Brothers's Wife	-	-	-	-	-	-	38	79	19	214	34	291	42	264
Uncle's Wife	-	-	-	-	-	-	182	33	59	68	34	178	56	234
Total‡	-	-	-	-	95	84	45	335	15	799	23	1,360	50	1675
Non-Multiple Family Household														
Wife	-	-	-	-	17	1,381	19	2247	23	2,059	20	1,098	45	468
Daughter	43	511	17	120	32	250	-	-	-	-	-	-	-	-
Widows	-	-	16	1,174	-	-	1	131	2	431	25	839	57	1,178
Total all Households‡	40	3,315	18	6,515	17	1,1725	17	1,1396	20	9,575	24	7,404	49	5,431

Table 7.6. *Male mortality by family relationship, 1792–1867 (deaths per thousand person-years)*†

Household Relationship	1-10 Rate	1-10 N	11-20 Rate	11-20 N	21-30 Rate	21-30 N	31-40 Rate	31-40 N	41-50 Rate	41-50 N	51-60 Rate	51-60 N	61-70 Rate	61-70 N
							Age (sui)							
Multiple-family household														
Head	-	-	10	100	7	543	9	1,319	20	2,152	34	2,622	58	2,343
Brother	-	-	11	444	7	1,428	7	2,246	16	2,466	32	1,508	60	663
Cousin	10	303	8	881	10	1,026	10	912	10	578	17	177	-	-
Uncle	-	-	16	127	15	272	19	427	37	535	108	389	208	154
Son	33	1398	9	3,650	6	4,415	10	3,489	18	1,530	23	353	37	107
Brother's Son	27	1,751	7	3,169	8	2,282	9	1,092	29	309	-	-	-	-
Cousin's Son	31	549	12	575	-	-	-	-						
Total‡	37	7,829	9	12,678	7	12,048	10	10,515	18	8,124	32	5,593	61	3,832
Non-multiple family household														
Total	34	1,699	8	3,961	8	3,482	12	3,665	19	3,767	37	2,664	61	1,783
Total All Households‡	36	9,528	9	16,639	7	1,553	10	14,180	18	11,891	34	8,257	61	5,615

†This calculation is restricted to registers 1792, 1795, 1798, 1801, 1810, 1813, 1816, 1819, 1828, 1837, 1840, 1843, 1855, 1858, 1861, 1864.
‡Totals include men in miscellaneous relationships, for example, grandson, as well as men in households where the head is dead. Calculations for detailed relationships are restricted to households where head is alive, and presented only if there were more than 50 person-years at risk.

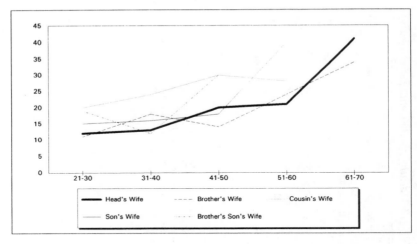

Figure 7.2. *Married female mortality in multiple-family households, by relationship*

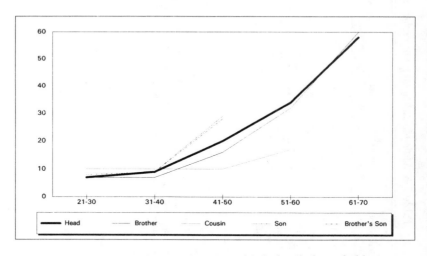

Figure 7.3. *Male mortality in multiple-family households, by relationship*

Table 7.7. *The price of children: married male
mortality in all households by children already born,
1792-1873 (deaths per 1000 person-years at risk)*

| Age (*sui*) | Number of children already born | | | | | |
| | 1–3 | | 4–6 | | 7–up | |
	Rate	N	Rates	N	Rate	N
21–30	8	4,229	-	-	-	-
31–40	10	7,059	15	930	18	55
41–50	23	6,060	14	1675	26	231
51–60	39	4,332	38	1428	61	181
61–70	60	2,603	68	762	75	159
71+	132	969	171	244	200	30

three, and those men with more children, that is more than seven, of at least 20 percent—a difference by 60 *sui* of 10 years in life expectancy. Children, in other words, came with a heavy price. Nevertheless, many men continued to have children even when the price of such parental investment was heavy enough to drag their overall well-being down.

Who was willing to pay such a price? As we might expect, the answer is heads and their heirs, that is, their eldest sons. Table 7.8 differentiates male mortality by household relationship, by birth order, and by the number of children. The results are quite complex. On the one hand, household heads, first sons, and uncles who had many children clearly suffered more from higher mortality than those who had fewer children. On the other hand, later born sons, brothers, cousins, and brothers' sons who had children clearly had lower mortality than those who did not. Household heads and proto-heads, in other words, were willing to have children whatever the drain on their resources. Other men who were not in the line of headship transmission only had children when they had the resources.

Household seniority, in other words, carried responsibilities as well as privileges. We can only speculate what the specific causes of higher head mortality were: too much work, too much play, or a combination of both.[11] Clearly, these privileges—early marriage

[11] Given the importance of exposure patterns to infectious disease mortality, and lifestyle patterns to chronic disease mortality, we may hypothesize numerous explanations for heads' higher mortality. As families' representatives to the "outside world," for example, heads would have been exposed to infection more frequently than other household members. They would have had more interactions with other village residents, and may even have been more likely to travel to Shenyang. Meanwhile, the burdens of having to manage the household's affairs and at the same time contributing labor may have worn them down physically and psychologically,

and many children—cut both ways. The theoretical hierarchy, in consequence, did not always translate into extended practice.

Household structure and demographic conflict

Individual demographic behavior was clearly shaped by Confucian principles of hierarchy. Nevertheless, while these principles provided a general paradigm of precedence and deference, different household members could still make competing claims for entitlements. Negotiation and compromise inevitably had to complement hierarchy and authority in household decision making.

Household structure often determined the outcome of such negotiations since different configurations of relationships had different lines of authority and allegiance. Household structure, in other words, modulated household hierarchy. Indeed, as we shall see, specific configurations could fundamentally distort the traditional hierarchy. Moreover, these distortions are reflected in demographic rates.

Such comparisons, of course, are increasingly complex since they attempt to locate behavior within four rather than three dimensions: adding household type to family relationship, generation, and age group. Once again it is important to remember that although these rates control for age in order to take into account individual mobility, they do not take into account the different possible household circumstances of people of the same age and different relationship. We again ignore simple households as they by definition have little hierarchy and no structure to differentiate.

Nuptiality: We begin with marriage, not only because marriage was the first demographic event of any significance, but also because marriage was an event over which households typically exercised considerable control. Table 7.9 measures the proportion of married men by household type, and by family relationship. The results differed considerably from the simple hierarchy described in table 7.2.

Three contrasts stand out. First, not only was there a hierarchy between household members, there was also a hierarchy

making them more vulnerable to infection. On the other hand, heads' privileges could have exacted a price as well by increasing their chances of chronic illness. On the *kang*, heads slept closest to the heating stove, so that while they may have been warmer than their kin, they may also have been more exposed to airborne pollutants. Their command of household resources may have allowed them to indulge in unhealthy behaviors, for example, consume alcohol. Given the lack of concrete data on behavior patterns, let alone cause-of-death, it is of course impossible to test any of these hypotheses.

Table 7.8. *Male mortality in multiple-family households by children already born, 1792-1867 (deaths per 1000 person-years at risk)†*

Relationship	Children already born	Age (sui)									
		21-30		31-40		41-50		51-60		61-70	
		Rate	N	Rate	N	Rate	N	Rate	N	Rate	N
Head	1-2 Children	13	188	5	684	21	957	33	1060	51	902
	3+ Children	71	18	22	253	19	894	37	1290	61	1066
Brother	1-2 Children	9	304	7	942	16	1048	35	705	65	225
	3+ Children	-	-	1	351	16	899	25	606	59	254
Uncle	1-2 Children	28	33	11	141	15	219	17	220	115	133
	3+ Children	-	-	24	38	23	118	50	236	97	212
Cousin	No Children	14	444	9	320	16	135	37	25	-	-
	1+ Children	7	177	13	441	9	391	18	34	-	-
First Son	No Children	7	300	13	359	7	124	0	27	-	-
	1+ Children	4	432	14	883	16	577	40	133	-	-
Later Son	No Children	7	629	12	336	25	110	-	-	-	-
	1+ Children	6	513	6	603	13	273	-	-	-	-
Brother's Son	No Children	7	763	10	334	31	67	-	-	-	-
	1+ Children	5	511	9	521	27	187	-	-	-	-

†This calculation is restricted to registers where immediately succeeding register is also available: 1792, 1795, 1798, 1801, 1810, 1813, 1816, 1819, 1828, 1837, 1840, 1843, 1855, 1858, 1861, 1864.

Table 7.9. *Percentages of men ever married by household type*
and family relationship, 1792-1873
(multiple family households only)†

Relationship	16–20 %	16–20 N	26–30 %	26–30 N	36–40 %	36–40 N	46-50 %	46-50 N
				Age (*sui*)				
Vertical Multiple-Family Households								
Head	-	-	100	15	100	26	100	146
Son	51	337	87	482	89	322	95	112
Grandson	22	184	74	62	-	-	-	-
Total‡	41	585	86	616	90	400	97	278
Horizontal Multiple-Family Households								
Head	-	-	95	78	95	233	98	348
Brother	32	115	79	312	90	491	92	446
Son	23	489	77	432	85	255	80	66
Grandson	25	122	-	-	-	-	-	-
Brother's Son	27	576	77	359	83	138	91	22
Total‡	26	1,521	78	1,372	89	1,242	94	948
Diagonal Multiple-Family Households Without Brothers								
Head	55	29	73	62	85	61	90	52
Cousin	41	119	73	139	90	102	91	55
Uncle	-	-	83	18	86	43	90	63
Son	33	60	61	41	88	77	-	-
Cousin's Son	35	65	69	36	100	13	-	-
Total‡	39	289	71	307	88	243	91	181
Diagonal Multiple-Family Households With Brothers								
Head	-	-	83	41	89	74	91	67
Brother	18	68	68	115	83	98	86	58
Cousin	33	138	73	147	81	108	95	39
Uncle	54	13	91	34	95	41	96	69
Son	25	71	75	40	94	14	-	-
Cousin's Son	42	50	78	18	-	-	-	-
Total‡	28	413	73	424	83	355	91	240

†This calculation is restricted to households where the head is currently
alive. Results presented only for relationship/age group combinations with
more than ten men at risk.
‡Totals also include miscellaneous relationships, for example, grandson, as
well as households where head is not alive.

between household types with vertical households at the top, households in the middle, and diagonal households at the bottom. As we might expect, the contrasts were greatest in the 16—20 age group with a gap of over 50 percent and narrowed considerably by the 46—50 age group to just under 10 percent. Even after 50, however, marital fulfillment did not increase with household complexity. The larger the number of contending factions, the fewer the marriages.

Second, seniority generally took precedence over proximity to the household head especially in the early age groups (16 through 30 *sui*). Thus while the proportions of married sons in vertical households were extremely large, their proportions in horizontal and diagonal households were much smaller—a difference of a factor of two in the 16—20 age group and a difference of a factor of one-third in the 26—30 age group. Instead brothers and cousins clearly married earlier and in greater numbers than sons; just as uncles married earlier and in greater number than household heads. Household setting, in other words, could be even more important a determinant of nuptiality than family relationship.

Third, while marriage clearly followed a distinct pecking order, the order of precedence changed with household type. In vertical households access to marriage was decided largely by birth order. Eldest sons married far earlier and in much greater numbers than non-eldest sons. In horizontal households, however, such preferential treatment virtually disappeared among sons and can only be found in the generation of the head. Heads still married earlier and more frequently than their younger brothers. However, even this preferential treatment fades somewhat in diagonal households where, controlling for age, uncles typically married in larger numbers than household heads. Each household possessed a clear hierarchy, but as household complexity increased, the dividing line between the haves and have-nots shifted outwards and upwards. Under certain circumstances, in other words, distant relatives did not have to wait. Indeed, they married first.

Fertility: Household structure, however, was a less important determinant of fertility. Table 7.10 measures the number of boys already born to married men controlling for age, household type, and family relationship.

The results are mixed. As in nuptiality, fertility decreased with household complexity. Children, moreover, were allocated at least partially according to seniority as well as proximity. In both vertical and horizontal households, older sons have more children

Table 7.10. *Boys already born by household type and family relationship, 1792-1873†*

				Age (*sui*)				
	16-20		26-30		36-40		46-50	
Relation	Boys	N	Boys	N	Boys	N	Boys	N
	Vertical Multiple-Family Households							
Head	–	–	0.73	15	2.26	27	2.39	148
Son	0.13	173	0.62	432	1.16	297	1.59	111
Total‡	0.13	216	0.60	484	1.24	329	2.00	260
	Horizontal Multiple-Family Households							
Head	–	–	0.83	75	1.48	224	1.76	357
Brother	0.16	37	0.51	249	1.19	450	1.66	434
Son	0.09	116	0.65	334	1.40	229	2.02	61
Brother's Son	0.10	159	0.55	282	1.02	120	1.50	20
Total‡	0.10	363	0.60	968	1.28	1026	1.72	872
	Diagonal Multiple-Family Households Without Brothers							
Head	0.19	16	0.70	47	1.25	52	1.96	53
Cousin	0.12	51	0.39	102	1.06	97	1.92	50
Uncle	–	–	0.75	16	1.28	406	1.80	59
Son	0.10	20	0.60	25	0.93	15	1.00	6
Cousin's Son	0.13	24	0.32	25	0.69	13	–	–
Total‡	0.13	115	0.50	222	1.11	223	1.87	173
	Diagonal Multiple-Family Households With Brothers							
Head	–	–	0.57	35	1.24	67	1.53	68
Brother	0.08	13	0.35	79	1.02	81	1.46	52
Cousin	0.06	47	0.45	111	0.86	92	1.32	41
Uncle	–	–	0.64	33	1.36	42	1.66	70
Son	0.22	18	0.39	31	1.89	18	–	–
Cousin's Son	0.10	21	0.57	14	–	–	–	–
Total‡	0.08	118	0.45	319	1.11	305	1.52	236
	Non-Multiple Family Households							
Head	0.14	35	0.54	224	0.98	494	1.25	530
Brother	0.20	5	0.24	21	0.61	56	0.79	58
Son	0.09	11	0.35	54	0.91	53	1.04	26
Total‡	0.13	54	0.49	313	0.94	619	1.19	636

†Calculations by relationship are restricted to households where the head is currently alive. Results presented only for relationship/age group combinations with more than ten men at risk.

‡Totals also include miscellaneous relationships, for example, grandson, as well as households where head is not alive.

Table 7.11. *Married female mortality in multiple-family households by household type and family relationship, 1792-1867 (deaths per thousand person-years)*

Age (sui)

Household Relationship	1-10 Rate	1-10 N	11-20 Rate	11-20 N	21-30 Rate	21-30 N	31-40 Rate	31-40 N	41-50 Rate	41-50 N	51-60 Rate	51-60 N	61-70 Rate	61-70 N
Vertical Households														
Head's Wife	-	-	-	-	18	72	9	74	20	493	29	737	32	972
Son's Wife	-	-	34	166	16	1,809	17	1,365	23	611	44	113	-	-
Total	-	-	35	202	17	2,168	15	1,528	21	1,111	31	851	34	696
Horizontal Households														
Head's Wife	-	-	-	-	12	330	11	951	20	1,223	14	1,190	48	570
Brother's Wife	-	-	0	55	10	1,058	18	1,672	14	1,569	23	842	43	281
Brother's Son's Wife	-	-	34	116	21	1,309	11	666	36	197	12	82	-	-
Son's Wife	-	-	10	133	15	1,261	13	1,103	16	379	-	-	-	-
Total	-	-	15	351	15	4,205	14	4,438	17	3,368	18	2,137	45	887
Diagonal Households With No Brothers														
Head's Wife	-	-	-	-	8	129	20	152	29	151	26	63	-	-
Cousin's Wife	-	-	-	-	14	342	32	334	26	141	36	55	-	-
Uncle's Wife	-	-	-	-	-	-	17	137	17	161	45	187	43	92
Son's Wife	-	-	-	-	3	122	-	-	-	-	-	-	-	-
Cousin's Son's Wife	-	-	-	-	14	72	11	62	-	-	-	-	-	-
Total	-	-	0	64	14	728	23	751	23	480	38	315	41	148
Diagonal Households With Brothers														
Head's Wife	-	-	-	-	17	121	30	100	27	187	0	66	-	-
Brother's Wife	-	-	-	-	11	266	20	300	32	190	7	51	-	-
Cousin's Wife	-	-	-	-	22	459	19	374	20	221	31	204	69	146
Uncle's Wife	-	-	-	-	17	81	9	149	-	-	-	-	-	-
Son's Wife	-	-	-	-	17	121	30	100	-	-	-	-	-	-
Brother's Son's Wife	-	-	-	-	4	81	-	-	-	-	-	-	-	-
Cousin's Son's Wife	-	-	-	-	41	89	-	-	-	-	-	-	-	-
Total	-	-	15	130	18	1,218	19	1,226	24	821	25	477	63	231

Table 7.12. *Male mortality in multiple-family households by household type and family relationship (deaths per thousand person-years)*†

Household Relationship	1-10 Rate	1-10 N	11-20 Rate	11-20 N	21-30 Rate	21-30 N	31-40 (sui) Rate	31-40 N	41-50 Rate	41-50 N	51-60 Rate	51-60 N	61-70 Rate	61-70 N
Vertical Households														
Head	-	-	-	-	0	55	0	86	28	382	32	745	56	976
Son	27	223	5	938	7	2,040	9	1,728	19	842	32	197	-	-
Total‡	46	1,474	5	2,171	6	2,590	8	1,905	22	1,227	32	942	55	1,023
Horizontal Households														
Head	-	-	-	-	11	211	11	802	18	1,318	36	1,547	64	1,145
Brother	-	-	13	263	10	1,065	8	1,844	17	2,138	31	1,375	63	690
Brother's Son	28	1551	6	2,824	8	2,066	10	973	26	287	7	139	41	57
Son	33	864	11	2,180	4	2,069	13	1,477	18	573	-	-	-	-
Total‡	37	4,097	6	6,649	7	5,837	10	5,186	18	4,325	32	3,108	61	1,836
Diagonal Households With No Brothers														
Head	-	-	0	60	6	167	14	237	27	223	55	104	77	65
Cousin	0	113	6	422	5	463	9	433	8	237	13	106	-	-
Uncle	-	-	-	-	-	-	21	129	27	208	29	250	86	159
Son	29	160	9	266	8	171	22	77	-	-	-	-	-	-
Cousin's Son	39	251	12	267	0	152	-	-	-	-	-	-	-	-
Total‡	31	642	10	1,087	5	1,015	12	967	19	711	31	467	78	254
Diagonal Households With Brothers														
Head	-	-	-	-	8	124	6	275	11	304	34	185	70	81
Brother	-	-	7	202	2	391	0	430	6	312	72	102	-	-
Cousin	18	189	9	485	12	553	14	484	12	326	31	64	-	-
Uncle	-	-	-	-	30	102	16	147	10	228	46	288	139	214
Son	37	182	6	336	22	193	8	127	-	-	-	-	-	-
Brother's Son	18	246	7	340	13	177	0	79	-	-	-	-	-	-
Cousin's Son	25	308	11	301	0	111	-	-	-	-	-	-	-	-
Total‡	25	1,075	10	1,790	11	1,656	7	1,586	9	1,228	44	665	97	385

†Calculations by relationship are restricted to households where the head is currently alive. Results presented only for relationship/age group combinations with more than 50 person-years at risk.

‡Totals also include miscellaneous relationships, for example, grandson's wife, as well as households where head is not alive.

than younger sons. Similarly, in horizontal and diagonal households, heads have significantly more children than brothers and cousins. Uncles have as many or more children than household heads of the same age. But these patterns do not seem really to change by household type. Indeed, with the exception of uncles, proximity seems to have been more important than seniority as a determinant of fertility. Thus in both horizontal and diagonal households, sons generally had more children than brothers and cousins, presumably because of their need to perpetuate the line. The entitlement to children, in other words, was different from the entitlement to marriage. Seniority may have allowed brothers to produce their heirs early; it did not lead them to increase the numbers of their children.

Mortality: Household structure appears to have had little influence on mortality. Tables 7.11 and 7.12[12] present results on mortality by sex, by age group, by family relationship, and by household type. Certainly the death rates for the household head's wife do not seem to follow any consistent pattern by household type. Nor do the death rates for the other female relationships.

Patterns of male death rates by household type, however, resembled those in multiple-family households overall. Once again, heads suffered far higher mortality than other household members. Similarly, in horizontal and diagonal households sons died earlier than both brothers' sons and cousins' sons. The price of children, in other words, was so high that it overrode whatever effects household structure may have had on mortality.

The only exception was in diagonal households, where the presence or absence of brothers had the strongest effect on the death rates of the household head. When the head was without brothers, he not only did worse than his cousins, but past age 40 his mortality was three to four times higher. In contrast, when brothers were present, the head not only did better than his cousins, but in several age groups his mortality was 50 percent lower. Isolated heads, in other words, even when surrounded by uncles and cousins, were able to enforce their claim to wives and children, but were not able to provide themselves with the resources necessary to enjoy these benefits. The realities of competition and coalition between household members reinterpreted the principles of hierarchy.

---

[12] In tables 7.11 and 7.12 we restrict our calculations by relationship to households where the head is currently alive. Results presented only for relationship/age group combinations with more than 50 person-years at risk. Totals also include miscellaneous relationships, for example, grandson's wife, as well as households where head is not alive.

In theory, all household members deferred to the authority of the household head. In reality, the distribution of resources also depended to some extent on the configuration of family relationships and the consequent patterns of alliance and antagonism. As a result, vital rates not only vary by family relationship, but also by household type. Specific configurations of family relationships could distort the canonical hierarchy.

Conclusion

Demographic events, such as marriage, birth, and death, were by no means simply a stroke of fate. On the contrary, they were intimately related to household structure, one of the most important forms of social organization in rural China. Family relationship and household composition clearly had important implications for individual lives. The wide differences in vital rates by family relationships depict a hierarchical society muted only by individual upward mobility over the life course.

This was especially true because of the opportunity structure presented by the Liaoning demographic system. Since there were not enough women, some men had to delay or postpone marriage indefinitely. Since married couples could control their fertility, some people had to delay child birth when times were tough or their claim on household resources low. Since couples could use infanticide to determine the gender as well as the number of their children, some preferred to have more boys; others preferred to have more girls.

These demographic decisions to marry, to bear children, to retire, and to depart were the product of a complex system of bargaining and shifting coalitions within the household. Moreover, these coalitions were formed according to household relationship and household structure. Household heads and their children were the most enfranchised. Distant coresident relatives were the most disenfranchised. Vertical households were the most canonical. Diagonal households were the most conflicted. In rural Liaoning the large complex household, in other words, was neither an autocracy nor a "happy family." Obedience and deference, even reinforced by affect and tradition, did not always command willing compliance.

Part 4

Banner organization and population behavior

with Chris J. Myers

While the household in rural Liaoning was largely a private institution, the banner system was an entirely public institution. Created by the Qing state in the early-mid seventeenth century, banner ranks delineated the framework of social organization above the household. Households were organized into lineage units called *zu* patterned after the Manchu *mukūn*. These lineage organizations functioned as units of civil, fiscal, judicial, and military administration and provided the lowest level of formal government in Liaoning.[1]

In contrast with Han civil society, however, the banner system did not restrict itself to affairs above the household level. Instead the banner system penetrated household organization down to the level of individual adult males called *ding*. Daoyi district was state land, and its people were not just state servants, but elite military servants. Every adult male in the area was therefore liable for military service as well as for a variety of local civil service positions. The Eight Banner registers that provide the bulk of our data accordingly record for each *ding*, detailed information on his obligation or ability to serve the state, as well as any specific occupational or organizational banner positions he might hold.

The banner system, therefore, provided many opportunities for individual advancement outside the household. We distinguish in Part Four between two overlapping banner hierarchies: the organizational and the occupational. On the one hand, men could rise to a position of leadership within the banner lineage organizations. On the other hand, men could also ascend to a number of formal artisanal, civil, and military occupations. In either case, just as demographic opportunities

---

[1] By contrast, these lineage organizations were far less important "within the passes" where the company or *niru* assumed many of these functions (Mark Elliott personal communication October 19, 1995).

varied by position in the domestic hierarchy, so they also varied by position in these banner hierarchies.

In contrast with household position, banner positions were supposed to be decided by ability. In theory, no local banner positions were hereditary. Lineage leaders, for example, were supposedly elected for their ability, honesty, and intelligence; just as military officers were supposedly promoted according to their ability, performance, and virility. In rural Liaoning the banner organization, in other words, provided a major opportunity for most peasants to transcend the fate dictated by their hereditary domestic circumstances.

In Part Four, we focus on the demographic consequences of the banner system. We divide our presentation into three chapters. We begin in Chapter 8 with a brief description of banner organization and individual status, especially entry to and exit from banner service. We then turn in Chapter 9; to an analysis of demographic rates by banner position, and assess the comparative influence of banner and household position on demographic behavior. Finally in Chapter 10, we compare the two paths—ability and heredity—by which bannermen could climb the ladder of success in rural China, and conclude with an assessment of their relative importance for individual fate and fortune.

8

Bannermen and banner organization[1]

(with Chris J. Myers and with the help of Yizhuang Ding)

In Daoyi, the most important organization above the level of the household was the Eight Banner system, in particular its occupational and organizational hierarchies. These overlapping hierarchies were the principal link between individuals and households on the one hand and the state on the other. The occupational hierarchy supplied the state with skilled manpower. The organizational hierarchy provided the local civil, fiscal, judicial, and military leadership, and in fact was the lowest layer of formal government administration in rural Liaoning.

The Eight Banner registers provide detailed information on the position of individuals within these two hierarchies, recording the obligations, occupations, and offices of every adult male every three years. These data are an important source not only for the study of the structure of rural social hierarchy, but also for the study of social mobility within that hierarchy. Furthermore, when combined with our knowledge of household relationships and household structure from previous chapters, they enable us to analyze the interactions between the occupational, organizational, and household hierarchies in our population.

In this chapter we describe both Eight Banner hierarchies. We do this because no similar study yet exists and because our understanding of rural banner society is consequently extremely rudimentary.[2] In

---

[1] Lee and Myers did the calculations for this chapter during the summer of 1989 as part of an unpublished study on social mobility and the life course in rural Liaoning. Lee rewrote and reorganized the text in the spring of 1991, while Campbell reedited the text in the summer of 1992. Ding Yizhuang provided invaluable last minute help elucidating the nature of banner hierarchy. We would like to express our thanks once again for her critical contribution.

[2] Previous studies of banner society, like the study of Chinese society, have focused either on the broad institutional outlines of banner organization (Ding 1992; Elliott

section I, we focus on the age pattern of entry to and exit from banner service, and the relationship with such life course events as marriage and headship. In sections II and III, we describe the occupational and organizational hierarchies. Finally in section IV, we provide some measures of career mobility within and between these two overlapping hierarchies.

Banner service

The basic unit of the Eight Banner occupational hierarchy in Daoyi was the adult male, or *ding*. Altogether, the Daoyi registers identify almost fifty different types of *ding*, listed in table 8.1. The most common are such broad categories as "young" (*youding*), "new" (*xinzeng ding*),[3] "healthy" (*zhuangding*[b]), "disabled" (*feiding*), "retired" (*tuiding*), "elderly" (*laoding*), and "escaped" (*taoding*). In addition, there are 2,500 more precise occcupational *ding* records.

The meaning of some of these generic *ding* statuses is opaque. For example, the precise differences between *tuiding*, *laoding*, and *laotui* are unclear.[4] Furthermore, because *ding* were defined by their obligation or potential for state service, not all occupations are necessarily identified.[5] For most men, we only know their generic *ding* status and that they were presumably peasants. Nevertheless, analysis of the age patterns and of the household and banner context of these *ding* statuses can tell us much about the individual male life course and the opportunities for banner mobility. We begin this section with entrance into banner service.

Entrance: Virtually all males began their banner service as "beginning" *ding* (*chuding*) or "new" *ding* (*xinzeng ding*), which apparently indicated their eligibility for banner positions.[6] In general, this occurred between 15 and 19 *sui*. In this section, we attempt to reconstruct

---

1993), or on urban elite populations, not rural peasant populations (Crossley 1990).

[3] "New adults" abruptly disappear from the registers after 1846, presumably a function of institutional reform.

[4] These terms are missing from the *Rules and Regulations of the Eight Banners* (*Baqi zeli*) and from the various editions of the *Rules and Regulations of the Qing* (*Da Qing huidian shili*).

[5] While shop keepers or peddlers, for example, are generally absent, these professions may not have been indigenous to the local population. Even today most commercial services in rural Liaoning are supplied by itinerant immigrants from Shandong.

[6] 76 boys are initially registered as "child" *ding* (*youding*) before becoming "able-bodied." They, however, are typically the only male in their household. The average child *ding* entered this status at 10 *sui* and exited at 17 *sui*. Over 90 percent of the boys with this status are also listed as child heads of households.

Table 8.1. *Frequency of banner occupational statuses among adult males*

In English	In Chinese	Cases	Persons
		Banner occupational status	
Commoners		*28,405*	*4,259*
New adult male	Chuding	2	2
New adult male	Xinzengding	1,639	1571
Young male	Youding	226	134
Able-bodied male	Zhuangding[b]	19,043	3,654
Disabled adult male	Feiding	4,882	914
Disabled adult male	Chen (fei)	16	16
Disabled retired adult male	(Chen) tui	57	18
Retired adult male	Tuiding	1,345	629
Old adult male	Laoding	1,184	485
Old and retired adult male	Laotui	11	11
Soldiers		*1,020*	*186*
Adult male soldier	Jia (ding)	916	174
Adult male soldier	Bingding	2	2
Retired soldier	Tuijia	64	20
Forcibly retired soldier	Getui jiading	29	10
Forcibly retired soldier	Getui bing	9	4
Artisans and			
miscellaneous occupations		*708*	*128*
Archer artisan	Gongjiang	32	8
Archer artisan—retired	Tui gongjiang	13	3
Artisan	Jijiang	253	61
Artisan—new	Xinzeng jijiang	1	1
Artisan—retired	Tui jijiang	160	39
Blacksmith	Kezi jiang	25	3
Blacksmith—retired	Tui kezi jiang	2	1
Dyer	Ranjiang	61	12
Dyer—retired	Tui ranjiang	9	4
Fisherman	Yuding	40	17
Fisherman	Daxilin yuding	7	2
Fisherman—retired	Daxilin yu tuiding	3	2
Funeral expert	Huaer jiang	27	6
Funeral expert—retired	Tui huaer jiang	14	3
Shepherd	Muding	11	5
Shepherd	Muzhang	4	2
Shepherd—retired	Tui muding	9	1
Tailor	Caifeng	20	4
Tailor artisan	Caifeng jiang	2	1
Tanner	Pijiang	12	4
Tanner—new	Xinfang ranjiang	1	1
Tanner—retired	Tui pijiang	2	1

Table 8.1. (cont.)

| In English | In Chinese | Banner occupational status | |
		Cases	Persons
Officials		*324*	*68*
Degree holder	Shengyuan	4	1
Degree holder—purchased	Juanna gongsheng	3	
Government student	Guan xuesheng	57	15
Government student— Retired	Tui guan xuesheng	42	8
Guard captain	Wei lingcui	4	1
Preceptor captain	Niru cuizhang	20	8
Preceptor captain	Shifeng cuizhang	3	1
Runner	Guanfu	34	8
Runner—new	Xinfang guanfu	2	2
Runner—retired	Tui guanfu	9	3
Scribe	Bitieshi	14	4
Scribe—new	Xinbu bitieshi	1	1
Sergeant	Xiaoqi wei	1	1
Student—Imperial Academy	Jiansheng	37	6
Student—Imperial Academy	Gongsheng	1	1
Subofficial	Zhishiren	52	17
Subofficial—orchard	Guoyuan zhishiren	4	3
Subofficial—quartermaster	Maimai zhishiren	2	1
Subofficial—retired	Tui zhishiren	8	1
Subofficial—textiles	Zhizao zhishiren	1	1
Subofficial—textile warehouse	Zhizao ku zhishiren	1	1
Tax preceptor	Lingcui	3	3
Tax preceptor—honorary	Dingdai lingcui	2	1
Tax preceptor	Niulu lingcui	3	2
Tax preceptor—retired	Tui lingcui	2	1
Warehouse clerk	Kushi	13	4
Warehouse clerk—new	Houbu kushi	1	1
Warehouse clerk—retired	Tui kushi	1	1
Other†		*304*	*201*
Escaped male	Taoding	92	65
Corvee laborer	Bangding	209	135
Exiled male	Faqian ding	3	2
Total		30,761	4,433‡

†These are excluded from all subsequent calculations involving banner occupation.

‡Smaller than sum of above entries because many individuals appear in more than one occupation during their lifetime.

Table 8.2. *Mean ages at ding status transitions in early adulthood, 1792-1846**

Transition to	Mean Age	Standard Deviation	N
"New" *ding*†	18.7	1.6	919
"Able-bodied" *ding*‡	21.8	2.6	1,088
Marriage	21.9	6.0	932

All ages are in *sui*.
* Registers: 1792, 1795, 1798, 1801, 1804, 1813, 1816, 1819, 1822, 1831, 1843, 1846. Information on "new" *ding* status is unavailable after 1846.
†*chuding, xinzeng ding*.
‡*zhuangding*[b]

the significance of the passage to *ding* status by comparing its timing with that of two other life course events common among young males, marriage and acquisition of household headship.[7] The goal is to determine whether the transition to formal *ding* status could affect or be affected by the timing of these important life course events. If *ding* status indicated adulthood in a formal, legal sense, we might expect it to be a prerequisite for marriage. Alternatively, it may have been granted early to those who married or acquired headship while still in adolescence.

A comparison in table 8.2 of the mean ages at which young men underwent transitions in these registers suggests a standard sequence. Men first registered as "new" *ding*, changed to "able-bodied" *ding* in the next register, and then married, either in that register or the one subsequent. According to table 8.2, the mean age of men acquiring "new" *ding* status was 18.7 *sui*, with a standard deviation of only 1.5 years. Men became "able-bodied" *ding* three years later, when they were 21.8 *sui*. Marriage occurred soon afterward, at 21.9 *sui*, but the standard deviation, 6 years, was high.

Variations on this standard sequence, however, were frequent. According to the tally of out-of-sequence transitions in table 8.3, approximately one-quarter of the men attaining "New" status in the

---

[7] For this analysis, we rely on data for young men in the twelve registers from before 1855 for which immediately preceding registers are still extant. Having the immediately preceding register available permits more precise measurement of the timing of the transitions of interest. We restrict ourselves to the pre-1855 registers, meanwhile, because they distinguish most new *ding* with the special terms mentioned earlier, *chuding* and *xinzeng ding*. In 1855 these two categories vanished abruptly.

Table 8.3. *Sequencing of ding status transitions in early adulthood,*
1792-1846*

Transition to	From	Percent	N
"New" *ding*[†]	married, no *ding* status	25	234
	unmarried, no *ding* status	<u>75</u>	<u>685</u>
	Total	100	919
"Able-bodied" *ding*[‡]	married with no *ding* status	2	26
	married "new" *ding*	24	264
	unmarried with no *ding* status	15	162
	unmarried "new" *ding*	<u>60</u>	<u>656</u>
	Total	100	1088
First marriage	unmarried, with no *ding* status	14	12
	unmarried "new" *ding*	18	169
	unmarried, other *ding* status	<u>68</u>	<u>636</u>
	Total	100	932

* Registers: 1792, 1795, 1798, 1801, 1804, 1813, 1816, 1819, 1822, 1831, 1843,
1846. Information on "new" *ding* status is unavailable after 1846.

[†]*chuding, xinzeng ding.*

[‡]*zhuangding*[b].

Table 8.4. *Household headship and the transition to ding status,*
1792-1846*

	Percent with headship	N	Mean Age of those with headship	Standard deviation
"New" *ding*[†]	4	36 of 919	19.0	2.0
"Able-bodied" *ding*[‡]	7	73 of 1,088	21.5	2.3

* Registers: 1792, 1795, 1798, 1801, 1804, 1813, 1816, 1819, 1822, 1831, 1843,
1846. Information on "new" *ding* status is unavailable after 1846.

[†]*Chuding, xinzeng ding.*

[‡]*zhuangding*[b].

twelve registers were already married. One-quarter of the men achieving able-bodied status were already married as of the preceding register. As for the passage from "New" to "Able-bodied", well over one-sixth of the men registering as "Able-bodied" for the first-time, had no banner status at all in the preceding register.

Acquisition of household headship similarly did not affect the timing of transition to *ding* status, even though one might expect headship to require changes in an individual's legal status. According to a count in table 8.4 of males who were already household heads in the register preceding their passage to "New" or "Able-bodied," a small but nevertheless appreciable proportion of men became household heads before they became *ding*. When they did acquire *ding* status, they did so at the same age as other males.

Adult *ding* status, in other words, appears solely to have been an indicator of whether an individual was physically capable of banner service. It seems not to have carried any other obvious legal or social connotations. The passage to *ding* status was determined largely by age, unaffected by when an individual acquired other responsibilities such as household headship. Acquisition of *ding* status also does not seem to have been a prerequisite for marriage, the other significant event in the life course of young males. Entry to *ding* status, in short, seems to have been a creation of the public banner hierarchy with no intentional overlap with private household hierarchy.

Exit: This was also the case with exit from *ding* status. As was the case with the transition to *ding* status, we do not know all the rules that dictated the timing of the transitions to "retired" (*tuiding*) and "elderly" (*laoding*). In theory, men became "elderly" at 60 *sui*.[8] It is unclear, however, whether retirement occurred automatically at specific ages and under specific conditions, or was the result of an evaluation of the individual's condition, either by himself or a representative of the state. Furthermore, other than knowing that they were no longer eligible for banner service, we do not know if individuals who retired or registered as elderly acquired any new rights or responsibilities, or were released from previous obligations.[9]

We accordingly attempt to reconstruct the meaning of the transitions to retirement and old age, by examining the demographic circumstances of men undergoing such transitions. For calculations involving the timing of these transitions, we rely on data in the sixteen registers that have an immediately preceding register. For other descriptive statistics of the men who have undergone these transitions, we use all available registers, because the precise timing of the transition is unimportant for such tabulations.

Our goal again is to identify whether or not there are specific conditions associated with movement into the categories of "retired" (*tuiding*) and "elderly" (*laoding*). If the statuses *tuiding* and *laoding* had some meaning outside the framework of the banner occupational hierarchy, we might expect transitions into them to be associated with

---

[8] According to one eighteenth-century text, for example, "men are excused from service when they reach 60." Jin Dechun (c. 1700), *Qijun zhi*.

[9] We surmise, however, that retirement did mean the cessation of formal government salary.

other transitions that occurred in old age. For example, retirement or registration as "elderly" might be associated with the marriage of adult sons, or perhaps widowhood.

Comparison of the mean ages at which men underwent transitions in table 8.5 indicates that men were classified as *tuiding* and *laoding* at different ages, and that there was considerable variation in the timing of both. Formal classification as *tuiding* occurred at a mean age of 61.6 *sui*, with a standard deviation of 9.4 years. Classification as *laoding*, meanwhile, took place at an average age of 67.9 *sui*, with a standard deviation of 7 years. That the timing of these two transitions varied so much suggests that, unlike the original transition to *ding* status, which tended to occur within one or two years of 17 *sui*, these were not arbitrary reassignments occurring at fixed ages.

As was the case with the transition to *ding* status, there do not seem to have been any obvious prerequisites for the transitions to *tuiding* and *laoding* status. Furthermore, other transitions do not seem to have been contingent upon them. Table 8.6 summarizes the relevant household circumstances of 900 men at the time when they were first registered as *tuiding* or *laoding*. According to these statistics, over one-half were still married. Over two-thirds of them lived with one or more surviving son, and in fact more than one-half lived with at least one surviving married son.

Comparison of the previous banner statuses of males newly classified as *tuiding* and *laoding* in table 8.7 suggests that different rules governed entrance into the two categories. Transitions from "retired" *tuiding* to "elderly" *laoding* were much more common than transitions in the other direction. Whereas one-quarter of retired individuals were reclassified as elderly in the next register, only one-tenth of elderly individuals were reclassified as retired in the next register. The most likely explanation is that whereas retirement was a formal change in status that meant exemption from banner service, elderly status indicated inability to serve.

The Banner occupational hierarchy

In any case, there are approximately 2,500 observations in table 8.1 of people with a precise occupation or title who served the state in an occupational capacity. These observations represent the experience of some 400 individuals. They include adult males in military posts (i.e. soldier, overseer, and commander), specific occupations (i.e. artisan, dyer, gardener, blacksmith, tailor, and tanner), and official positions

Table 8.5. *Mean age of ding status transitions*
in late adulthood†

Transition to	Mean age	Standard deviation	N
Marriage of eldest son	48.1	7.9	472
Retired (*tuiding*)	61.6	9.4	424
Elderly (*laotui, laoding*)	67.9	7.0	280

†Registers 1789, 1792, 1795, 1798, 1801, 1804, 1813, 1816, 1819, 1822, 1831, 1840, 1843, 1846, 1858, 1861, 1864, 1867.

Table 8.6. *Household circumstances of adult*
males making the transition to retirement and
old age, 1774-1873

		%	N
Marital Status	Never married	11.8	108
	Married	58.0	530
	Widowed	30.2	276
	Total	100	914
Household Structure†	Simple	30.6	270
	Complex	69.4	611
	Total	100	881
Surviving Sons	Present	62.1	568
	None	37.9	346
	Total	100	914

†For this calculation registers before 1792 are excluded because they have no information on household structure.

(i.e. government student, runner, and scribe). They also include adult males in such other professions as laborer, fisherman, and shepherd.

These 400 men with specific occupations or titles were among the elite of rural banner society in Daoyi. Either because of their family background or their innate ability, they had acquired talents or qualities which the state found useful and which distinguished them from the rest of the able-bodied *ding*. In Chapter 9, we will examine how these individuals translated such social and economic privilege into demographic privilege. We restrict ourselves here to a description of the positions themselves.

Table 8.7. *Transitions in the banner occupational hierarchy*†

Status in previous register	Status in Current Register			New Status of Individuals Who Change‡								
	Change %	No Change %	N	'New' or 'Able-Bodied' %	Soldier %	Artisan %	Official %	Retired %	Elderly %	Disabled %	Exit %	N
'New', 'Able-Bodied'	21.8	78.2	19,641	35.1	2.4	1.7	0.4	9.8	4.1	12.6	33.9	4,275
Soldier	15.7	84.3	867	5.2	1.5	2.2	18.4	12.5	0.7	0.7	58.8	136
Artisan	24.4	75.6	484	9.3	0.0	4.2	1.7	41.5	0.0	0.0	43.2	118
Official	29.5	70.5	244	2.8	11.1	1.4	33.3	12.5	0.0	0.0	38.9	72
Retired	43.7	56.3	1,793	6.5	0.3	0.3	0.1	4.1	25.5	0.9	62.4	784
Elderly	39.7	60.3	1,112	9.3	0.0	0.0	0.0	10.9	0.0	0.9	78.9	441
Disabled	19.8	80.2	4,891	16.0	0.2	0.7	0.1	18.7	9.9	0.6	53.8	969
Total	23.4	76.6	29,032	26.0	1.7	1.3	1.0	11.1	7.0	8.2	43.7	6,795

†This calculation is restricted to males who are alive and present in a register before 1873 and have a status recorded both in that register and either die before the next register or have a status recorded in that register as well.

‡Individuals identified in the columns on the left as changing status but who remain within the same category in the right of the table (i.e. entries along the diagonal) have changed their detailed occupation, but remained within the same broad category. For example, men whose new and old statuses were both in the broad category 'New', 'Able-bodied' to 'New', 'Able-bodied' (35.2% of the 'New', 'Able-bodied' who change status) consist primarily of men who changed from 'New' to 'Able-bodied.' The men whose new and old statuses were both 'Official' (33.3% of the men listed as 'Official' who changed status) comprised a diverse set of transitions, most commonly from Subofficial (*zhishiren*) to some other position. For example, there were three cases where men changed from Subofficial to Preceptor Captain (*niru cuizhang*).

For the purposes of our analysis, we divide these individuals into three categories—soldier, artisan, and official—according to precise occupation or title.[10] The soldiers are those individuals identified as *jiading* (soldiers). The artisans include both the individuals listed as *jijiang* (artisans) and some of those listed with a specific craft. The officials, meanwhile, comprise salaried military officers such as commanders (*xiaoqiwei*) and sergeants (*lingcui*), local civil functionaries such as tax preceptors (*cuizhang*), subofficials (*zhishiren*), and scribes (*bitieshi*), as well as individuals with honorary or purchased titles.[11]

Soldiers were distinguished by their physical prowess. Individuals who wished to become army officers during the Qing had to pass an exam in which they were required to perform feats of strength, marksmanship, and swordsmanship (Miyazaki 1976). The same qualifications applied even to ordinary bannermen. According to an early eighteenth-century text, "Soldiers are selected from among the able-bodied adult males *zhuangding*[b]) according to their stature (five feet and above), and their ability to ride and shoot." [12] An early nineteenth-century text elaborates: "Missing members of the Vanguard (*qianfeng*) and non-commissioned officers (*lingcui*) are recruited from among the cavalry and infantry. Missing cavalry and infantry are selected from the artisans, the irregulars, and the other *ding*. The Banners report the number of missing soldiers to the military authorities who in turn summon all the eligible men to the parade ground. The men all wear wooden placards inscribed with their banner affiliation, age, and military and technical experience. The generals and commanders then select the soldiers and officers according to their performance at riding and shooting, their experience, and their economic status, giving priority to those with many dependents."[13]

---

[10] Soldiers include *jiading*, and *bingding*. Artisans include *jijiang, kezi jiang, huaer jiang, gongjiang, caifeng* and *ranjiang*. Officials include civil titles such as *zhishiren, guan xuesheng, guanfu, kushi, bitieshi, jiansheng* and *gongsheng* and military positions such as *xiaoqiwei, lingcui*.

[11] These positions are generally lower in rank than banner officials "within the passes." Moreover, some such as *cuizhang* and *xiaoqiwei* while common among the banner reserve population in northeast China, do not appear to have existed at all "within the passes." This is partly due to the fact that bannermen "outside" the passes were liable to the state for different taxes from those "inside" the passes. See Brunnert and Hagelstrom 1910, 323—336 and Isett 1996.

[12] Jin Dechun (c. 1700), *Qijun zhi* (Liaohai congshu edition, 4.2a).

[13] This well-known text comes from Xi Qing (c. 1810), *Heilongjiang waiji* (Heilongjiang renmin chuban she 1984, 3.36). Xi Qing was a member of the Xilinjueluo clan and a bannerman in the Manchu Bordered Blue Banner. The book records his personal observations from a trip to Heilongjiang in 1806. It is important to note that according to his observations, banner soldiers were selected according to need as well as ability.

Because the Eight Banner system did not distinguish clearly between civil and military administration, officers and to a lesser extent soldiers are likely to have had authority over what we might consider civil affairs. For example, they are likely to have been involved in law enforcement.[14] In Mongolia, which remained under a banner system until as late as 1910, the military officers had a variety of police-administrative duties, such as tracking down deserters and apprehending criminals.

Artisans and technicians were distinguished by their mastery of a craft. But in contrast with civilian craftsmen, they too worked for the military. Like the common rank and file, they too were chosen by examination from the entire population at large. Moreover, like military specialists everywhere, their rank and pay were higher than those of common soldiers.[15] Many of their crafts, for example blacksmithing and tailoring, are likely to have been of commercial value. This combination of income and expertise guaranteed prestige as well as privilege among the local community.

Most of the individuals we refer to as officials, meanwhile, were local functionaries who had earned titles in connection with their work. Like soldiers and artisans, many officials such as scribes and clerks were supposed to have been selected by formal tests. According to the Guangxu (1875-1907) edition of the *Rules and Regulations of the Qing* (*Da Qing huidian shili*), "All officials are chosen by examination (*kaoxuan*). Scribes (*bitieshi*) and clerks (*kushi*) should be selected from among the government students (*guan xuesheng*)."[16] Although a small number of individuals purchased titles, it was for the most part only after their relatives had already succeeded in merit-based positions. By the time the Yang family of Dingjia fangshen purchased our population's first honorary *jiansheng* degree in 1828, for example, family members had already served as soldiers, civilian subofficials, and military commanders for several decades.

---

[14] Brunnert and Hagelstrom 1910, 447.

[15] According to the Guangxu edition of the *Rules and Regulations of the Qing*, "within the passes," for example, the monthly wages for the rank and file were 1.5 taels of silver compared with as much as 4 taels for artisans (*Da Qing huidian shili*, Zhonghua shuju edition, juan 254.pna).

[16] Zhonghua shuju edition, 1994, 769.

Table 8.8. *Household groups (zu) by number of individuals
and number of households in the group, 1774-1873*

Number of Individuals	Group (zu)	
	n	%
1	342	7
2–4	1,061	22
5–9	1,585	33
10–14	904	19
15–19	434	9
20–24	212	4
25–29	138	3
30+	95	2
Total	4,769	100
Households		
1	1,793	38
2	1,198	25
3	783	16
4	416	9
5	298	6
6	158	3
7	123	3
Total	4,769	100

The Banner organizational hierarchy

The 1,000 group leaders (*zuzhang*) in Daoyi had similar earning potential. The banner administration organized all households into groups
called *zu* modeled after Manchu lineage organizational units called
mukūn. Zu were not lineage organizations based on descent from a
common male ancestor. Rather, they functioned as the basic units
of state civil, fiscal, judicial, and military administration in Daoyi
district. Group leaders accordingly occupied the lowest rung in the
Eight Banner system's formal organizational hierarchy.

The groups varied considerably in size. Although most *zu* were
originally organized to include three to five households or more,
many inevitably shrank, the victims of random drift. According to
the distribution of group sizes in table 8.8, many leaders presided
over groups of only one household, namely their own. Other groups,
however, were much larger. There were, for example, 123 observations
of groups with more than seven households. And it is in these larger
groups that we would expect group leaders to have been especially
powerful and perhaps demographically privileged.

The leaders of these groups were charged with the task of carrying out administrative work associated with the official functions of the group. Like the *jiazhang*[b] in the *baojia* system typical of China proper, the leader was responsible for collecting taxes and recruiting corvée laborers from the households over which he ruled.[17] In addition, his duties included the compilation of the population registers, approving marriages, ruling on inheritance, and ratifying household divisions.[18] Moreover, regardless of the size of his group, he was considered one of the community leaders and was formally consulted by the banner commanders over policy issues. According to Fuge, a nineteenth century Manchu, "The common banner men are administered by group leaders (*zuzhang*). These men are selected for office from among the retired officials or the more respected members of the community. They discuss freely all public and private matters with the Company Commander *zuoling*. Although they do not have a formal government rank or salary, they have the status of officials."[19] A late nineteenth-century compendium elaborates: "The Eight Banners appoint group leaders to lead the Group. They are established beneath the Company Commanders (*zuoling*) to manage and control the group members. Moreover, if the group is small and composed of only one household they can be merged together. The Lieutenant-General (*dutong*) should select the group leaders from the civil officials (*guan*), the imperial or government students (*gongjian* and *shengyuan*), or the military commissioned and non-commissioned officers (*hujun, lingcui*)."[20]

In contrast with household heads, household group leaders were, therefore, selected on the basis of ability. Ideally, they were chosen on the basis of their education, honesty, and competence.[21] The position was elective, and could be given or taken away according to the will of the group membership. The rules governing the selection of leaders

---

[17] In contrast with banner populations "within the passes," banner households in northeast China regularly provided corvée labor called *bangding*. These terms, however, are restricted to the 1774, 1780, and 1786 registers. They do not appear after the reforms of 1789. See Wang Zhonghan 1988 for a discussion of *bangding*.

[18] At least based on Shirokogoroff's early twentieth century observations of their modern equivalents in Heilongjiang (1926, 50–54).

[19] *Tingyu congtan* (Zhonghua shuju 1984, 132). Fuge was a bannerman in the Han Bordered Yellow Banner who worked in the imperial court administration during the Xianfeng (1851–1861) and Tongzhi (1862–1874) reign periods.

[20] This passage is from the Guangxu (1875–1907) edition of the *Rules and Regulations of the Qing* (*Da Qing huidian shili*, Zhonghua shuju edition, 1994, 758). According to Liu Xiaomeng, however, the passage dates back to an official edict in 1725 (Wang Zhonghan, 1995, 754).

[21] See Shirokogoroff 1926:50-54.

were in fact flexible enough that some groups of households had more than one head at a time.

In spite of these rigorous requirements, group leadership appears to have been a relatively common experience among older adult males in Daoyi. Table 8.9 shows the age profile of position in the organizational as well as occupation hierarchies. While one-eighth of the men observed over the age of 15 served as leaders, the proportion increased steadily with age, to one-quarter of the men between 55 and 59. In Daoyi, in other words, leaders were chosen also for their maturity. Since many leaders ruled groups consisting of only one household, a significant proportion were household head as well as group leader. Their status, therefore, included the role of household leader as well as elder, and community leader.

In later chapters we will analyze the demographic behavior of these leaders to determine the extent to which they were able to translate their power into demographic privilege, comparing their experience with that of the individuals in the occupational hierarchy. We will also examine how the position of leader was transmitted within the group, looking for evidence of selection based on ability as opposed to inheritance. We devote the rest of this chapter, however, to a description of social mobility within these banner hierarchies, as people moved, changed occupations, and assumed organizational as well as occupational responsibilities.

Banner career mobility

Beyond   recording information about individual status at specific points in time, the banner registers also provide detailed information on changes in individual status. In theory, any entrance or exit from *ding* status required state recognition. Similarly, any change in formal status from an "able-bodied" male to a soldier or from a soldier to a commander had to be registered. Changes in status did not have to be explicitly annotated in the registers to be included in our analysis, though, because we can also detect them by comparing the linked records of individuals across time.

We begin with the age profile of banner occupation. The distribution by age of banner occupational category in table 8.9 has several salient features. First, while the proportion of group leaders increased with age, the proportion of men who were soldiers, artisans, or officials was fairly constant across almost all age groups. Second, the only major exceptions were what we would expect: the proportion of men

Table 8.9. *Banner occupational and organizational status: percent distribution by age for adult males, 1774-1873*

Age group	'New' or 'Able-'bodied	Soldier	Artisan	Official	Retired	Elderly	Disabled	Total	Occupational Hierarchy			N
									No status	Group leader	Total	
16-20	92.8	1.1	0.1	0.9	0.0	0.0	5.2	100	98.7	1.3	100	2,552
21-25	86.6	2.1	0.5	0.6	0.0	0.0	10.3	100	97.0	3.0	100	3,798
26-30	80.7	3.9	1.6	0.7	0.2	0.0	12.8	100	94.0	6.0	100	3,709
31-35	77.4	3.8	1.6	0.9	0.7	0.0	15.5	100	89.7	10.4	100	3,430
36-40	74.5	3.5	2.1	1.0	1.1	0.0	17.8	100	84.8	15.2	100	3,402
41-45	72.0	3.4	2.5	0.9	1.6	0.0	19.6	100	81.0	19.0	100	3,109
46-50	65.8	3.8	2.7	1.1	2.5	0.1	23.9	100	77.7	22.3	100	2,628
51-55	62.0	2.4	2.5	1.1	4.3	0.3	26.5	100	75.7	24.3	100	2,160
56-60	51.2	2.8	2.1	1.0	12.1	2.1	28.7	100	75.1	24.9	100	1,842
61-65	22.5	3.0	1.8	1.0	38.8	13.2	19.7	100	76.0	24.0	100	1,415
66-70	9.3	3.0	1.2	0.3	48.0	28.6	9.6	100	78.7	21.3	100	991
71-75	8.7	1.5	0.9	0.7	34.5	48.9	4.8	100	81.6	18.5	100	542
76+	7.7	0.5	0.5	0.0	18.6	69.5	3.1	100	75.1	24.9	100	574
Total	68.3	3.0	1.6	0.9	6.0	3.9	16.2	100	86.1	13.9	100	30,152

Table 8.10. *Banner occupational and organizational status: percent distribution by age for adult males, 1774-1873*†

Status in current register	None	Status in next register			
		Group leader	Exit‡	Total	
	%	%	%	%	N
None	86.7	3.6	9.9	100	25783
Group Leader	9.1	80.0	10.8	100	3998
Total	76.1	13.9	10.0	100	29781

†This calculation is restricted to men who are alive and present in a register previous to 1873, and have already reached *ding* status.

‡Exits occur either through death or disappearance.

who were disabled increased steadily with age, and the proportion of men who were elderly or retired increased dramatically beginning from age sixty onwards.

Although individuals who changed occupation were most likely to move to a new position within the same general category of service, for example from one generic *ding* status to another, there were also individuals who moved between categories.[22] According to table 8.9 the most common transitions for soldiers, artisans and officials were movements from generic *ding* status and movements to retired/elderly status. Movements from disabled status back to generic *ding* status were common as well, as were movements from disabled status to retired or elderly status. There was also movement from disabled status into retired or elderly status, but few cases where the reverse was true.

Moreover, there appears to have been a system of promotion and possibly even demotion within the banner occupational hierarchy that crossed over from military to civil office and back again. Seventeen soldiers (*jiading*) became civilian subofficials (*zhishiren*),[23] two of

[22] Some of these positions, of course, were hierarchical. According to the 1739 edition of the General History of the Eight Banners (*Baqi tongzhi*), for example, "Any empty *kushi* or *lingcui* positions should be chosen by long tradition (*jiuli*) from among the government students"; "Any empty scribeships should be chosen by long tradition from among the government students or the clerks (43.812).

[23] Subofficials were called *baitangga* in Manchu Chinese. According to recent scholars, "While the position literally meant 'useful,' these men like the yamen runners in China proper had no formal government office, but served in minor local civil positions." (Shang *et al.* 1990, 33).

whom later switched back. Seven other soldiers were promoted to the rank of commissioned officer (*niru cuizhang*), four of whom eventually switched back. And four civilian subofficials rose to become commanders.[24] A total of twenty-three people were involved in these movements, sometimes moving more than once.

Movements within the occupational hierarchy, in other words, were more varied and their timing less predictable than movements within the household hierarchy. Whereas transitions from one household relationship to another always occurred in a fixed progression and only under very specific circumstances, transitions within the occupational and organizational hierarchies could in theory be from one of any number of statuses to another, could take place at almost any time, and could occur for a variety of reasons.

Meanwhile, turnover in the organizational hierarchy was heavy. Table 8.10 indicates that one-twentieth of those commoners who survived to the next register would rise in rank to group leadership. Similarly, one-fifth of the men observed as leader would lose the position before the next register, one-half of these through death or disappearance and one-half through retirement. Turnover could occur for any number of reasons, including the retirement or death of a leader, or the division or merger of household groups.

Conclusion

In Daoyi, every adult male was a "bannerman" as well as a household member. Banner positions, however, unlike household positions were earned by ability not by heredity. While many adults, of course, remained commoners, a significant proportion did rise through the banner hierarchy to positions of authority and even wealth. And, as we shall see in Chapter 9, the rewards of banner position were considerable. Soldiers, artisans, and officials all received stipends, and in some cases earned hefty salaries. Moreover, like household position, these benefits produced demographic advantages.

---

[24] In theory, all subofficials were eventually promoted to a formal salaried civil rank after five years of service. See the 1739 edition of the *General History of the Eight Banners*, edited by E'Ertai (*Baqi tongzhi*, Heilongjiang chuban she, 1988:835).

9

Banner hierarchy and demographic privilege[1]
(with Chris J. Myers)

In Daoyi, all together 1,400 men rose in the banner hierarchy: 400 in the occupational hierarchy and 1000 in the organizational hierarchy. These men in theory were the elite of rural banner society. They were assumed to be the most capable. They were stipulated to be the best paid. And they were supposed to be the most powerful. If they were as privileged in fact as they were in theory, this should be apparent in their demographic behavior. We have already seen in Chapter 7 how marriage, fertility, and even mortality were related to position in the domestic hierarchy. In this chapter we explore how they were also related to position in the banner hierarchies.

We divide our chapter into two sections, each with its own methodology. In section I, we follow the arithmetic methodology used in Chapter 7 to analyze the distribution of privilege within the household, calculating measures of demographic performance—the proportion married, and the number and sex ratio of children "born"—according to the various categories of banner service. In section II, we introduce logistic regression to compare the effects of position in the banner and household hierarchies on demographic behavior and determine their relative importance.

In so doing, we differentiate not only the degree of demographic privilege enjoyed by the household and banner hierarchies over ordinary men, but also the degree of privilege within these hierarchies. Thus we see whether artisans were above soldiers, and whether civil officials were on equal footing with military officials. While we have a clear understanding of the normative ordering of position within

---

[1] This paper has its origins in a paper written by Myers during the summer of 1990 and reorganized by Lee in the spring of 1991 entitled "Social mobility: the ladder of success in rural China." Campbell subsequently rewrote and reorganized this chapter during the summer of 1992, redoing the previous calculations and adding several others as well.

the household, our knowledge of the banner hierarchy is much less complete. We only have the broad principles in the prescribed rules and regulations of the Eight Banners which place military officials at the top of the banner hierarchy followed by civil officials, soldiers, and then artisans. Unfortunately, much of our data on comparative income among the Eight Banner occupations are for the urban garrisons in China proper and are not directly applicable to rural Liaoning society.[2] We have very little information in particular on provincial civil salaries.[3] And we do not know even in theory how banner organizational hierarchy compared with banner occupational hierarchy. In contrast with Chapter 7, which tested the hypothesis that differentials in demographic behavior would reflect Confucian norms about family organization, the analysis here is necessarily descriptive and exploratory.

Banner position and demographic privilege

In both sections, we organize our analyses according to the ordering of the demographic events of interest in the typical male life–course. We therefore begin with the relationship between banner status and the probability of marriage. We follow with an analysis of banner status and fertility, looking not only at the number of registered births, but at their sex ratio as well. We conclude in section II with an analysis of mortality when we compare the household and banner hierarchies.

A word of caution is in order regarding causal inference. The relationship between banner status and demographic behavior causality cannot be as clear as was the case in the household hierarchy. The variables analyzed in previous chapters were all determined externally to the individual. Banner status, however, was in theory more dependent on individual characteristics which may have had a sep-

---

[2] Salary data, where available, are one index of their relative rankings. According to the *Rules and Regulations of the Qing (Da Qing huidian shili)*, Beijing noncommissioned officers (*lingcui*) earned a monthly salary of 3 taels of silver as well as an annual allowance of 48 *hu* of grain. Provincial soldiers earned 1–2 taels of silver a month, as well as a monthly allowance of 9 *dou* of soy in winter and spring and 6 *dou* of soy in summer and autumn, and an annual allowance of 30 *shu* of hay. Artisans (*gongjiang* and *tiejiang*) earned 1 tael of silver a month.

[3] According to the 1739 edition of the *General History of the Eight Banners ((Baqi tongzhi)*, for example, government students from the Han Army Banners earned 1 tael of silver a month, the same salary as artisans (47.917). But this seems to be for the late nineteenth century and for the Beijing population. According to Xi Qing's observations in *Heilongjiang waiji*, the government students there earned only 2 taels of silver a year.

Table 9.1. *Percent of men ever married by position in the household and banner hierarchy, 1792-1873*†

	16—20		26—30		36—40		46—50	
	%	N	%	N	%	N	%	N
Household Hierarchy								
Single Family HH Member	10	575	45	759	67	928	73	822
Multiple Family HH Member	41	1,697	78	2,524	87	1,853	92	1,032
Multiple Family HH Head	57	60	87	204	93	409	97	614
Total	34	2,332	71	3,487	82	3,190	87	2,468
Banner Organizational Hierarchy								
Single HH Group Member	40	284	70	394	76	246	81	171
Single HH Group Leader	86	7	84	45	88	123	94	107
Multiple HH Group Member	33	2,016	70	2,888	81	2,445	85	1,733
Multiple HH Group Leader	52	25	84	160	92	376	95	457
Total	34	2,332	71	3,487	82	3,190	87	2,468
Banner Occupational Hierachy‡								
Soldiers	85	26	96	137	98	111	100	106
Artisans	33	3	90	52	94	67	95	78
Officials	59	22	88	26	100	39	100	41
Commoners	33	2,281	70	3,272	81	2,973	86	2,243
Total	34	2,332	71	3,487	82	3,190	87	2,468

Age group (in *sui*)

†There are fewer observations in the 16-20 *sui* group than in later age groups because analysis is restricted to men with a banner status reported.

‡See Table 8.1 for the specific occupational statuses included in each of the categories. Because this is a measure of cumulative demographic behavior, retired are included in the occupational category from which they retired.

arate and independent effect on demographic behavior. Individuals with status may have been more likely to be from wealthy families or favored household relationships. Until Chapter 10 where we identify the determinants of attainment in the banner hierarchies, we can only say that we have observed correlations, even though we frequently use words like "effect."

Nuptiality: In Chapter 7 we saw that marriage was a sensitive measure of privilege in rural Liaoning. For males, marriage was not universal. Access to marriage was determined by access to resources. Within the household hierarchy, resources were allocated according to one's proximity to the household head. Thus the closer you were to the household head, the more likely you were to marry. If service in the banner hierarchies was associated with an increased availability of resources, that should also be reflected in the proportion married.

Success in the banner hierarchies was indeed associated with success at marriage. Group leaders married earlier and in higher proportions than men who were not group leaders. In table 9.1, which presents the proportion of men ever married by status within the banner occupational and organizational hierarchies, the difference in the proportion married between the top and the bottom of the organizational hierarchy is over 30 percentage points for the 16–20 *sui* age group. Even in the 46–50 *sui* age group, the difference is still at least 10 percentage points.

Men with banner occupations also married earlier and in far higher proportions. Once again, the differences are particularly acute among the younger age groups. In the 16–20 age group, for example, 85 percent of all soldiers and 59 percent of all officials were already married, compared with 33 percent of ordinary bannermen, a difference of over 100 percent.[4] While the differences narrow with age, they remain significant even in the later age groups. Thus while only 86 percent of all ordinary bannermen aged 46–50 were married, 95 percent of artisans and 100 percent of all soldiers and officials were married. Whatever their age, men with a profession were more likely to marry than the rest of the population.

Soldiers and officials, however, were more likely to marry than artisans. They were also the only individuals in the banner hierarchies who were more likely to marry than multiple-family household heads. Soldiers and officials were in fact the only men in the population to achieve universal marriage. All officials were married by the 36–40 *sui* age group, as were all soldiers by the 46–50 *sui* age group. As we discussed in Chapter 5, marriage in rural Liaoning was hypergamous. Income was apparently one dimension of male attractiveness. Perhaps so were physical and official powers.

Fertility: Chapter 7 showed that in rural Liaoning, completed fertility was also an indicator of privilege. Measured as the number of boys already born at different ages, it accounts for the cumulative effects of differences in both age at marriage and fertility within marriage. Within the household, individuals with the most privilege and the most status had the most children.

As we might expect, the higher the position in the banner organizational hierarchy, the greater the completed fertility. Table 9.2 summarizes the number of boys already born by household relationship for married men age 16 through 50 *sui*. Just as household heads had more children than household subordinates, so group leaders had more children than other group members. Multiple-household group leaders aged 46–50 *sui* had 1.92 boys while other members of multiple-household groups had only 1.56 boys. Single-household

---

[4]   There are hardly any artisans in this age group (three) so we do not include them in this comparison.

Table 9.2. *Boys already born by position in the household and banner hierarchy, ever-married men 1792-1873†*

	Age group (in *sui*)							
	16-20		26-30		36-40		46-50	
	Boys	N	Boys	N	Boys	N	Boys	N
Household Hierarchy								
Single Family Household Member	0.13	60	0.59	341	1.00	625	1.23	607
Multiple Family Household Member	0.20	709	0.64	1,978	1.24	1,628	1.71	953
Multiple Family Household Head	0.21	34	0.84	178	1.49	382	1.94	599
Total	0.20	796	0.65	2,482	1.22	2,625	1.64	2,149
Banner Organizational Hierarchy								
Single Household Group Member	0.18	113	0.53	278	1.04	192	1.46	143
Single Household Group Leader	0.33	6	0.66	38	1.13	108	1.84	101
Multiple Household Group Member	0.20	670	0.64	2,047	1.17	1,988	1.56	1,482
Multiple Household Group Leader	0.29	14	0.99	134	1.61	347	1.92	433
Total	0.20	796	0.65	2,482	1.22	2,625	1.64	2,149
Banner Occupational Hierarchy								
Soldiers	0.32	22	1.02	132	1.76	109	2.57	106
Artisans	0.00	1	0.96	47	1.78	63	2.42	74
Officials	0.08	13	0.91	23	1.97	39	2.17	41
Commoners	0.20	760	0.62	2,280	1.17	2,414	1.55	1,928
Total	0.20	796	0.65	24,820	1.22	2,625	1.64	2,149

†See notes to Table 9.1.

Table 9.3. Children already born by position in the household and banner hierarchy, ever-married men 1792–1840†

	Age group (in *sui*)											
	16-20			26-30			36-40			46-50		
	Boys	Girls	N	Boys	Girls	N	Boys	Girls	N	Boys	Girls	N
Household Hierarchy												
Single Family HH Member	0.18	0.15	40	0.63	0.39	241	1.10	0.51	439	1.31	0.75	409
Multiple Family HH Member	0.23	0.12	418	0.73	0.42	1,215	1.32	0.78	963	1.70	0.98	501
Multiple Family HH Head	0.24	0.14	21	0.97	0.50	124	1.49	0.78	241	1.95	1.03	407
Total	0.23	0.13	479	0.73	0.42	1,580	1.29	0.71	1,643	1.66	0.92	1,317
Banner Organizational Hierarchy												
Single HH Group Member	0.18	0.09	56	0.52	0.34	128	1.12	0.61	82	1.24	0.97	71
Single HH Group Leader	1.00	0.00	2	0.73	0.59	22	1.26	0.65	77	1.69	0.77	61
Multiple HH Group Member	0.23	0.13	417	0.72	0.42	1,348	1.21	0.70	1,264	1.61	0.88	919
Multiple HH Group Leader	0.25	0.00	4	1.18	0.59	82	1.77	0.81	220	1.94	1.10	266
Total	0.22	0.13	479	0.73	0.42	1,580	1.29	0.71	1,643	1.66	0.92	1,317
Banner Occupational Hierarchy												
Soldiers	0.33	0.25	12	1.12	1.42	81	1.86	2.21	58	2.39	2.61	61
Artisans	0.00	0.00	1	0.89	0.61	36	1.79	0.60	47	2.40	1.08	53
Officials	0.00	0.00	3	1.00	0.64	14	2.10	2.14	21	2.13	2.43	23
Commoners	0.22	0.11	463	0.70	0.36	1,449	1.24	0.63	1,517	1.58	0.80	1,180
Total	0.22	0.13	479	0.73	0.42	1,580	1.29	0.71	1,643	1.66	0.92	1,317

†See notes to Table 9.1.

group leaders had 1.84 boys, versus 1.46 for other members of single-household groups.

In the occupational hierarchy, differentials were even more pronounced. Once again, soldiers seem to be the most privileged. By the 46—50 *sui* age group, soldiers have one more male child on average than men with no banner occupation. Married artisans have almost as many children as married soldiers, while married officials are midway between soldiers and the population at large. Also in contrast with the results from marriage, all of the men with a detailed banner occupation do better than multiple-family household heads.

Sex preferences and demographic strategies: In rural Liaoning, soldiers, artisans and officials had more boys than other villagers, but diverged dramatically when it came to girls. According to the breakdown by occupation of sex of children in table 9.3, soldiers and officials were most likely to let a girl live. Indeed, looking at the completed fertility of married men in the 46—50 *sui* age group, the sex ratio of children born to soldiers was 0.94 while that of officials (including military officials) was 0.88. In other words, they had more girls than boys. In contrast, the sex ratio of children born to artisans was 2.22, even higher than the 1.89 sex ratio of children born to multiple-family household heads and the 1.98 sex ratio of children born to commoners. Surprisingly, given their higher incomes, son preference was strongest among artisans.

The comparison of sex ratios, in other words, enables us to differentiate demographic strategies by occupation. Artisans were chosen by expertise; officials by bravery and leadership; and soldiers by strength. We should not be surprised if their demographic goals differed. Soldiers married early, had many children, and apparently did not care about the sex of their surviving children. Artisans married later and produced twice as many surviving sons as daughters. While the Liaoning demographic system provided ample opportunities for parents to tailor their families according to their circumstances, not every one took equal advantage of these opportunities. Moreover, as we have seen, some strata were more reactive; others were more proactive.

We cannot, of course, reconstruct the demographic reasoning behind such behavior in any detail. Still, we can surmise that it was based on a combination of rationales. Individual character may have been most important. Artisans may have been more practical and more inclined to plan their behavior. Officials may have been more wealthy and had no need for such constraints. Soldiers were presumably more "physical" and the least inclined to think of the demographic

Table 9.4. *Overlap in the household and banner hierarchies, 1792-1873*†

Position	Household hierarchy			Organizational hierarchy				Occupational hierarchy				N
	single family HH member %	multiple family HH member %	multiple family HH head %	single HH group member %	single HH group head %	multiple HH group member %	multiple HH group head %	soldier %	artisan %	official %	other %	
Household Hierarchy												
Member of Single-Family Household				4.5	3.5	79.1	12.9	0.9	1.1	0.4	97.6	8,020
Member of Multiple-Family Household				13.2	2.3	78.5	6.0	3.6	1.2	1.0	94.3	15,407
Head of Multiple-Family Household				6.6	6.0	63.7	23.7	4.2	2.8	1.2	91.8	4,877
Total				9.6	3.3	76.1	11.0	2.9	1.5	0.8	94.8	28,304
Organizational Hierarchy												
Member of Single-Household Group	13.3	74.8	11.9					0.5	1.3	0.2	98.0	2,715
Leader of Single-Household Group	30.0	38.4	31.5					4.1	1.6	0.4	93.8	926
Member of Multiple-Household Group	29.5	56.1	14.4					2.3	1.1	0.9	95.7	2,1543
Leader of Multiple-Household Group	33.2	29.8	37.0					9.0	3.6	1.2	86.3	3,120
Total	28.3	54.4	17.2					2.9	1.5	0.8	94.8	28,304
Occupational Hierarchy†												
Soldier	9.0	66.5	24.5	1.6	4.6	60.0	33.9					832
Artisan	21.0	45.5	33.5	8.8	3.7	60.1	27.4					409
Official	14.2	61.5	24.3	2.5	1.7	80.8	15.1					239
Commoners	29.2	54.1	16.7	9.9	3.2	76.8	10.0					26,824
Total	28.3	54.4	17.2	9.6	3.3	76.1	11.0					28,304

†This calculation is restricted to men aged 16 *sui* and above. Retired individuals are included among commoners, regardless of which occupational category they retired from.

consequences of their actions. Economic factors may have been almost as important. While all men with a banner occupation lived better than the vast majority of all commoners, their trades had different needs. Artisans were engaged in craftsmanship. Their children, especially their male children, may have contributed to their production.[5] Soldiers and officials had administrative duties which only they could fulfill. The number and sex of their children was not relevant to their work.

Banner hierarchy, household hierarchy and demographic privilege

Since the household and banner hierarchies overlap, it is important to distinguish their relative influence on demographic behavior. Many individuals held positions in more than one hierarchy. Table 9.4 tabulates the percentage of individuals in each hierarchy who have a position in one of the other hierarchies. The most common overlap was between the household hierarchy and one of the banner hierarchies. Two-thirds of the men in the organizational hierarchy were also household heads, as were over one-third of the men in the occupational hierarchy, including half of all artisans. Similarly one-third of all men in the occupational hierarchy also served in the organizational hierarchy. In rural Liaoning, in other words, many men in authority could draw on a variety of sources for their power.

Such overlap, of course, poses a problem for inference about the effect of position in the various hierarchies. Bivariate crosstabulations such as those in tables 9.1, 9.2 and 9.3 cannot rule out the possibility that the apparent effects of being a household head are really the result of a disproportionate number of household heads also having a banner position. Conversely, they cannot exclude the possibility that the apparent effects of having a banner position are actually the result of a disproportionate number of men in banner service also being household heads.

To parcel out the effects of position in each of the different hierarchies, we turn to multivariate logistic regression.[6] Logistic regression differs from the ordinary least-squares regression with which readers may be familiar in that the dependent variable is dichotomous. It indicates for each observation whether or not a specific condition is true or

---

[5] We of course realize that male and female children could have been equally productive. However, given the bias toward males in traditional Chinese society, couples are likely to have believed that boys could contribute more labor than girls.

[6] Logistic regression is described briefly in Appendix B and in more detail in Aldrich and Nelson 1984.

false. In most cases, it indicates whether or not an event of interest has occurred. The logistic regression estimates coefficients which describe the change in the log-odds of the event occurring associated with unit changes in each of the independent variables. The percentage change in the odds associated with a unit change in the independent variable a_n can be approximated from the estimated coefficient b_n as follows:

(1)   Percent change in odds = $100*(\exp(b_n)-1)$

The relative importance of different independent variables can be assessed by comparing their coefficients. In general, if the coefficient estimated for one variable is larger than the coefficient estimated for another, that indicates that, all other things being equal, the effect of a unit change in the former is larger than the effect of a unit change in the latter. Similarly, if the coefficient estimated for one categorical variable is higher than another, the implication is that the effects of being in the former category are greater than being in the latter. A coefficient can be tested for statistical significance by dividing the standard error into it and treating the result as a t-statistic.[7]

Nuptiality: We begin in table 9.5 with an analysis of marriage. The dependent variable indicates whether or not an individual has ever been married. When the coefficient estimated for an independent variable is positive, that indicates a positive association with the odds of ever having been married. A negative coefficient indicates an inverse association. In this and other regression analyses we include a categorical variable for each age group to ensure that differences in the age composition of population subgroups do not generate spurious differentials in the odds of ever being married.

To provide an example of how coefficients are interpreted, we use the results in table 9.5 to examine the effects on odds of marriage of being a household head. The dependent variable in this analysis is an indicator of whether or not an individual has ever been married. Chapter 7 and table 9.1 both demonstrated that household heads married earlier and in higher proportions than other household members. The estimated coefficients in table 9.5 confirm that these findings were not an artifact of the overlap between household headship and banner position apparent in table 9.4, but rather an independent effect of being a household head. All things being equal, including position

---

[7] In our tables, in addition to starring coefficients according to their level of significance, we present the standard errors and the associated t-statistics. The reader can use his or her own standard to determine whether or not the result is statistically significant. Normally, a t-statistic of 1.96 indicates significance at the 0.05 level.

Table 9.5. *Logistic regression of marital status on position in the household and banner hierarchies, males 1792-1873*

Variable	Estimated Coefficient	Standard Error
Age (reference category: 16—20 sui)		
21—25	0.90***	0.06
26—30	1.59***	0.06
31—35	2.11***	0.07
36—40	2.31***	0.07
41—45	2.46***	0.07
46—50	2.72***	0.08
Household Context (Reference Category:		
Single-Family Household Member)		
Multiple Family Household Member	1.45***	0.04
Multiple Family Household Head	2.01***	0.09
Banner Organizational Hierarchy (Reference Category:		
Single-Household Group Member)		
Single Household Group Leader	1.09***	0.16
Multiple Household Group Member	0.22***	0.06
Multiple Household Group Leader	1.21***	0.10
Banner Occupational Hierarchy (Reference Category:		
No Banner Occupation)		
Soldier	2.02***	0.22
Artisan	1.13***	0.22
Official	1.48***	0.27
Constant	-2.08***	0.08
-2 * Log Likelihood	20,620	
Degrees of Freedom	21,146	
N	21,160	

Notes:
1. * = significant at 10% level, ** = significant at 5% level, *** = significant at 1% level.
2. Dependent variable is 1 if male is either married, widowed or remarried in current observation, 0 otherwise.
3. Retired individuals are included in the occupational category from which they retired. See Table 8.1 for definitions of occupational status categories.

Table 9.6. *Logistic regression of fertility on position in the household and banner hierarchies, males 1792-1873*

Variable	Estimated coefficient	Standard error
Age (Reference Category: 16—20 sui)		
21—25	0.55***	0.15
26—30	0.59***	0.14
31—35	0.58***	0.14
36—40	0.40***	0.15
41—45	0.04	0.15
46—50	-0.29*	0.16
Household Context (Reference Category: Single-Family Household Member)		
Multiple Family Household Member	0.20***	0.07
Multiple Family Household Head	0.17*	0.10
Banner Organizational Hierarchy (Reference Category: Single-Household Group Member)		
Single Household Group Leader	0.03	0.18
Multiple Household Group Member	0.03	0.09
Multiple Household Group Leader	0.27**	0.12
Banner Occupational Hierarchy (Reference Category: No Banner Occupation)		
Soldier	0.54***	0.11
Artisan	0.36**	0.18
Official	0.35	0.23
Constant	-2.20***	0.171
-2 * Log Likelihood	9,653	
Degrees of Freedom	10,909	
N	10,923	

Notes:
1 . * = significant at 10% level, ** = significant at 5% level. *** = significant at 1% level.
2. This calculation was restricted to registers where the immediately preceding register was available.

3. Dependent variable is 1 if there were any male births within the last three years, 0 otherwise.

4. Retired individuals were not included in the occupational categories from which they retired. See Table 8.1 for definitions of occupational status categories.

in the banner hierarchies and age, the odds of a multiple-family household head being married were 75 percent higher than those for other multiple-family household members.[8]

The effect of being a group leader was larger than that of being a multiple-family household head. Controlling for age as well as position in the household and occupational hierarchies, group leaders in single-household groups had three times the odds of being married (197 percent higher) than other members of their groups. Similarly, their colleagues in multiple-household groups had 169 percent higher odds of being married than other members of their groups. Recalling the cautionary note at the beginning of the chapter, we should note that this is evidence of demographic privilege but not necessarily of causality. Group leaders were selected, or elected, on the basis of unobserved individual traits, such as character, intelligence, and popularity, which may also have made them more marriageable, independently of whether or not they actually had a banner position.

Position in the occupational hierarchy was even more influential than position in the organizational hierarchy, a reflection of the benefits of having a steady income in a hypergamous society such as Daoyi. The odds of a soldier being married were nine times (802 percent higher) those of men without banner occupation. Officials came next: their odds were 339 percent higher. Artisans' odds were 209 percent higher. Again, we have to qualify our results. Because occupations were distributed according to individual characteristics, the men with occupation may have been unusually capable individuals who would have married in high proportions even without a banner position.

Fertility: Table 9.6 presents the results of our analysis of the fertility of married men. Once again, the dependent variable is dichotomous. We set it to 1 if the subject has had any male children in the time since the previous register, 0 otherwise. Female births are excluded so that data from the entire century under consideration can be used.[9] In order to standardize the length of the time period being considered at three years, the analysis is restricted to the sixteen registers where the immediately preceding register is also available.

As was the case with marriage, banner occupation was more important than position in either the household or organizational hierarchies. Soldiers and artisans had much higher marital fertility than either officials or men with no banner occupation. Within the

---

[8] Here and elsewhere we derive these comparisons by subtracting the coefficient for members of multiple-family households (1.45) from the one for heads of multiple-family households (2.01), exponentiating, subtracting one, and multiplying by 100.

[9] Female children were incompletely recorded, especially after 1840. See Appendix A.

organizational hierarchy, only leaders of multiple-group households had appreciably higher fertility. Within the household hierarchy, meanwhile, the difference between the fertility of multiple-family household heads and that of other household members does not seem to have been significant.

Explanations for differences in cumulative fertility observed earlier apparently varied according to hierarchy. The weakness of the results for the household hierarchy implies that differences in the completed fertility of married men according to their household relationship were largely the result of differences in age at marriage. The strength of the results on fertility for the occupational hierarchy and certain parts of the organizational hierarchy, however, suggests that the higher completed fertility of soldiers, artisans, and multiple-household group leaders was at least partly due to higher fertility within marriage.

Sex preferences: To elaborate on the findings in table 9.3 on the sex ratio of cumulated births, we also conduct a logistic regression of the sex of recent births. The analysis is restricted to married men with at least one birth in the past three years. We only use the ten registers between 1792 and 1840 where the immediately preceding register is also available. We code the dependent variable as 1 if the number of girls born in the last three years was equal to or greater than the number of boys born, 0 otherwise. A positive coefficient for an independent variable therefore indicates an increase in the proportion of female births, a negative coefficient a decrease.

Just as was the case with nuptiality and fertility, position in either the organization or occupational hierarchy affected sex preferences much more than position in the household hierarchy. In the organizational hierarchy, according to table 9.7, the leaders of multiple-household groups were especially likely to favor boys. Independently of whether or not they were household heads, multiple-household group leaders had 25 percent lower odds of having at least as many girls as boys in the last three years than other members of multiple-household groups. Even though group leaders were supposed to be selected according to ability, some perhaps hoped that they could transmit their position to a son, and behaved accordingly.

The results for the occupational hierarchy reiterate the findings for soldiers and officials in table 9.3. Soldiers were much more likely than other men to have girls. The odds of a soldier having at least as many girls as boys in the past three years were three times (209 percent higher) those of men without occupation. For officials, the odds were also three times (312 percent higher) those of the reference category.

Table 9.7. *Logistic regression of sex of recent births on*
position in the household and banner hierarchies,
ever-married males with one or more births in the last
three years, 1792-1840

Variable	Estimated coefficient	Standard error
Age (Reference Category: 16—20 sui)		
21—25	-0.49*	0.27
26—30	-0.56**	0.27
31—35	-0.65**	0.27
36—40	-0.66**	0.28
41—45	-1.00***	0.31
46—50	- 1.06***	0.34
Household Context (Reference Category: Single-Family Household Member)		
Multiple Family Household Member	0.13	0.07
Multiple Family Household Head	0.11	0.10
Banner Organizational Hierarchy (Reference Category: Single-Household Group Member)		
Single Household Group Leader	-0.14	0.40
Multiple Household Group Member	-0.27	0.23
Multiple Household Group Leader	-0.57**	0.29
Banner Occupational Hierarchy (Reference Category: No Banner Occupation)		
Soldier	1.13***	0.19
Artisan	-0.19	0.37
Official	1.14***	0.37
Constant	0.02***	0.350
-2 * Log Likelihood	2,029	
Degrees of Freedom	1,625	
N	1,639	

Notes:
1. * = significant at 10% level, ** = significant at 5% level, *** = significant at 1% level.
2. This calculation was restricted to registers where the immediately preceding register was available.
3. Dependent variable is 1 if the number of female births within the last three years was equal to or greater than the number of male births, 0 otherwise. Positive coefficients, therefore, correspond to more female births.
4. Retired individuals were not included in the occupational categories from which they retired. See Table 8.1 for definitions of occupational status categories.

Table 9.8. *Logistic regression of mortality on position in the household and banner hierarchies, 1792-1873*

Variable	Estimated coefficient	Standard error
Age (Reference Category: 16—20 sui)		
21—25	0.27	0.24
26—30	0.21***	0.24
31—35	0.56**	0.23
36—40	0.87***	0.22
41—45	1.20***	0.22
46—50	1.55***	0.22
51—55	1.84***	0.22
56—60	2.42***	0.21
61—65	2.47***	0.22
66—70	2.90***	0.22
71—Up	3.42***	0.21
Household Context (Reference Category:		
Single-Family Household Member)		
Multiple Family Household Member	-0.09	0.07
Multiple Family Household Head	-0.04	0.07
Banner Organizational Hierarchy		
(Reference Category: Single-Household Group Member)		
Single Household Group Leader	-0.29	0.18
Multiple Household Group Member	0.22**	0.11
Multiple Household Group Leader	-0.16	0.13
Banner Occupational Hierarchy		
(Reference Category: No Banner Occupation)		
Soldier	0.13	0.18
Artisan	0.41**	0.21
Official	0.61**	0.27
Constant	4.28***	0.23
-2 * Log Likelihood	8,673	
Degrees of Freedom	20,443	
N	20,463	

Notes:
1. * = significant at 10% level, ** = significant at 5% level, *** = significant at 1% level.
2. This calculation was restricted to registers where the immediately succeeding register was available.
3. Dependent variable is 1 if the individual dies within the next three years, 0 otherwise.
4. Retired individuals were not included in the occupational categories from which they retired. See Table 8.1 for definitions of occupational status categories.

The behavior of artisans, meanwhile, was largely indistinguishable from that of other married males, perhaps for the reasons discussed earlier.

Mortality: In our final calculation, we apply logistic regression to the study of mortality differentials by position in the banner hierarchies. The dependent variable is once again dichotomous, in this case an indicator of whether or not an individual will die within the next three years. Positive coefficients are therefore associated with an increased hazard of mortality, negative coefficients with a decreased hazard. To standardize the length of the time periods, we restrict our analysis to the sixteen registers where an immediately following register is also available.

The results of our calculations show that position in the banner hierarchies had a stronger effect on death rates than position in the household hierarchy. According to table 9.8, leaders of multiple-household groups had especially low mortality. After controlling for age and position in the other hierarchies, the odds that a multiple-household group leader would die in the next three years were one-half (46 percent lower) those of other multiple-household group members. The most likely explanation is that good health was a selection criterion for group leadership. People presumably were loath to elect "sick" leaders to manage the affairs of their household group.

Meanwhile, the overall odds of a member of a multiple-household group dying in the next three years were 24 percent higher than the odds of a member of a single-household group dying. Why the mortality in multiple-household groups was higher than mortality in single-household groups is not clear. The members of multiple-household groups were actually more likely to be wealthy, given that according to table 9.5 they were more likely to be married. It may be that multiple-household groups were distinguished by some unknown environmental factor, perhaps geographic location, which affected their mortality but not their nuptiality and fertility, over which they had more control. Households, for example, may have been more likely to constitute a group if they were immediately adjacent to each other. Higher density may have resulted in a less hygienic living environment. The greater potential sources of infection in a multiple-household group simply exposed them to more risk than in single household groups.[10]

---

[10] This was certainly the case in England and France where roughly similar phenomena have been observed by Walter and Schofield 1989. They surmise that the higher mortality of multiple-group households is purely a function of the multiple sources of infection.

In the occupational hierarchy, the otherwise privileged officials and soldiers actually had higher mortality. The odds of an official dying in the next three years were almost 84 percent higher than those of commoners without occupation. The odds of a soldier dying in the next three years, meanwhile, were 50 percent higher. Given the high fertility of soldiers and officials, such differentials may reflect the price of children observed in Chapter 7. Alternatively, such high mortality may reflect greater geographic mobility. Both groups included officers and administrators whose duties were likely to require them to travel throughout Daoyi District as well as into nearby Shenyang, thus exposing themselves to greater chance of infectious disease.[11]

Conclusion

Overall, demographic behavior was much more strongly associated with banner position than with household position. Whether one is referring to nuptiality, fertility, sex preferences, or mortality, the difference between those with banner position and those without was much wider than the difference between those with household headship and those without. Moreover, these differences by banner position persisted even when we used logistic regression to control for the potential effects of overlap between the hierarchies.

These results are concrete evidence that men with banner position represented an elite in rural Liaoning. Even though Chapter 5 showed that there was a shortage of potential brides in Daoyi, men with banner position married earlier and in higher proportions. Some groups even achieved universal marriage. Men with banner position also had more children, some because of their early marriage, others—soldiers and officials—because of higher marital fertility. They also differed from the population at large and each other in the treatment of daughters. Soldiers and officials were especially likely to allow girls to live, but multiple-household group leaders and artisans were not. Multiple-household group leaders had lower mortality than other members of their groups, but officials and soldiers had higher mortality.

In contrast with our analysis of household hierarchy and demographic privilege in Chapter 7, we do not know if the distinct patterns of banner hierarchy and demographic privilege outlined in Chapter 9 can be accounted for entirely by banner position. As we saw in Chapter 6, household position was assigned without regard to individual

---

[11] Another possibility that cannot be ruled out is that such excess mortality was the consequence of unrecorded military engagements. We have no evidence, however, to suggest that this was the case.

characteristics and was beyond individual control. Thus differentials according to household position were indeed the effects of household hierarchy. Position in the Eight Banners, by contrast, was distributed according to individual ability to test well and to be selected either by peers, in the case of the organizational hierarchy, or by superiors, in the case of the occupational hierarchy. It is entirely possible, therefore, that individuals with banner position were from families with the resources to educate and train them and the influence to ensure their selection. Group leaders, for example, may come largely from the pool of household headmen. Artisans may come largely from the pool of artisan sons.

In the next chapter, we compare the backgrounds of individuals with banner status to determine how representative they were of the population at large. If wealth and household position were indeed prerequisites for banner position, much of what we have observed in this chapter may have been the result of selection effects. If, however, men with banner position were drawn from the population at large, then banner position was independently meaningful as a route for social and economic mobility in rural Liaoning, an alternative ladder to fortune, bypassing fate.

10

Two types of social mobility[1]

(with Chris J. Myers)

Throughout Chinese history, heredity and ability inevitably overlap. On the one hand, the Chinese state rewarded achievement with hereditary rights and privileges. On the other hand, Chinese parents rewarded what ability their children had, through a system of familial education and parental, especially maternal, dedication (Hsiung 1994). As a result, in late imperial China, as in contemporary China, nurture could supply what nature lacked. Privileged children consequently often did far better than other children their age.

This was especially true in rural Liaoning, where position in the traditional household hierarchy was dictated largely by heredity.[2] Bannermen followed a life course from one family relationship to another in a fixed progression determined at the time of their birth by their parentage and their birth order. The timing of relationship transitions depended on two events over which individuals had virtually no control: when household heads died, and when households divided. In consequence, within the household system there was little opportunity for social mobility.

In contrast, there was considerable mobility outside the household in the banner hierarchies of occupation and organization. According to the rules and regulations of the banner system, bannermen could earn position in the occupational and organizational hierarchies through their ability, regardless of their position in the household hierarchy. Under ideal circumstances, talented men fated by the circumstances

---

[1] This paper has its origins in a paper written by Myers during the summer of 1990 and reorganized by Lee in the spring of 1991 entitled "Social mobility: the ladder of success in rural China." Campbell subsequently rewrote and reorganized this chapter during the summer of 1992, redoing the previous calculations and adding several new ones as well.

[2] The reader will recall that by heredity, we refer to characteristics fixed at the time of one's birth. See Chapter 2.

196

of their birth to a life at the bottom of the household hierarchy could still rise in social mobility. In rural Liaoning, the Eight Banners, in other words, could have been the rural equivalent of the elite "ladder of success" (Ho 1959).

Regulation and reality may have differed. Whether or not the occupational and organizational hierarchies really allowed talented individuals to advance regardless of parentage would have depended on the degree to which the Han Martial Banners preserved traditional Han Chinese concerns with kinship. In the face of a long tradition of nepotism, adherence to the stated meritocratic principles of the banner system would have been difficult. Even though the state may have intended banner positions to be open to all, it is easy to imagine that prominent families would have attempted to use their influence to monopolize them. If such tendencies prevailed, then in Daoyi, as elsewhere in China, low-level official positions may have been the preserve of a local elite, inaccessible to able young men from undistinguished backgrounds.

This chapter investigates whether individual advancement in the banner hierarchies was according to merit, as was intended, or according to family background, as might be expected. It is divided into three sections, each of which examines one facet of heredity in the banner hierarchies of organization and occupation. Section I assesses the importance of parental position and birth order. Section II examines the importance of having a prominent or wealthy family background. It closes with an analysis of all acquisitions of position in the banner hierarchies, distinguishing according to whether position was inherited from one's father, from a member of one's household, or acquired independently. Section III assesses the role of other influential family advantages unrecorded in the household registers. Using fertility as a proxy for privilege, it compares the behavior of men before and after they acquire banner position to see whether or not they were already well-off to begin with. We conclude in the epilogue with an overall assessment of fate and fortune in rural Liaoning and in late imperial China at large.

Parental background

Household hierarchy: In Chapter 6 we saw that individuals only acquired household headship by inheritance or household division. Both paths favored eldest sons. Han banner households followed strict primogeniture principles. Only the eldest son of a household head was eligible to inherit.[3] If a deceased head had no sons, headship passed to his eldest brother, that is his father's eldest surviving son. Meanwhile, when a linking relative passed away and the household divided, the head of the new household was generally the deceased link's eldest surviving son or brother.

Heredity, in the form of relationship at birth and birth order, clearly predestined certain individuals to be household heads. Table 10.1 calculates the percentage of men between 40 and 49 *sui* who are household heads according to household relationship at first appearance and birth order. As would be expected, sons of heads were substantially more likely to become heads themselves. Of the men "born" as son or grandson to a household head, 40 percent are heads, compared with only 5 percent of those "born" as cousins. As would also be expected, first-born and only-born males enjoyed a dramatic advantage over their later-born counterparts: 78 percent of heads' eldest sons were head compared with 16 percent of heads' younger sons. The closer the relationship to the household head, and the fewer the elder siblings, the greater the probability of becoming head.

Inheritance, of course, did not always proceed as expected. Random luck, working through mortality, could still play a role in determining who would be a head. In table 10.1, more than eighty first-born sons of household heads were still not heads by the time they were in their forties. These men, who had been destined at birth to be heads, had the misfortune to be the heirs of especially long-lived household heads. Meanwhile, almost an equal number of later-born sons of household heads were heads. These men, who had not been destined for headship but who acquired it anyway, were lucky in the perverse sense that all the other heirs that had stood in their way were dead.

Organizational hierarchy: Heredity should have been a far less important determinant of banner position. Banner positions in rural Liaoning were meant to be earned, not inherited. Virtually all adult males were eligible for office, regardless of their parentage or their birth order. In the organizational hierarchy, group leaders were elected by popular acclamation. They were ostensibly chosen solely on the basis of personal characteristics such as ability, energy, honesty,

---

[3] This was not true in other banner households and may be a result of Han cultural traditions. Mongol banner households generally followed an ultimogeniture principle whereby the youngest son inherited headship. "Manchu" banner households often followed a utilogeniture principle whereby the most capable son inherited headship (Ding Yizhuang personal communication).

and intelligence. The only characteristic beyond individual control that might have mattered would have been seniority, for the respect it could command. The effects of relationship at birth and birth order either should have been negligible or, to the extent that they shaped personal character, indirect.

Banner regulation and banner reality coincided in the organizational hierarchy. Table 10.2 calculates the percentage of men between ages 40 and 49 who are group leaders, dividing them according to household relationship at first appearance and birth order. The difference between the proportion of first sons and later sons with group leader status was 11 percentage points, much smaller than the 60 point difference between them for household headship. The difference by relationship at birth was equally small. The widest gap was between grandsons and brothers, who differed by 12 percentage points. In the household hierarchy the widest gap, that between sons and cousins, had been 39 percentage points.

According to table 10.2, almost half of the men in Daoyi had better chances of succeeding in the organizational hierarchy than in the household hierarchy, even though there were far more household heads than group leaders. The vast majority of them were later-born males, who accounted for more than 43 percent of males overall. Whereas only 12 percent of them were household heads between ages 40 and 49, 15 percent were group leaders. The remainder were distant relatives of the head, for example, men born as cousins. An individual whose first appearance was as a cousin was more likely to be a group leader than a household head, by a margin of 19 percent to 5 percent.

Occupational hierarchy: Heredity should have been even less important for banner occupation than banner organization. Criteria for office depended solely on ability, with no role for popularity or seniority. As was the case at the highest levels of the government bureaucracy, standardized tests were used to provide an objective criterion for determining fitness for service. If the system worked as intended, any effects of heredity would have been indirect, for example, as the result of parents systematically focusing their limited resources on helping specific children acquire the necessary qualifications.

The occupational hierarchy appears to have worked as intended. Table 10.3 calculates the percentage of men between ages 40 and 49 who have banner office, dividing them according to household relationship at first appearance and birth order. There is little evidence of bias according to birth order, although there are differences according to the total number of sons born. The difference between first-born

Table 10.1. *Percentage of men aged 40-49 sui who are heads of households by relationship at birth and birth order*†

| Relationship at birth | Birth order | | | | | | | |
| | Only boys | | First boys | | Later boys | | Total | |
	%	N	%	N	%	N	%	N
Son	59.4	123	78.3	341	15.7	479	44.0	943
Grandson	62.0	121	49.3	479	6.4	314	36.2	914
Brother	0.0	6	0.0	0	22.2	18	16.7	24
Brother's Son, Grandson	60.2	83	53.0	387	12.8	351	36.5	821
Cousin	0.0	7	10.0	10	50.0	40	5.3	57
Cousin's Son, Grandson	56.3	16	33.3	45	20.7	29	33.3	90
Total	58.2	356	57.4	1,262	12.4	1,231	38.0	2,849

Table 10.2. *Percentage of men aged 40-49 sui who are group leaders by relationship at birth and birth order*†

| Relationship at birth | Birth order | | | | | | | |
| | Only boys | | First boys | | Later boys | | Total | |
	%	N	%	N	%	N	%	N
Son	13.0	123	29.3	341	18.0	479	21.4	943
Grandson	28.1	121	32.8	479	11.2	314	24.7	911
Brother's Son, Grandson	14.5	83	22.5	387	13.1	351	17.7	821
Cousin	0.0	7	40.0	10	17.5	40	19.3	57
Cousin's Son, Grandson	0.0	16	26.7	45	3.5	29	14.4	90
Total	17.4	356	28.5	1,262	14.5	1,231	21.1	2,849

Table 10.3. *Percentage of men aged 40-49 sui who have a banner office*†*by relationship at birth and birth order*‡

| Relationship at birth | Birth order | | | | | | | |
| | Only boys | | First boys | | Later boys | | Total | |
	%	N	%	N	%	N	%	N
Son	0.0	123	6.2	341	7.1	479	5.8	943
Grandson	4.1	121	9.4	479	7.0	314	7.9	914
Brother	0.0	6	0.0	0	0.0	18	0.0	24
Brother's Son, Grandson	8.4	83	6.5	387	8.3	351	7.4	821
Cousin	0.0	7	0.0	10	7.5	40	5.3	57
Cousin's Son, Grandson	0.0	16	11.1	45	6.9	29	7.8	90
Total	3.4	356	7.6	1,262	7.3	1,231	7.0	2,849

†Banner office is defined to include soldiers, artisans, and officials. ‡This calculation is restricted to men whose births are recorded in 1792 or later registers.

sons and later-born sons is negligible: 6 percent of first born have an occupation versus 7 percent of later-born sons. Nor is there any evidence of bias according to household relationship. The proportion with an occupation ranged from 5 percent, for the individuals who first appeared as cousins, to 8 percent, for the individuals who first appeared as grandsons.[4]

As was the case in the organizational hierarchy, certain individuals were actually more likely to succeed in the occupational hierarchy than in the household hierarchy. While only 6 percent of the men who first appeared as later-born grandsons headed a household, 7 percent of them had a banner occupation. Similarly, while only 5 percent of the men who first appeared as later-born cousins headed households, almost 8 percent had occupations. For many men in Daoyi, in other words, it was more realistic to hope for position in the banner hierarchies than it was to hope to head a household of one's own.

The only substantial exception is a difference in the proportion of men with banner occupation according to the number of siblings. An only son was much less likely to have a banner occupation than a son with brothers, perhaps a function of his greater household responsibilities and/or his lack of support from other bannermen, perhaps too a reflection of the state's reluctance to select soldiers and officers from families with few children.[5] Such differences may also reflect differences between households, not differences within households. A disproportionate number of the sons with brothers were from multiple-family households.[6] Multiple-family households were wealthier and may have been better able to provide their sons with the educational, social, or physical endowments that would single them out for success in the banner occupational hierarchy.

Heredity in a narrow sense was not as important in the banner hierarchies as it was in the household hierarchies. Within families, the distribution of banner positions did not depend on birth order and parentage in the same way that the distribution of household relationship did. Whereas formal rules regulated the transmission of status from generation to generation in the household hierarchy,

---

[4] The only exceptions were the individuals who first appeared as brothers: none of them acquired banner office, at least not between the ages of 40 and 49. This discrepancy is the likely result of the unusual household context of individuals who had first appeared as brothers. They tend to have been from households with child heads, which were generally single-family households which had recently experienced the death of a head.

[5] See footnote 11 in Chapter 8.

[6] According to Chapter 7, fertility in multiple-family households was higher than fertility in single-family households.

criteria other than household relationship and birth order seem to have been paramount in the selection process.

Family background

Nevertheless, heredity in a broad sense may still have been important in rural Liaoning banner society. The histories of two prominent families, the Yang and the Su, suggest that while parentage may not have been a factor in the distribution of positions within families, it was a factor in the distribution of positions among families. These two families dominated the upper reaches of the banner occupational hierarchy for much of the century under consideration, accounting for many of the *lingcui* and all of the honorary degrees.

The Yang family who moved from Daoyi to Dingjia Fangshen seem to have been *the* elite family in Daoyi and surrounding communities. The Yangs began their climb to prominence in 1792 when Yang Demei became a subofficial (*zhishiren*). At that time Demei, a former soldier, lived in a multiple-family household headed by his eldest brother, Chengmei. Demei's other brothers Tingmei, Yimei, and Taoqi all lived there with their families. Chengmei later passed away without leaving an heir and his next younger brother, Tingmei, inherited. By 1810, Tingmei's son Fa had become a noncommissioned officer (*lingcui*), one of two recorded in that register. From that time onward, whenever there were any noncommissioned officers recorded in the registers, at least one of them was a Yang.

In the 1830s, the Yang brothers and their descendants exploded onto the rural Liaoning scene. By 1828, the upwardly mobile Yangs had accumulated enough wealth to purchase an honorary degree for Changshan, Tingmei's fourth son and Fa's younger brother. This was the beginning of a spree of similar purchases. In 1837, Changshan was joined by Demei's eldest grandson Wende and Yimei's eldest grandson. At the same time, Taoqi's third son Chengxi became a scribe (*bitieshi*). By now, every branch of the family had at least one person with a degree or office.

The Yang household entered a period of instability in 1840 when Fa, by now the household head, passed away. The situation in the household must have been precarious. There were about seventy individuals living in the same household, but there were no linking senior relatives who according to Chapter 6 bind households together. The last of the original brothers, Demei, had passed away between 1837 and 1840. By 1846 the original household had divided into four, one for each of the original brothers' descendants.

Of the four new households, the one comprising Tingmei's descendants prospered the most. Tingmei's fourth and fifth sons, Changshan and Shuangshan, were particularly favored. Two of Changshan's sons, Chunling and Decang, acquired honorary degrees, while a third, Heling, became a scribe. Meanwhile, Shuangshan's sons Decheng and Dean both purchased or earned degrees. Decheng eventually became a noncommissioned officer. Decheng's eldest son Jisheng later became a clerk (*kushi*). Except for Taoqi's son Chengxi, who in 1867 rose to become a salaried officer, none of the other Yangs acquired any degrees or offices after the household divisions of the 1840s.

Individuals born into the Su family also enjoyed unusual success when it came to attaining high office. According to a special annotation in the 1786 register, their deceased father had been a runner and their grandfather a businessman (*zuo maimai*). The first Su to acquire office in our registers was Yutai, a former subofficial, who became a non-commissioned officer in 1798. In 1816, Su Tingdong, another former subofficial, rose to be a noncommissioned officer. Later, several subofficials were appointed from the Su family, such as Tingfu, Jiyuzanbu and Kuicheng. Eventually, Jiyuzanbu rose in 1873 to become a noncommissioned officer. Interestingly enough, Yutai, Tingdong, and Jiyuzanbu came from disparate branches of the original family.

All together, the Yang and Su families together accounted for 32 of the 70 subofficial records in the registers. The two families also accounted for 20 of the 40 observations of noncommissioned officers. The Yangs, meanwhile, had a lock on degrees. Of the seven individuals with *jiansheng* or *gongsheng* degrees, only Dong Yilibu was not a Yang. Clearly, if one wanted a top office in rural Liaoning, it helped to be born into the right family.

While these two families dominated the upper reaches of the banner hierarchies, the social situation in rural Liaoning was fluid. This fluidity derived from the availability of the banner system as a route for individual social mobility. Paradoxically, the history of the Yang family provides some of the best evidence of this. Examples of several other individuals who achieved banner position in the course of the century under consideration are also illustrative. The earlier exhaustive analysis of the circumstances surrounding the acquisition of occupations is the best proof of how open the banners were.

Although the Yangs dominated the upper reaches of the banner hierarchies in rural Liaoning in the nineteenth century, in the eighteenth century they lived in relative obscurity. The only person with a banner occupation was Yang Demei himself, who became a soldier in 1786, although according to an annotation in the register, Demei's deceased father had been a soldier. Yet as we have seen, it was Demei's brief stint as runner (*kushi*) in 1792 and Fa's service as a noncommissioned officer (*lingcui*) in 1810 that ushered in an extended period of remarkable prosperity for the family. Yangs in later years benefited from their family situation, but only because the banners had been open enough in the first place to admit Demei and Fa.

There are other conspicuous examples of individuals who achieved high office in the banners and then prospered. The two individuals in our data set who took concubines are interesting examples. The first was Ren Huaide, the son of a government student, who became a *lingcui* in 1858 and remarried some time between 1859 and 1861. The second was Wu Guangshun, an overseer's nephew and third son of a retired soldier, who became a *lingcui* in 1864, and remarried some time between 1862 and 1864. Strangely enough, both men died a few years after taking a concubine, a fatalistic tale reminiscent of Chinese fiction.

While the histories of specific families and individuals are interesting and suggestive, it is only by surveying the family background of men attaining status in the banner hierarchies that we can determine whether positions were kept within certain families, or open to all. To measure the extent to which banner statuses were handed down from father to son, we begin in table 10.4 with an examination of intergenerational mobility.[7] For men in the household, occupational, and organization hierarchies, each column in table 10.4[8] presents the percentage whose fathers ever attained a specified status.[9] If a banner status was handed down from father to son, a high proportion of the fathers of men with that status should also have had that status. For a banner status awarded according to ability, the percentage of men

---

[7] This calculation was restricted to the 4,336 men who made at least one live appearance in 1792 or a later register, and whose fathers appeared alive at least once in 1792 or a later register.

[8] In each row, men were only included in the analysis if they appeared live at least once in the specified position in 1792 or a later register, and had a father who made at least one live appearance in 1792 or a later register. Figures are for individuals not observations, thus a man appearing more than once in a given position is counted only once. Percentages therefore represent the proportion of men attaining the position specified in the row heading whose father made at least one live appearance in the position specified by the column heading.

[9] Because the calculation tabulates fathers by whether they ever attained each status during their lifetime, not by whether or not they had status at the time of their son's attainment, the percentages include cases where the father's loss of status—either through death, retirement, or movement to another status—was not immediately followed by a son's attainment of it.

Table 10.4. *Intergenerational mobility in the household and banner hierarchies*

| Position | Occupational Hierarchy | | | | Organizational Hierarchy | | | Household hierarchy | | | |
	Soldier %	Artisan %	Official %	Soldier, artisan or official %	Single-hh group leader %	Multiple hh group leader %	Any group leader %	Single-family hh head %	Multiple-family hh head %	Any hh head %	N
Occupational Hierarchy											
Soldier	30.0	10.8	20.0	45.4	7.7	29.2	32.3	24.6	57.7	63.1	130
Artisan	6.6	27.9	3.3	34.4	9.8	36.1	44.3	31.1	52.5	65.6	61
Official	31.3	6.3	27.1	52.1	6.3	29.2	29.2	27.1	45.8	54.2	48
Soldier, Artisan or official	23.0	14.8	16.1	43.3	7.8	32.3	36.4	25.8	53.0	61.3	217
Organizational Hierarchy											
Single HH Group leader	6.9	6.9	0.0	13.8	37.4	28.1	50.3	38.4	56.2	69.5	203
Multiple HH Group leader	5.9	6.0	1.4	12.4	8.5	38.0	42.1	34.1	61.1	73.0	563
Any group Leader	5.7	6.1	1.2	12.2	15.7	36.5	44.9	34.7	59.2	71.5	671
Household Hierarchy											
Single-family HH head	3.1	3.7	1.4	7.4	7.4	25.9	30.7	46.0	46.2	72.0	706
Multiple-family HH head	7.9	5.0	2.7	13.6	9.2	32.3	37.1	26.2	65.8	73.7	707
Any HH head	5.5	4.2	2.1	10.3	8.1	28.7	33.3	36.1	55.8	72.7	1148
All Men	7.2	4.4	2.6	12.8	9.5	29.9	34.5	26.8	46.1	56.3	4336

Percent of men whose father was observed at least once as

with that status whose fathers also attained that status should be close to that of men overall.

Heredity dominated transfer of position in the household hierarchy, as we might have expected. Of the men who headed a household at some point in their life, 72.7 percent were the sons of household heads. Similarly, 65.8 percent, or two-thirds, of the heads of multiple-family households had a father who had headed a multiple-family household. The remainder acquired headship either by departing from the household and forming a new one or, in a few cases, by inheriting from a head who had no sons of his own. The residual category of men acquiring headship through departure is relatively unimportant, given that we already know from Chapter 6 that strict rules governed who departed and who could head the households they formed.

In the banner hierarchies of organization and occupation, whether or not one's father had a position was much less important. For example, more than one-half of the men who became group leaders were the sons of men who had never been a group leader. In multiple-household groups, where there were more men to choose from, almost two-thirds of group leaders were the sons of men never observed as a group leader. Similarly, in the occupational hierarchy, more than half of the individuals who acquired a status as soldier, artisan, or official were the sons of men who never appeared in any of these categories. While having an elite family background may have helped if one aspired to a banner occupation, it was clearly not a precondition. In Daoyi, there was room at the top even if one was not surnamed Yang or Su.

Being the son of a father with banner status did matter more for some occupational categories than for others. It was least important among artisans, for whom manual dexterity and technical skill would presumably have been the most important qualifications. Two-thirds of the men who became artisans were the sons of men with no occupation. At the opposite extreme, it was most important among officials. More than one-half of all officials were the sons of men who had been a soldier, artisan, or official at some point in their lives. Soldiers, meanwhile, occupied the middle ground. Indeed, the widespread availability of low-ranked positions as soldier compensated for the domination of the upper ranks of the official positions by the Yangs and the Sus.

The percentages, in other words, not only include men whose fathers had status, but also those whose uncles, great uncles, or

Table 10.5. *Household background and position in the banner hierarchies*

Percent of men observed at least once as coresident with a member of a preceding generation ever observed as

| Position | Occupational hierarchy | | | | Organizational hierarchy | | | N |
	Soldier %	Artisan %	Official %	Soldier, artisan or official %	Single-household group leader %	Multiple-household group leader %	Any group leader %	
Occupational Hierarchy								
Soldier	46.2	20.0	36.9	65.4	10.8	63.9	64.6	130
Artisan	19.7	44.3	9.8	55.7	13.1	63.9	72.1	61
Official	60.4	20.8	58.3	77.1	25.0	75.0	77.1	48
Soldier, artisan, or Official	41.0	27.2	32.7	64.5	14.8	66.4	69.6	217
Organizational Hierarchy								
Single HH Group leader	12.3	13.3	3.0	23.7	50.3		70.0	203
Mutiple HH Group Leader	12.8	12.1	4.1	23.1	14.4	46.8	65.4	563
Any Group Leader	12.2	12.4	4.0	23.0	22.7	60.2	67.2	671
All Men	17.3	12.3	7.33	27.1	20.3	60.0	66.1	1336

Notes: For the sake of comparability with the preceding table, the same criteria were used for determining which men to include in the analysis in each row. Percentages therefore represent the proportion of men attaining the position specified in the row heading observed at least once to be coresident with a member of a preceding generation who was observed at least once in the position specified by the column heading. The household hierarchy was omitted because, tautologically, everyone had to be observed at least once coresident with a household head.

grandfathers had status. Table 10.5 examines the household context of men with banner status. For men in the household, occupational, and organizational hierarchies, the columns present the percentage who at some point in their life were coresident with a man of his parents' generation or an earlier one who had status at some point in his life.[10] The percentages, in other words, include not only men whose fathers have had status, but whose uncles, great-uncles, or grandfathers had status. For banner statuses that were monopolized by particular families, the percentages of men in that status who at some point in their life were coresident with a man who had status should be high. For open statuses, the percentages should be low.

Although family background was important in the organizational and occupational hierarchies, according to table 10.5 there was still room for men from families with undistinguished histories of banner service. Two-thirds of soldiers, artisans, and officials were at some point in their life coresident with somebody who had been in one of the three categories, and two-thirds of multiple-household group leaders were at some point coresident with someone who had been a multiple-household group leader. By implication, one-third of the men attaining position in the occupational and organizational hierarchies could be claimed to be "new men," in the sense that no senior member of a household in which they lived ever had a status in their hierarchy.

Wealth and privilege

In rural Liaoning, social structure was defined by the formal hierarchy of household and banner organization. Moreover, position within each hierarchy was characterized by distinctive patterns of demographic behavior. Early marriage and many children were two of the most visible benefits of status and power. As we saw in Chapter 9, the probability of marriage was 20 to 200 percent greater for men with household or banner position. Moreover, banner position was more important than household position, and banner occupation was more important than banner organization. The hierarchy appears to have been driven partly on the basis of wealth since only artisans, soldiers, and officials drew salaries.

What is not clear, however, is the extent to which wealth begat wealth. The previous section showed that banner positions were open to individuals from families where no one had banner office. The calculations there, however, could not exclude the possibility that

[10] The percentages include senior relatives who had status even before they were coresident with the index male.

men with banner positions came disproportionately from wealthier families. Presumably, elite families would have been more capable than other families of producing talented, or at least educated, individuals qualified for banner service. Thus family background could have been an important consideration for individuals seeking banner office, even if positions were awarded on the basis of ability. If ability was not important, but wealth and personal connections were, then such families would have enjoyed even more of an advantage.

To resolve whether or not individuals who achieved office were characterized by a privileged family background, we turn to an analysis of fertility. We use recent fertility behavior as a proxy for privilege. Chapter 7 showed that within the household, children were distributed according to proximity to the head. Chapter 9 showed that fertility was related to banner status, either because acquiring banner status had an effect, or because individuals with banner status were privileged to begin with. The assumption of the analysis that follows is that individuals from a privileged family background have higher fertility than those from other backgrounds.

Using logistic regression, we compare the recent fertility behavior of individuals before and after they acquire banner office. The dependent variable, an indicator of whether or not an individual has had any male births within the last three years, is intended to capture the short-term fertility response to changes in individual circumstances. We include categorical independent variables describing age and the means by which banner position was acquired. The coefficients estimated for them describe how the recent fertility of the men in each category compares with that of men in a reference category, with positive values indicating higher fertility, negative values indicating lower fertility, and 0 indicating no change. In the case of age, coefficients represent fertility relative to that of men between 16 and 20 *sui*. In the case of banner position, they represent fertility relative to that of men who never have position.

On one hand, we expect that if men with banner position were privileged to begin with, acquiring a position should not affect their marital fertility. Their fertility should have been high to begin with, and should have remained high. The fertility of individuals who have a position should therefore be similar to the fertility of individuals who do not have one now, but will in the future. The fertility of both groups, reflected in the estimated coefficients, should be higher than the fertility of men who never achieve banner position.

On the other hand, if banner positions were open to men from all walks of life, acquiring a position should result in an increase in marital fertility. The fertility of individuals with a position should be higher than the fertility of individuals who do not have one now, but will in the future. Moreover, the fertility of individuals who do not have a position now but will in the future should be indistinguishable from that of individuals who never acquire a position.

According to the results of our analysis, summarized in table 10.6, the effect of having a position in the organizational hierarchy depended on how one acquired it. Men who inherited group leader status from their father enjoyed a boon: although their fertility before inheritance was indistinguishable from that of men who never had office, their fertility after inheritance was significantly higher. Whereas the coefficient for men who would inherit group leader status in the future was 0.02 and statistically insignificant, the coefficient for men who had inherited was 0.29 and highly significant, suggesting a 31 percent increase in their odds of having had at least one male child in the last three years. Meanwhile, men who succeeded a leader from another household may have been selected on the basis of their wealth, or perhaps their fertility: before succession, their fertility was significantly higher than that of other men, as indicated by a coefficient of 0.42.

These results raise the possibility that household groups differed in the way they selected group leaders. Some, most likely the smallest ones, may have allowed group leader status to pass from father to son, without regard to personal characteristics. In such household groups, becoming group leader had its perquisites, as reflected in the statistically significant coefficient 0.29 in table 10.6, but the households from which leaders were drawn were otherwise undistinguished, reflected in the insignificant coefficient 0.02. Other household groups may have awarded group leader status according to a man's perceived success in managing his own family's affairs. Wealth measured by fertility, or perhaps even fertility itself, might have been one index of management skills, accounting for the higher fertility observed among men who acquired group leader status from someone other than their father.

Having a position in the banner occupational hierarchy, however, had a definite and positive effect on fertility that was incompatible with the possibility that occupations were dominated by wealthier families. In table 10.7, the coefficients for the fertility of married men who did not have office but would have it in the future suggest that their fertility was similar to that of men overall, or in the case of men

Table 10.6. *Logistic regression of marital fertility on means by which group leader status is acquired, 1792—1873†*

Variable	Estimated coefficient	Standard error
Age (Reference: 16—20 sui)		
21—25	0.65	0.14
26—30	0.65	0.14
31—35	0.65	0.14
36—40	0.55	0.14
41—45	0.18	0.15
46—50	-0.17	0.16
Will Acquire Group Leader Status From‡		
Father	0.02	0.22
Other Household Member	0.49*	0.26
Outside Household	0.42**	0.20
Already Acquired Group Leader Status From‡		
Father	0.29***	0.09
Other Household Member	0.15	0.13
Outside Household	0.14	0.10
Constant	-2.15	0.3
-2 * Log Likelihood	8,330	
Degress of Freedom	9,545	
N	9,557	

†Based on male births only. Dependent variable = 1 if any male births within previous three years; 0 otherwise. Calculation restricted to registers where immediately preceding register was available, and to records of ever-married males observed at least once in or after 1792 whose fathers were also observed at least once in or after 1792.
‡Reference category: individuals who never acquire group leader status. Source of group leader status is assumed to be father if he was ever observed as a group leader. It is assumed to be another household member if the father was never a group leader, but the index individual was coresident at least once with a member of a preceding generation who was a group leader at some point in their life.

Table 10.7. *Logistic regression of marital fertility on means by which Banner occupation is acquired, 1792–1873*†

Variable	Estimated coefficient	Standard error
Age (Reference: 16—20 sui)		
21—25	0.65***	0.14
26—30	0.65***	0.14
31—35	0.66***	0.14
36—40	0.57***	0.14
41—45	0.20	0.15
46—50	-0.16	0.16
Will Acquire Banner Occupation From‡		
Father	-1.68*	1.02
Other Household Member	-0.71	1.05
Outside Household	-0.17	0.62
Already Acquired Banner Occupation From‡		
Father	0.47***	0.13
Other Household Member	0.53***	0.17
Outside Household	0.33**	0.14
Constant	-2.14	0.13
-2 * Log Likelihood	8,316	
Degress of Freedom	9,545	
N	9,557	

†Based on male births only. Dependent variable = 1 if any male births within previous three years, 0 otherwise. Calculation restricted to registers where immediately preceding register was available, and to records of ever-married males observed at least once in or after 1792 whose fathers were also observed at least once in or after 1792. ‡Reference category: individuals who never acquire banner occupation. Source of occupation is assumed to be father if he was ever observed as with an occupation. It is assumed to be another household member if the father never had a banner occupation, but the index individual was coresident at least once with a member of a preceding generation who had an occupation at some point in their life.

who would inherit from their father, slightly lower. Thus the men who acquired occupations were not characterized by an especially privileged background, at least as measured by their marital fertility before attainment. After they acquired their occupations, though, they had substantially higher marital fertility, regardless of how they obtained their position. Banner occupation made men privileged, not vice versa.

The relationships between banner occupational status and demographic privilege observed in Chapter 9 were apparently causal. The correlation between status and privilege was not the result of a selection effect where already privileged individuals were the ones most likely to acquire an occupation. Individuals prospered as a result of having a banner occupation. The banner occupational hierarchy was a ladder of success in rural Liaoning that could be climbed by men from almost any family or place within the family.

Conclusion

The emphasis in the banner hierarchies really seems to have been on ability. In the first section of this chapter we saw that differentials in attainment according to household relationship and birth order were much narrower than in the household hierarchy. In the second section, we saw that an individual could still acquire position in the banners even if no one else in his family had a position. In the third section, we just saw that the individuals acquiring banner occupations were not distinguished by a privileged background. It seems that even if banner positions were few in number, they were at least open to everyone.

That the ability-based banner hierarchy could coexist with a heredity-based household hierarchy helps explain the contradictory beliefs about individual fate held by the Chinese. On one hand, the Chinese believed in a rigid system of inheritance where status was acquired and transmitted on the basis of relationship at birth and birth order. On the other hand, the Chinese lived in a society where prestigious official positions were awarded through a national examination system open to most men.

The Chinese accepted two social myths that on the surface seem diametrically opposed. They recognized the role of heredity and fate in human affairs. According to this conception, social mobility was beyond the realm of individual control. Whether or not an individual succeeded in life depended on a combination of family background and luck. Yet at the same time, the Chinese believed that individuals could exercise at least some control over their own destiny. Through hard work and serious study, an individual could rise to a station in life well above the one for which he was destined in his household.

The dual importance of heredity and ability had concrete implications for the peasants of Liaoning. As we saw in earlier chapters, the most fundamental aspects of demographic behavior, including marriage, childbearing and death, were all tied to position in the household and banner hierarchies. Position in these hierarchies was in turn affected by both heredity and ability. Individuals unable to satisfy goals for marriage or number of children because of their position in the household hierarchy could still hope to achieve them by succeeding in the banner hierarchy.

The coexistence of the household and banner hierarchies also fulfilled psychological needs for order, meaning, and hope. Banner and household structures defined local social structure and individual place in that order, while banner and domestic rituals infused individual existence with additional meaning. At the same time, banner opportunities motivated individual aspirations. Individuals (mostly men) who were condemned to a low station in life by the circumstances of their birth could realistically hope for success. As a result, peasants in rural Liaoning, like their urban elite counterparts, also sought to climb a "ladder of success."

Epilogue

Prospects, implications, and comparisons

There is no such thing as a representative community. This is as true for China as elsewhere. Nevertheless, Daoyi was hardly unique. There were many similar military farming communities in late imperial China. Military state lands called *qidi* under the Eight Banner Armies, or *tuntian* under the Green Standard Armies, represent 5—10 percent of all registered land during the eighteenth century.[1] Some of these lands were regular banner estates, similar to Daoyi, or military estates under similar military administration. Others were imperial or noble estates under imperial household or noble household control. While there are no aggregate population statistics for these state farm populations in Liaoning or for that matter any other province,[2] their national proportions were probably roughly similar to that of the registered cultivated acreage, that is, 5—15 million people in the middle of the eighteenth century, i.e. somewhere between the national populations of England and France.

Prospects

Like the men and women of Daoyi, the social organization and population behavior of these state farm populations can be reconstructed in great detail. Thousands of household registers, similar to the twenty-five that provide the bulk of the data for this book, have been discovered in the historical archives of Beijing, Heilongjiang, Inner

---

[1] According to Liang Fangzhong 1980, the registered cultivated acreage during the eighteenth century ranged from 600 million to 800 million *mu*, of which 30—60 million *mu* were banner lands or army lands (380—381, 420—421). These numbers do not include the banner estates or other estates around Beijing.

[2] A very rough estimate, based on the surviving household registers in the Liaoning Provincial Archives, would be a banner population of around 0.5 million people c. 1750.

Mongolia, Jilin, and Liaoning (Finegan and Telford 1988). Others may survive elsewhere as well. In Liaoning alone, these registers record some 5 million observations for approximately 1 million individuals who lived during the eighteenth and nineteenth centuries.[3] Other archival materials record a variety of other information on the institutional, legal, and social history of many of these communities,[4] as do a number of elaborate lineage genealogies.[5] Future research will, therefore, be able to compare our description of social stratification and population behavior in Daoyi with a wide variety of other communities and populations from elsewhere in northeast China.[6]

And even in the Chinese interior as well. Most bannermen lived in garrison towns and cities scattered throughout China proper as well as greater China.[7] Together with their dependents, they numbered in the millions and represent the majority of the banner population. While these military families unlike their Liaoning counterparts were not peasants, they lived under similar military institutions with virtually identical occupational and organizational hierarchies. Household registers, organized more or less identically to the household registration

---

[3] Tsay Sue-mei, working with James Lee, Jeff Svare, and Melvin Thatcher, has recently produced a catalog of 3318 such complete registers from the Liaoning Provincial Archives available on microfilm from the Genealogical Society of Utah. In addition, the Liaoning archives have several thousand incomplete registers. The Genealogical Society of Utah is also filming several thousand complete registers from the Heilongjiang Provincial Archives which we hope to catalog soon.

[4] These materials are scattered in various archives and libraries in Beijing (Lee and Guo 1994), Shenyang (Tong 1984), and Tokyo (Guan, Tong, and Wang 1987). See Isett 1996 for a marvelous first attempt to pull some of these materials together.

[5] Beginning in the middle of the eighteenth century, all regular banner populations were required to compile formal lineage genealogies modeled after the genealogy of the Niuhulushi. Several of these genealogies have been collected by Li Lin who has published several selections (1988a, 1988b, and 1992). See too the imaginative, if non-demographic, use of other more conventional sources by Pamela Crossley to reconstruct the history of one Manchu lineage garrisoned in Hangzhou (1990).

[6] We are, in fact, embarking on such a comparison as part of a larger project on comparative population and family history organized by Hayami Akira. Specifically, we have begun a longitudinal study of two other rural communities in Liaoning. One is a community from Kaiyuan County organized under the imperial household. The other is a community of tenant farmers from Gai County organized under one of the banner noble households. To date we have coded six of the Kaiyuan registers dated 1789, 1792, 1795, 1798, 1801, and 1804, and twenty of the Gai registers dated: 1762, 1789, 1792, 1807, 1813, 1816, 1819, 1825, 1828, 1831, 1834, 1837, 1840, 1843, 1846, 1849, 1852, 1855, 1858, and 1861.

[7] The best studies of the Eight Banner garrison armies—Ding 1992 and Elliott 1993—are quite recent. See too Luo Ergang's 1984 revised history of the Green Standard Army, an even larger military population which should have been similarly registered. See too Crossley 1990 for a history of the Hangzhou banner garrison and especially Han 1988 for a study of the banner settlement in and around Beijing.

system in northeast China, and lineage genealogies, document their population history in at least as great detail as the peasants of Daoyi.[8] Recent studies of these documents based largely on the genealogical archives of the Qing imperial lineage have also contributed much to our knowledge of Chinese social and demographic behavior during the late imperial period.[9] They show that the distinctive fertility and mortality behaviors identified in Daoyi were equally prevalent at the top of Qing society as at the bottom.

Implications

Moreover, this tradition of state military organization, state population registration, and state rural penetration reaches back over millennia of Chinese history. State farms date back to the early first millennium BC (Yang and Lee 1990). Historical records from the Qin, Han, and Tang attest to the ability of the state to settle military households, organize production, register population; and restructure society.[10] Our study therefore has implications not only for rural Liaoning, and for banner society at large, but also for other areas of China, as well as other periods of Chinese history.

Indeed, while the exact proportions and processes are still a matter of fierce debate, it is commonly accepted that before the late Ming, the vast majority of Chinese peasants lived under tenurial conditions roughly similar to the peasants of Daoyi.[11] Tied to the land, they too where forbidden to migrate freely and could not leave their immediate communities. As a result, they like the peasants of rural Liaoning were forced to control their population processes. Numerous qualitative materials attest to the prevalence of population behaviors (primarily

---

[8] Thousands of such household registers, for example, are readily available for the city of Beijing. Finegan and Telford 1988 describe the registers stored in the First Historical Archives available on film from the Utah Genealogical Society. In addition, hundreds, at the very least, of other household registers are available in the library of the Chinese Academy of Science.

[9] See in particular the essays in Lee and Guo 1994 as well as Lee, Campbell and Wang 1993, Lee, Wang, and Campbell 1994, and Wang, Lee, and Campbell 1995.

[10] Lee 1978 provides a short state of the field essay of these early policies and institutions. Ironically here too a number of population records survive written on Han wooden strips and on Tang and Song manuscript rolls.

[11] Legal restraints on migration date at least as far back as the late first millennium BC and were only gradually abolished in the second millennium AD. Beginning in southeast China in the twelfth century and culminating in an edict affecting the entire empire in the eighteenth century, the imperial court abrogated all laws tying tenants to the land. By the mid-fifteenth century, the Ming government even gave up its attempts to confine the Chinese to hereditary occupational groups and geographical areas (Lee 1978).

deliberate low female survivorship and low marital fertility) roughly similar to late imperial Daoyi from as early as the first millennium BC.[12] These demographic mechanisms consequently enabled China to maintain low population growth at an aggregate annual level below 5 per 10,000 until early modern times.[13] The Malthusian adjustments we have described for Daoyi, in other words, perpetuated a homeostatic demographic regime in China for over 1.5 millennia.

While demographic trends in rural Liaoning may be representative of a substantial proportion of Chinese before the mid-Ming and in northeast China during the Qing, they were not representative of the majority of people during the late imperial period. Beginning in the eighteenth century the Chinese demographic system changed. Between 1750 and 1950, China's population quadrupled from 150 to 580 million—an annual growth rate of 7 per 1,000. This period of population growth was the consequence of successive waves of migration to settle the Chinese periphery and to urbanize the Chinese interior. Frontier expansion combined with commercialization and consequent urbanization to redefine the social and economic parameters of China's previous demographic system. Constrained by the banner system, these processes largely ignored Daoyi and the other banner estates. As a result, in spite of these communities' close proximity to the city of Shenyang, they remained not only rural, but demographically anachronistic, representative of an era gone by.

They were also representative of an era to come. As idiosyncratic as Daoyi's situation was, due to the constraints of the banner system, its demographic indices are in line with those of Chinese populations during the first half of the twentieth century. Male and female life expectancies at age 5 in Daoyi, 43.8 and 37.2 respectively, are close to the 40.0 and 36.9 estimated for north China in the late 1920s (Barclay *et al.* 1976).[14] In Taiwan during the early years of Japanese occupation, male life expectancy at age 5 ranged between 35.9 and 40.0, while

---

[12]   See for example Chen 1989 on the early second millennium AD and especially Liu 1994a and b and 1995a on the late first millennium B.C. and on 1995b the first millennium A.D. We would like to thank Angela Leung for bringing Chen to our attention and Lai Huimin for bringing Liu to our attention and making copies of her articles available to us.

[13]   The population of China is commonly estimated to be 60 million people at the beginning of the first century AD and at most 120 million people by the beginning of the sixteenth century AD (Zhao and Xie 1988, 42, 360). This implies an annual growth rate of 46 per 100,000—virtually no growth at all.

[14]   We compare life expectancies at age 5 because the underregistration of deaths below that age requires the imposition of assumptions about the level of mortality. Thus the results of comparisons of life expectancy at birth might reflect differences in assumptions as much as they do differences in the true level of mortality.

female life expectancy at age 5 ranged between 38.8 and 44.7 (Barclay 1954, 154). As for fertility, the adjusted total marital fertility rate in Daoyi, at 6.3 was only marginally higher than that estimated for north China as a whole in the late 1920s: 5.86.[15] Relatively small numbers of children ever born and surviving children, comparable to the levels observed in Daoyi, were actually a common finding in many of the small-scale studies carried out in China during the first half of this century.[16]

The results from Daoyi are most important not for the specific estimates of demographic rates they provide, however, but for what they reveal about the range of options available to Han Chinese peasants everywhere who had to reconcile their demographic behavior to the limitations of their specific institutional and economic circumstances. That the positive and preventive checks in a Han Chinese peasant population could be so sensitive to such a wide range of factors, including short-term fluctuations in price, long-term increases in Malthusian pressure, and individual location within the household and banner hierarchies, suggests a much larger role for increases in fertility, as opposed to reductions in mortality, in explaining the rapid increase in China's population during the late imperial period.

At the same time, the existence of the two preventive checks may also explain why Chinese fertility has declined so rapidly in recent years. As Wang, Lee, and Campbell 1995 point out in their analysis of fertility in the Qing imperial lineage, the remarkably rapid fertility declines observed in Chinese populations during this century are much less puzzling in light of evidence that Liaoning peasants before this century also deliberately limited their fertility in response to changed circumstances. Fertility limitation was already within the "calculus of conscious choice" of the Chinese peasantry (Van de Walle 1992), so that only changed incentives and new technology were necessary for rapid reductions in birth rates. While the intensity of demographic behavior in Daoyi was undoubtedly specific to this and similar communities, the Chinese demographic system with two types of positive check and two types of preventive check was representative of Chinese population behavior at large.[17]

---

[15] Calculated from age-specific rates of "North" married women aged 15—49 in table 5B on p. 614 of Barclay *et al.* 1976.

[16] See, for example, Lamson 1935 and Lennox 1919. Lamson 1935 is particularly interesting because it shows that, as was the case in Daoyi, the privileged, or at least the better-educated, had more children than the less privileged.

[17] Recent work in Tokugawa, Japan has revealed that of these positive checks, infanticide may have played an important role in the Japanese demographic systems as well. See Saito 1992, Skinner 1993, and Smith 1997, as well as the essays in Lee and

Similarly, findings on household behavior in Daoyi increase our understanding of domestic processes in Han Chinese populations during the Qing and early twentieth century. The general understanding of Han Chinese household formation in Qing China acutely resembles our description of Han banner household organization in rural Liaoning. In Taiwan, the only other rural population to be analyzed in any detail, households were equally complex during the early twentieth century and followed a domestic cycle much like that in eighteenth- and nineteenth-century Liaoning with similar tensions between household members.[18] The distribution of power and privilege according to proximity to the head, reconstructed in Chapters 6 and 7 through the differentiation of demographic rates according to household relationship, resonates with qualitative descriptions of the hierarchical household in such novels as Ba Jin's *Family* (*Jia*).

As for social mobility, while Han rural society at large may not have been as meritocratic by design as Manchu rural society in Liaoning, many civil institutions also attempted to identify and develop human talent. Ho Ping-ti (1962) and others have studied the proliferation of clan and village schools beginning from the late Ming. Evelyn Rawski and others have studied the early education and popular literacy. According to their estimates, by the middle of the nineteenth century as many as 30 percent of the male rural population in China may have been functionally literate (Rawski 1979, 140).

It is, therefore, difficult to say whether banner villages were more or less mobile than other Chinese villages. In some ways they were actually less mobile. The two major avenues for upward mobility in most late imperial Han villages were closed in Daoyi. Bannermen could not legally emigrate; nor could they engage in trade. As a result, the process of land concentration and expropriation were probably slower in rural Liaoning than elsewhere in China proper. Land speculation and land sales were theoretically illegal, especially to nonbanner populations. Rural banner society was consequently more stable, but also more stagnant than other villages. According to the land reform records that survive for Daoyi from 1948, the proportion of landless peasants in Daoyi was quite low (10 percent) compared with many villages elsewhere in China proper.

The current understanding of late imperial and early modern Chinese history is that, until the 1949 revolution, the state gave up

---

Saito, forthcoming.

[18] Cohen 1976 and M. Wolf 1968 are two vivid ethnologies of Taiwanese households in the middle of the twentieth century. See too the many works of A. Wolf and Pasternak cited earlier.

much of its ability to penetrate rural society, especially compared with such early governments as the Qin and Han and Wei and Tang dynasties.[19] Our study, however, suggests while this may be true for much of China proper, there were also large regions of the Chinese countryside—northeast China, north China (especially around Beijing), and northwest China—where the late imperial state penetrated deeply into the fabric of rural society.[20] In these areas, the state was able to reach down to the individual level and restructure households, occupations, even entire village communities in accordance with the state vision of rural society.[21]

Comparisons

In China, parallel but contradictory ideologies of hierarchy and ability coexisted at both the national and local levels, resulting in a form of social organization fundamentally different from the West. Individual rights and responsibilities were rigidly defined according to position in fluid hierarchies. Although individual actions were tightly constrained in the short term by hierarchical context, individuals could also act over the long term to change their circumstances. At the national level, this was apparent in the coexistence of a rigid hierarchy of official positions and a merit-based system for assigning individuals to official positions. At the local level, this was apparent in the coexistence of rigid hierarchies of family relationships and banner positions with a merit-based system for assigning individuals to banner positions.

The result was a society that was at once highly ordered and highly elastic. On the one hand, all individuals were integrated into society by the assignment of rights and responsibilities according to location within clearly defined hierarchies. On the other hand, the state held out hope for advancement within some of these hierarchies. Individuals dissatisfied with their lot in life could always satisfy themselves with the hope that they, or their progeny, could achieve a better one.

---

[19] This view was first expressed by Chinese scholars during the Republican period, but has been developed since largely by Western historians. See Fei 1953 for an example of such early Chinese views and the essays in Esherick and Rankin 1990 for a succinct summary of the state of this field in the West.

[20] A number of Chinese studies have recently focused on the history of these state lands. See in particular the detailed essays by Guo Songyi and Lin Yongkuang in Wang *et al.* 1991 2.228-424 for the Qing period and Li Shutian 1993 for Manchu land use. Guo Songyi 1991, 291-344 covers some of the same material although in less depth.

[21] Guo Yunjing 1984 provides one of the better summaries of Qing economic policy. See too Wang Zhonghan's thoughtful 1985 essay.

It may be this duality of order and elasticity that underlies the recent, rapid development of East and Southeast Asian societies and economies. Whereas discussions of these societies' recent behavior often emphasize state concern with order and individual concern with collective well-being, a more plausible explanation may be that they continue an ancient tradition of using highly articulated hierarchies to link individuals to society at large, and at the same time provide for movement within these hierarchies. In such a setting, individuals have both a sense of belonging and a sense of hope. Individuals have incentives both to work for the good of society and for their own good.

Such a pliant but integrative system stands in dramatic contrast with that of the West, which, while at least as mobile, is far less cohesive. Social mobility has tended to occur through the operation of the abstract and diffuse market, not through the actions of a concrete and highly centralized state. Meanwhile, many of the other structures that once helped to integrate individuals into society at large and provide meaning for their day-to-day lives, for example, family, religion, and voluntary organizations, were either never as pervasive and all-encompassing as in China, or have diminished in importance (Bellah *et al.* 1991). The result is an atomized social system in which individuals may be sustained by their hope for a better future for themselves or their descendants, but do not share such aspirations or concerns for society at large.

Appendix A

Sources and methods for the population and family history of rural Liaoning[1]

Background

For almost half a century, two advances in population and family history have been central to the rapid expansion of quantitative, social scientific history. First in the late 1950s, demographers developed a body of analytical techniques known as family reconstitution to calculate demographic rates from records of weddings, baptisms, and burials (Gautier and Henry 1958). Then in the late 1960s, a group of historians and anthropologists proposed and propagated a series of analytical classifications of household structure to measure changes in household complexity (Hammel and Laslett 1974; Laslett and Wall 1972). These two sets of techniques were among the first quantitative methods of social scientific analysis that were easily accessible to nearly all historians. Together they inspired many historical studies of fertility and mortality, marriage and migration, household structure and household formation, individual and domestic cycle. The results have produced a new set of objective measures of life in the past. At the same time, they have provided generalizable standards with which to compare the historical experiences of societies in different parts of the world.

Such studies have greatly expanded our appreciation of history from below. On the one hand, population history has not only defined the patterns of demographic behavior among the common people, but has also redefined our understanding of many social customs and economic conditions. On the other hand, family history not only

[1] James Lee began this appendix in New York in September 1988; He completed the first draft in Taibei in July 1990 and the final draft in Ann Arbor in July 1994. Cameron Campbell worked with him during the summer of 1990, and made some minor revisions in the fall of 1994. R. B. Wong was with James Lee in 1988, and we are grateful for his help.

has shown what types of households and household formation were common in the past, but has also shed new light on the organization of production, the transmission of property, and the rise of familial affect. European historians, in particular, have linked such changes to the transition from feudalism to capitalism.[2] They have shown how this process was inextricably tied to both changes in demographic rates from high to low fertility as well as changes in household function from a unit of production to a unit of socialization. In consequence, much of our theoretical understanding of the modern transformation of the Western world is rooted in population and family history.

Chinese scholars have, of course, long been aware of the centrality of family and household in Chinese society. In China, the concepts of family and household date back to prehistory (Ho 1975). The importance of the family was reaffirmed by Confucius and further elaborated by Mencius in the fifth and fourth centuries BC respectively. Indeed Mencius elevated the centrality of the family by making three of the five fundamental human relationships familial: those of father and son, elder brother and younger brother, husband and wife.[3] Ever since, Chinese have modeled their behavior according to a social hierarchy of parents over children, senior relatives over junior relatives, and men over women. Historians of China have accordingly invested great efforts to define both the formal kin structure and the corresponding system of behavioral norms in traditional society (Freedman 1966). But because of the lack of nominative data, there has been little study of formal family and household structure, even in the late imperial period.

Chinese scholars have also long recognized the importance of population history to the Chinese past, if only because there have always been so many Chinese. Indeed the dramatic rise in population from 150 million in 1700 to almost 500 million by 1900 is probably the most frequently noted achievement of the late imperial period, the economic implications of which are still being investigated and explained (Chao 1986; Elvin 1973; Ho 1959; Huang 1985 and 1990; Liu 1986; Perkins 1969). Nevertheless, despite such research we still know very little about the demographic characteristics of late imperial China. We have as yet very few precise measures of fertility, mortality, and nuptiality. Without these measures we cannot fully understand Chinese population history nor can we place that history within the

---

2 See, for example, the influential books by Alan Macfarlane (1978, 1987) and Emmanuel Todd (1982, 1985).

3 The other two relationships, ruler—minister and friend—friend, while not explicitly familial are certainly paternalistic.

context of world history. Until very recently, it was fair to say that the Chinese of the late imperial period were among the least known of any major historical populations.

The change has been sudden. New data and new methods have begun to illuminate China's historical demography. Major advances in China, as in Europe, have been inspired by the discovery and analysis of nominative records. Two types of sources have been especially important. The first are genealogies which required the development of new techniques of analysis for incomplete data (Harrell 1995; Liu 1992).[4] The second are household registers which offer more complete information, but also require a far more laborious process of data entry and linkage. To date, most research has concentrated on genealogical demography. Research on household registers has been confined almost solely to Taiwan during the Japanese occupation (1895–1945) (Pasternak 1983; Wolf and Huang 1980). Preliminary research on such sources already has advanced our knowledge about population behavior in China (Lavely, Lee, and Wang 1990).

Household registers of the Eight Banners

For the first time, we use household registers to reconstruct the population and family history of a rural Chinese population living in the eighteenth and nineteenth centuries. Most of the 12,000 farmers we study lived in Daoyi tun and surrounding villages (Baodao tun and Dingjia fangshen) just north of the present-day city of Shenyang, along the main road to Chahar. While we have very little specific information about the history of these communities, we know that during the Qing they were incorporated as "Han-martial" (*hanjun*) units of the Eight Banners, the military organization responsible for much of the authority of the late imperial state.[5] As part of the Eight Banners, the villages were covered by its household registration system.

To the best of our knowledge, the Eight Banner household registers are the most extensive and detailed records of a Chinese peasant population in the late imperial period. The Qing relied heavily on these

---

[4] Liu Ts'ui-jung (1978) was perhaps the first contemporary historical demographer to use genealogies to reconstruct the population history of China. See Telford 1986 for a detailed description of the types of data found in Chinese genealogies and Harrell 1987 and Telford 1990 for an evaluation of their data quality.

[5] The Eight Banner organization was not just a military system but an ethnic one as well. These villages were designated communities for the personnel of the Chinese *hanjun* banners.

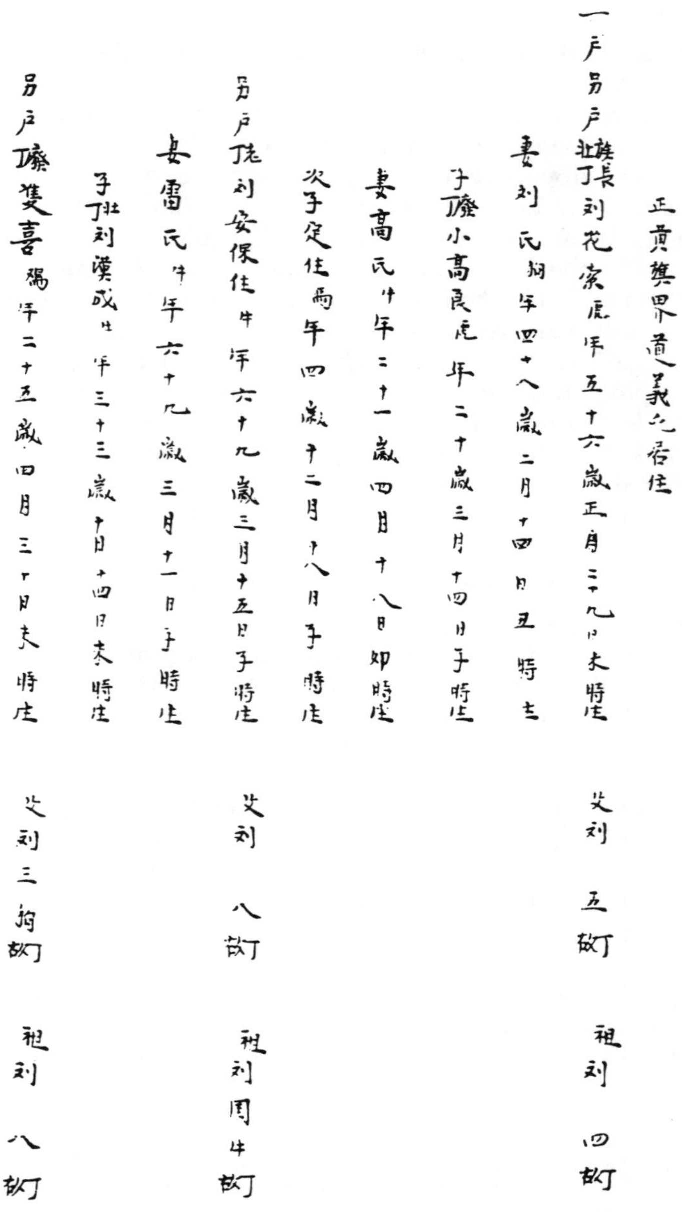
正黄旗界首義屯居住

一戶另戶壯丁族長劉花家虎年五十六歲正月二十九日未時生 父劉五故 祖劉四故

妻劉氏狗年四十八歲二月十四日丑時生

子壯丁小高良虎年二十歲三月十四日子時生

妻高氏牛年二十一歲四月十八日卯時生

次子定住馬年四歲十二月十八日子時生

另戶壯丁劉安保住牛年六十九歲三月十五日子時生 父劉八故 祖劉周牛故

妻雷氏牛年六十九歲三月十一日子時生

子壯丁劉漢成牛年三十三歲十月十四日未時生

另戶壯丁雙喜猴年二十五歲四月三十日未時生 父劉三狗故 祖劉八故

Figure A.1. *Sample page from the Eight Banner register*

registers for civilian and military administration. They accordingly devised a remarkable system of internal cross-checks to ensure consistency and accuracy. First, they assigned every person in the banner population to a residential household (*linghu*) and registered them on a household certificate (*menpai*). Then they organized households into clans (*zu*), and compiled annually updated clan genealogies (*zupu*).

Finally, every three years they compared these genealogies and household certificates with the previous register to compile a new register. They deleted and added people who had exited or entered in the last three years and updated the ages, relationships, and occupations of those people who remained. Each register, in other words, completely superseded its predecessor. Thanks to such efforts, these registers provide far more comprehensive and accurate demographic data than the *baojia* registration system common elsewhere in China.[6]

Figure A.1 shows a typical page from the Eight Banner registers. The data include information for each individual on sixteen variables: village, lineage, household, relationship to household head, sex, marital status, banner rank, banner status, name, age, year of birth (one of the twelve animal signs), month of birth, day of birth, hour of birth (one of twelve branches), recent vital events (out-marriage, emigration, death) and physical disability (if any). For household heads we also have his or her father and grandfather's names and occupations; or for widows her husband's name and occupation.

Strengths and weaknesses of the Eight Banner registers

The Eight Banner registers have many advantages over genealogies as sources for Chinese historical demography and social history. First, the registers are state records of village populations at specific points in time, a cross between a continuous registration system and a regular census. In contrast, genealogies are generally privately compiled retrospective reconstructions of the male patronym. Thus while most genealogies do not record female births and are often limited to those couples who have produced male heirs, household registers are contemporaneous records of the entire population regardless of fertility history, sex or marital status.[7]

---

[6] See Jiang 1993 and Skinner 1987 on the *baojia* system, and its problems.

[7] Since genealogies were frequently compiled retrospectively, most females would have already married out by the time of compilation, and would not be considered members of the lineage. Meanwhile, individuals without heirs had no one in the next generation to preserve and update the genealogy for their branch of the family. The most prominent exception to this and other statements about Chinese genealogies is, of course, the genealogy of the Qing imperial lineage, described in detail in Lee,

Second, household registers report complete information on vital events, whereas even in the better genealogies such data are at best incomplete, not just for females, but for males as well. The differences between the two sources are most pronounced in the earliest age groups, where the underrecording of vital events in genealogies is the most severe. Thus in contrast with genealogies, household registers can be used to calculate complete life tables for both males and females. We can also calculate many standard nuptiality and fertility indices such as age at marriage, proportions married, age-specific fertility, children ever born, birth intervals, and age at last birth. These rates allow us to compare easily the mortality, nuptiality and fertility experiences of our population with other populations.

Third, household registers can be used to estimate vital rates right up to the time of the last register, whereas in most genealogies data from the last hundred years of observation has to be discarded. Because vital information is incomplete in most genealogies, it is impossible to determine if people born during the last hundred years of observation who have no recorded death date are alive or dead at the end of the observation period. Any mortality calculations that included these individuals would therefore be flawed.[8] Moreover, whatever their date of birth, when either a husband or a wife has no date of death, the duration of their marriage cannot be measured. Any fertility calculations that included these individuals would also be inaccurate.

Many of the differences between these two sources would not matter if the incompleteness of reporting in genealogies was randomly distributed and could be compensated for. Unfortunately, the completeness of reporting in most genealogies depends on social status and location: the lower your status, the fewer recorded male descendants, or the more you migrate, the less likely your information is to be complete (Telford 1986, 1990). Eight Banner household registers, in contrast, do not have such problems. For the most part, the data are complete for all village inhabitants, regardless of their status, their fertility, or their migration history. What shortcomings do exist seem to be distributed randomly through the population, and do not affect comparisons between subgroups.

Campbell, and Wang 1993. The imperial lineage genealogy is unusual, however, in that it was maintained by the state, and thus had an elaborate bureaucracy dedicated to its upkeep.

[8]   This problem is common to virtually all genealogical materials, whatever the society. For an analogous example using Mormon genealogical data see Clayton Pope 1989.

We have of course found some problems and inconsistencies in these data, but the proportion of discrepancies for most variables are at most a few percent: death (1 percent),[9] out-marriage (1 percent),[10] changes in occupation (3 percent),[11] age (6 percent),[12] and maiden surname (6 percent).[13] Moreover, such variables as male surname, sex, animal year of birth, and family relationship have an error rate of less than one tenth of one percent, a stunning achievement for a registration system that required repeated hand transcription of thousands of cases.[14]

Although we can correct most inconsistencies by comparison with entries in other registers, some resist correction. For example, while we had almost no problems with an individual's sex, when they did occur they were intractable. There are all together seven cases

[9] This represents 62 of 5,150 recorded deaths, 61 of these miscoded deaths being repeated recordings of someone's death in successive registers, presumably through clerical error. Interestingly, half (31) of these errors were concentrated in two registers, 1816 and 1828. In these cases, we simply exclude the second record from calculations. The only exception was a Chinese "Rasputin," Song Qishi, who was reported dead in 1810, alive in 1813, 1816, and 1819, and dead for good in 1822. In his case we excluded the first record from our calculations.

[10] This represents 16 of 1,138 marriages, 15 of these 16 miscoded marriages also being repeated records, in successive registers presumably through clerical error. Moreover, once again, the 1816 and 1828 registers account for half (8) of the problem out-marriages. In these cases, we simply exclude the repeat record from calculations. However, there is one exception, a young lady named Liu Daniu, whose out-marriage was recorded in the 1816 register, who reappeared in the 1819 register, and married again in the 1822 register. In this case we decided to count both marriages as it is conceivable that her first marriage ended quickly and she returned to her natal household.

[11] Of these 5,841 changes in banner status, these 153 seem improbable since they require a reversal of the aging process. Of these 153 cases, 38 were men who went from "retired" to "healthy," 55 were men who went from "elderly" to "retired," and 21 were men who went from "elderly" to "healthy." The remainder were mainly "elderly" and "retired" men who changed to such other younger statuses as soldier or artisan.

[12] Based on tables B.1 and B.2, 6—8 percent of the reported ages (plus or minus one year age discrepancy) in each register or age group were inconsistent with the majority of the other reported ages for that person. There was no pattern according to time. However, older individuals, over age 55 and especially over age 75, showed a distinct tendency to exaggerate their age.

[13] In 200 of 3,091 in-marriages, wives changed their maiden name. We suspect that in most of these cases the wife with the original surname died and the husband remarried without registering his new wife properly. The new wife carried on the previous wife's household record, changing only the maiden name.

[14] Only 5 of the 6,326 men recorded in our data changed their surname while under observation. Families changing their surname tended to be recent arrivals adapting surnames common in Daoyi district. Many men changed their given names upon attainment of adult status, or switched back and forth between Manchu and Han Chinese names. Given names of married women were not recorded.

where an individual apparently changes gender. Four of these are boys at birth who later become young women and marry out of the household—perhaps a subterfuge to hide an illegal departure. Two are girls at birth who soon turn into boys and die or disappear. Finally, there is Liu Yingchun, the incestuous transsexual.

The bizarre story of Liu Yingchun began when he registered in 1810 at the age of 8 *sui* as the grandson of the household head (eldest son's second son). His father died before 1813 and he was raised by his mother during his adolescent years. Then between 1817 and 1819 two things happened. First, his 67-year-old grandfather, the head of the household, died and his elder brother, Erxiaoer, inherited the headship. Second, Yingchun apparently changed gender and married Erxiaoer, thus simultaneously violating taboos against endogamous marriage, incest, and transsexuality. Although their marriage is recorded in both the 1819 and 1822 registers, Yingchun and his/her husband disappeared sometime between 1823 and 1828 (perhaps driven from the village) so we cannot reconstruct their fertility history.

Such bizarre incongruities are the exception, not the rule. We can correct most discrepancies by systematic comparison of registers and can even fill in other missing information. Most importantly, for example, while entrances are not specifically annotated in the registers, we can identify births, immigration, and in-marriages by comparison with preceding registers. We can also identify any changes in social structure, social position, marital status, and physical condition and create variables accordingly.

Unfortunately certain other missing information continues to elude us. Month, day, and hour of birth, for example, are reported so erratically after 1804 as to defy any precise analysis of birth seasonality. Whereas age and animal year of birth were recorded with great consistency throughout the century under consideration, after 1804 the month, day, and hour of birth reported for individuals frequently changed from register to register.[15] Since the number of births re-

---

15 Month of birth is an excellent example. In 1795, 2,723 out of 2,724 individuals reported the same month of birth as they had in 1792. In 1798, 2,398 out of 2,652 (90.4 percent) had the same month of birth recorded as in 1795. In 1801, 2,579 out of 2,741 (94.1 percent) were consistent with the previous register. In 1804, 2,545 out of 2,693 (94.5 percent) were still consistent with the previous register. The figures are much lower in later registers: only 1,260 out of 2,630 (47.9 percent) are consistent in 1810, and 1,887 out of 2,903 (65 percent) in 1813. After 1831, the reporting of month at birth seems to become almost random. Only in 1858 and 1873 are more than 16 percent of reported months of birth consistent with those in previous registers. The reasons for the increasing inconsistency in the reporting of month, day, and hour

ported in the earlier registers are sufficient to analyze seasonality, we restricted our calculations of seasonality of birth in Chapter 3 to those that were registered between 1792 and 1804.

Three other data weaknesses stand out. First, the precise ages at entrance and exit are often unreported or reported incorrectly. Thus if an individual has entered or exited since the previous register, we have no way of determining in which of the three intercensal years he or she did so. Exact age at marriage, migration, or death, therefore, eludes us. Except for births, we only know the three-year period during which events occur.[16] In consequence, we can calculate rates by single years of age or period only for births. For events such as marriage, migration, household division, and death we are restricted to calculating rates for broader age groups and wider time periods.[17]

Second, registration is incomplete in the very early age groups and among females. Indeed, according to our calculations in Chapter 4, we are missing over one-fifth of all males and over one-half of all females, a consequence of high early mortality and late registration. According to table A.1, almost no one is registered below 2 *sui*. The mean age at first appearance for both sexes is only 6 *sui*, that is slightly less than 5 Western years of age. Many children who die before 6 *sui* simply do not appear in our records.[18] Girls were the most likely not to be registered, especially after 1840. In figure A.2, which groups the 200,000 person-years under observation in our population by age-group and sex, there are many more males than females at virtually every age group (below age 65), a function both of differential mortality and differential registration.

However, except for female underregistration these omissions, at least before 1840, do not appear to follow any selective bias. Moreover, such bias as there is appears to be uniform by time and household position. Thus mean age at first appearance summarized in tables A.2

---

of birth are unclear. One possibility is that peasants frequently changed their date, but not year, of birth out of astrological considerations, raising the possibility that predictions based on supposed constants like the *"bazi"* were very much open to manipulation and that peasants could easily *"gaiyun"*—change their fate.

[16] For births we can calculate year of entrance from the current year and reported age in *sui*.

[17] Recorded age in general is age in the year of register compilation, not in year of entry or exit.

[18] When calculating age-specific rates of mortality and nuptiality, we compensate for the unavailability of exact year of death or marriage by assuming that the events on average occurred in the midpoint of the three-year interval. Thus when calculating a numerator for age-specific rates, we attribute one-third of the events to each of the preceding three years, and time at risk accordingly. See the chapters on mortality and fertility for a detailed explanation.

Table A.1. *Age at first appearance ("birth"), 1774-1873*

Age	Females	Males	Totals
0	20	32	52
1	18	58	76
2	142	423	565
3	228	644	872
4	234	627	861
5	215	663	878
6	186	553	739
7	153	363	516
8	112	281	393
9	93	230	323
10	54	148	202
11	46	107	153
12	37	106	143
13	27	63	90
14	26	46	72
15	15	29	44
16	18	22	40
17	8	18	26
18	3	8	11
19	7	5	12
20	1	5	6
21	1	9	10
Total	1,644	4,440	6,084
Mean	6.1	5.8	5.9

All ages in *sui*. By sui the Chinese meant to indicate the number of calendar years during which a person had lived. People are accordingly one *sui* at birth and two *sui* at the next New Year. *Sui* are, therefore, on average one and a half years higher than Western years of age.

and A.3 is quite consistent by sex, time, and household relationship. As a result, the data although incomplete are nevertheless sufficient for demographic analysis of behavior patterns within the population, although our overall estimates of fertility and mortality fall short of actual levels.

Third, fully one-quarter (nine) of the registers from the century under consideration are damaged or lost.[19] In consequence, our record of demographic events for twenty-seven years is incomplete, especially the nine years from 1846 to 1854. On the one hand, our record of entrances for these missing years is necessarily incomplete. On the other hand, whenever a register is missing we cannot tell how the people who disappeared during that period did so, making it impossible to distinguish between emigration, out-marriage, and death.

[19] In 1994 the Liaoning Provincial Archives discovered at least one of these missing registers dated 1870 as well as several undated registers. Although it is too late to include them here, we hope to code and analyze these registers in a future article.

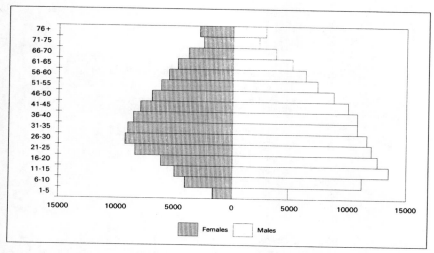

Figure A.2. *Age and sex distribution of the registered population,*
in person-years

Thus for the most part we restrict our analyses to years where adjacent registers are available. For example, because many women could also leave the registers through out-marriage, we must restrict female mortality calculations to years where we have consecutive registers.[20] Analyses of changes in household structure are similarly restricted because there is no way of knowing what form a household took in a missing register. There were some exceptions, however. Because emigration was rare and male out-marriage impossible, we can assume that males who disappeared during these gaps died, and estimate male mortality accordingly.[21]

Record linkage and analysis

Our analysis was made possible not only by the availability of new data, but also by the availability of new technologies for linking, manipulating, and analyzing such data. On its own, the raw data

---

[20] The sixteen intercensal periods for which we have successive registers are 1792–1795–1798–1801–1804, 1810–1813–1816–1819–1822, 1828–1831, 1837–1840–1843–1846, 1855–1858–1861–1864–1867. Our calculations of female life expectancy therefore cover only fifty-four years of the century under observation.

[21] Our calculations of male life expectancy include thirty intercensal periods (1774–1777 –1780–1783– 1786–1789–1792–1795 – 1798–1801 –1804 –1807 –1810 – 1813–1816 –1819 –1822 –1825 –1828 –1831 –1834 –1837 –1840 –1843 –1846, 1855–1858 –1861 –1864 – 1867–1870 –1873) and cover virtually the entire century.

Table A.2. *Frequency and mean age of children at first registration*†

	Females	Mean age	Males	Mean age
1774	-	-	-	-
1780‡	114	4.8	231	5.1
1786‡	151	4.6	283	4.8
1792‡	141	4.3	215	4.2
1795	59	4.3	120	4.3
1798	86	5.6	129	4.5
1801	68	4.6	126	5.3
1804	115	5.9	199	5.8
1810‡	114	6.7	211	6.2
1813	64	5.2	118	5.3
1816	36	5.2	93	5.0
1819	37	6.0	86	7.5
1822	66	4.5	165	4.8
1828‡	140	6.4	351	5.9
1831	65	5.3	130	4.1
1837‡	96	6.0	274	5.7
1840	39	4.4	114	4.3
1843	20	4.4	93	4.0
1846	27	3.5	91	3.8
1855‡	42	7.6	331	7.4
1858	9	3.0	114	4.0
1861	14	4.1	142	4.6
1864	10	3.9	162	5.2
1867	12	7.3	175	5.7
1873‡	27	6.6	288	6.2

†Registers were compiled every three years. Most numbers, therefore, represent the cumulated events over a three-year intercensal period. Due to missing registers some numbers, however, represent the calculated events over six years, and in one case, over nine years. To differentiate these numbers we use the ‡symbol.

All ages in *sui*. By *sui* the Chinese meant to indicate the number of calendar years during which a person had lived. People are accordingly one *sui* at birth and two *sui* at the next New Year. *Sui* are, therefore, on average one and a half years higher than Western years of age.

would have been sufficient only for the calculation of summary statistics describing distributions of characteristics at three-year intervals. By linking individual records across time and then making use of database software to manipulate them, it was possible to open new horizons in terms of the types of questions that could be investigated. We followed both individuals and households over time, using basic event history techniques to investigate how their behavior responded to changes in their characteristics and their context.

Tracking individuals from register to register was straightforward. Households were usually listed in the same order in each register, thus links between consecutive observations of the same individual could be made during coding, either by machine or by hand. When problems did arise, it was generally because an individual or a household was out of sequence, having jumped to a new location in the register. These problems were resolved by comparing lists of unlinked individuals in the previous register with lists of unlinked individuals in the current register. In almost all cases, a match could be made on name and age alone.

Record linkage resolved many shortcomings of the data. To pinpoint to within three years the timing of otherwise unannotated events, such as succession to household headship, we compared the data in records at the beginning and end of each three-year interval. Meanwhile, to identify and correct discrepancies in recorded data, for each individual we tracked eight sets of variables: name, age, sex, occupation, family relationship, marital status, vital events, and household structure. We checked each discrepancy against the original raw data and corrected mistakes in transcription and record linkage.[22]

Once individuals were successfully linked from register to register, we constructed personal histories for all 12,000 of them, setting the stage for an event history analysis.[23] From these personal histories, we derived for each individual indices of past, present, and future demographic and life course events as a function of occupation, social position, household structure, and family relationship.[24] We then

---

[22] If the discrepancy was in the original data we made no corrections. Our purpose was to produce a set of machine-readable data as close to the original manuscript data as possible.

[23] Among these personal histories are complete life histories, from birth to death, for some 4,000 men.

[24] Lawrence Anthony originally wrote several programs in C to analyze mortality and household structure. These programs set our standards in terms of data organization and format. Subsequently, most of the programming was done in one version of dBase or another by Cameron Campbell or Chris Myers.

Table A.3. *Age at first appearance
by relationship to household head*

Relationship	Age	N
Heads' Children	6.2	1,542
Siblings' Children	6.0	1,039
Cousins' Children	5.6	326
Heads' Grandchildren	5.1	1,429
Siblings' Grandchildren	4.7	451
Cousins' Grandchildren	4.8	49

reattached these time-varying indices to the original triennial observations. From the newly constructed observations, we could measure the effects of different explanatory variables on the probability of the event of interest occurring in the next three-year interval.

Not only did we link individuals' records to each other, but we also linked them to the records of parents, spouses, children, household members, and lineage members. In our analysis, this allowed us to make use not only of information from each individual's original records, but from their relatives' records as well. Thus we created considerable contextual information on household and family which we added to each of our individual observations. The resulting files allowed us to take an approach in our analysis which focused on events at the individual level and their covariance with a number of contextual economic, demographic, household, and family variables.

Meanwhile, by aggregating individual records into household records and then linking these household records over time, we were able to take the household itself as a unit of analysis. Just as we used linked individual observations to measure the probabilities of marriage, birth, and death, we used linked household observations to measure the probabilities of formation, transformation, and division. Furthermore, just as we could measure the effects of different contextual variables on the probabilities of individual demographic events occurring, we were also able to measure the effects of different contextual variables on the probabilities of household events occurring.

We were careful not to let technology form a barrier between us and the data. At every stage of this process, we were very aware that an overreliance on the seductive array of regression routines proffered by modern statistical packages could be dangerous. Given the nature of our data, repeated regressions on different combinations of dependent and explanatory variables would have been guaranteed to come up with much that was statistically significant, but not substantively meaningful. Only when a pattern held under close scrutiny of cross-tabulations or rates, did we run a regression, logistic or otherwise. Thus, what regressions we do present are not for ourselves, but for the readers for whom we want to summarize our results in a brief and easy-to-understand format. We describe these regression methods and some other statistical techniques in Appendix B.

In general, we approach historical demographic analysis as an experimental science. Whenever we investigate a new topic we examine the relevant data through simple cross-tabulations and frequency counts and then compute appropriate demographic indices. Based on these examinations, and our prior knowledge and experience of Chinese history and society, we then construct hypotheses about population behavior in Daoyi. Once we have chosen an appropriate hypothesis, we then rely on database technology to create the needed variables for each individual or household record. We test our hypotheses by calculating appropriate rates or cross-tabulations from the new, more detailed variables to see if our theories hold under more careful scrutiny. Many did not. While we could confirm that some of our conjectures about rural life in these villages are indeed facts, we also had to consign many (literally and figuratively) to the dustbin.

Appendix B

Statistical techniques

In this appendix, we attempt to explain briefly the two statistical techniques we use that may not be familiar to our readers: life tables and logistic regression. The explanations we provide are meant simply to give the reader an idea of what we are doing and are thus not very detailed nor very rigorous. Readers seeking more detailed explanations should consult the works listed as references.[25] We assume that readers have already been exposed to elementary statistical methods such as linear regression and correlation, and do not explain them here.[26]

Life table analysis

In Chapter 4, we rely on life table measures of mortality. Life tables summarize age-specific death rates by sex and from them calculate life expectancies and other indices at various ages. For the purposes of comparison between populations or over time, life table measures are more useful than crude death rates because they are unaffected by the age distribution. For example, whereas two populations with identical age-specific death rates but different age distributions are likely to have different crude death rates, they will have identical life expectancies.

Life table notation is standardized: $_nm_x$ normally denotes the death rate per thousand person-years at risk between ages x and $x + n$, and $_nq_x$, corresponds to the probability of dying by age $x + n$ conditional upon being alive at age x. Life expectancy at age x, e_x, is the number of additional years an individual can expect to live conditional upon living to age x. For example, e_5, is the number of years a five-year-old

---

[25] For logistic regression, readers are referred to Aldrich and Nelson 1984. For life tables, readers are referred to Shryock *et al.* 1971, and Chiang 1968, and 1984.

[26] Readers not familiar with linear regression and correlation may find introductions in almost any introductory statistics textbook.

can still expect to live. Meanwhile, l_x, commonly included in tables but mentioned only rarely in the text, is the probability of surviving from birth to age x, denominated in 100,000.

An appropriate technique to calculate life tables, given our data's similarity to a triennial population census, is by the intercensal death rates of age cohorts (Shryock *et al.* 1971). In a closed population recorded in a pair of censuses, the sole determinant of the size of an age group at the time of the second census is the size of that cohort in the first census, and the level of fertility and mortality during the period between the two censuses. Thus from the age distributions of a population in two successive censuses, the probabilities of dying during the intercensal period can be calculated for each age group. From these death probabilities may be computed the full range of mortality measures, and a period life table constructed.[27]

The arithmetic of this method is simple and straightforward, but two essential requirements for its use—that the population is closed to migration and that ages are reported correctly and consistently—are in practice often difficult to fulfill. In many historical populations, entries and exits are poorly recorded, making it impossible to distinguish deaths from emigrations. Because movement into and out of Daoyi was strictly controlled—all entrances and exits were annotated—we are able to satisfy the two requirements here by individual record linkage and subsequent data manipulation.[28] Specifically, we take three steps to analyze mortality. First we trace each individual though every register, linking individuals by hand. In table 2.1 we list as "disappearances" the individuals we could not trace from the preceding register or otherwise account for. The number was quite small.

Second, we close our population to migration. We exclude all immigrants and emigrants from the population at risk. Although people do occasionally disappear between consecutive registers, we identify these missing persons by machine. Table 2.1 summarized the number of these disappearances in each register. In the 15 registers for which the immediately preceding register was available, there were

---

[27] Period life tables represent the experience that a hypothetical cohort would experience if the age-specific death rates observed during the period of interest were held constant over the entire lifetime of the cohort. By contrast, cohort life tables, for example, those for the Qing imperial lineage in Lee *et al.* 1993, represent the age-specific mortality rates actually experienced by a specific cohort, followed from birth.

[28] Appendix A describes the processes by which records were linked and the data cleaned.

Table B.1. *Discrepancies between reported age and corrected age*

Errors	+4 or more	+3	+2	+1	None	-1	-2	-3	-4 or more
1774	1.2	0.8	0.4	1.4	87.1	2.4	1.7	1.1	3.4
1780	1.3	0.8	0.6	1.7	85.5	3.1	2.0	1.0	3.6
1786	1.6	0.5	1.2	1.5	88.4	2.6	1.9	0.4	1.8
1792	0.6	0.3	0.5	1.0	91.6	1.5	1.7	0.6	1.7
1795	0.6	0.2	0.6	0.9	93.2	1.5	1.0	0.6	1.2
1798	0.8	0.2	0.5	1.1	92.5	1.3	0.8	0.6	1.8
1801	1.2	0.3	0.7	1.1	91.6	1.9	1.1	0.6	1.4
1804	1.7	0.5	0.9	1.2	89.6	2.0	1.5	1.0	1.4
1810	1.2	0.5	0.7	1.3	92.1	1.3	0.6	0.9	1.4
1813	1.4	0.5	0.7	1.2	92.9	0.8	0.7	0.8	1.0
1816	1.0	0.5	0.7	1.2	91.4	1.3	0.7	1.4	1.6
1819	1.7	0.6	0.8	1.4	89.2	1.6	0.9	1.3	2.4
1822	1.6	0.6	0.8	1.7	88.3	2.1	1.1	1.2	2.6
1828	1.1	0.6	1.0	1.6	87.5	2.5	1.3	1.5	2.9
1831	1.6	0.6	0.7	1.8	89.7	1.6	0.7	1.4	1.9
1837	1.2	0.5	0.5	1.3	91.8	1.5	0.5	0.9	1.5
1840	0.9	0.5	0.6	1.1	92.7	1.1	0.1	1.0	1.7
1843	0.8	0.6	0.7	0.9	92.7	1.2	0.4	1.1	1.5
1846	0.8	0.5	0.7	1.2	92.4	1.2	0.5	1.0	1.5
1855	0.7	0.4	0.6	1.3	92.1	1.0	0.3	1.0	2.4
1858	0.3	0.3	0.4	1.1	94.0	1.0	0.2	0.9	1.4
1861	0.8	0.3	0.4	1.3	93.6	0.9	0.4	0.9	1.3
1864	1.5	0.3	0.3	1.6	91.6	1.0	0.3	1.6	2.1
1867	2.0	0.5	0.4	2.1	88.4	1.8	0.5	0.9	2.8

Age differences in *sui*. By *sui* the Chinese meant to indicate the number of calendar years during which a person had lived. People are accordingly one *sui* at birth and two *sui* at the next New Year. *Sui* are, therefore, on average one and a half years higher than Western years of age.

Table B.2. *Discrepancies in age reporting by age group (percent)*

Age group	-5.00	-4.00	-3.00	-2.00	-1.00	0.0	1.00	2.00	3.00	4.00	5.00	Total
1-5	.5	.1	.6	.5	1.6	94.3	1.8	.4	.2	-	-	3512
5-10	.6	.1	.4	.4	1.1	92.7	2.0	1.0	.8	-	.5	5589
10-15	1.0	.2	.3	.6	.9	91.3	2.0	1.2	.9	.5	1.2	5954
15-20	1.3	.2	.4	.7	1.3	91.2	1.4	1.0	.8	.3	1.5	6268
20-25	1.4	.2	.4	.5	1.1	91.9	1.5	.8	.7	.4	1.0	6925
25-30	1.4	.1	.3	.5	1.0	92.1	1.2	.8	.7	.4	1.5	6777
30-35	.9	.1	.4	.5	1.1	92.3	1.3	.7	.7	.3	1.8	6425
35-40	1.1	.1	.4	.5	1.0	92.5	.8	.6	.7	.2	2.0	6185
40-45	.9	.2	.5	.6	1.4	91.5	1.5	.6	.8	.1	1.8	5643
45-50	1.2	.2	.6	.8	1.6	91.2	1.2	.6	.8	.2	1.5	4940
50-55	1.2	.2	.8	.8	1.4	90.6	1.3	.5	.7	.5	2.1	4259
55-60	1.1	.3	.6	1.0	1.9	89.3	1.6	.5	1.1	.5	2.1	3709
60-65	1.4	.5	.9	1.1	2.1	88.1	2.0	.4	1.5	.4	1.7	3074
65-70	1.3	.4	.9	.8	2.3	88.1	1.5	.6	1.9	.3	1.8	2292
70-75	1.2	.4	.9	.7	2.2	85.5	2.2	.6	3.0	.5	2.7	1383
76+	5.8	.5	.6	1.3	1.6	75.5	2.6	1.7	4.2	.8	5.3	1650

Age differences in *sui*. By *sui* the Chinese meant to indicate the number of calendar years during which a person had lived. People are accordingly one *sui* at birth and two *sui* at the next New Year. *Sui* are, therefore, on average one and a half years higher than Western years of age.

only 364 cases where an individual recorded three years before was missing from the current register. On average, 22 people disappeared during each three-year intercensal period. The vast majority of these people are either very old or very young. When they are male, we believe that they disappeared by an unannotated death and, therefore, include them in the population at risk.[29]

Third, we correct errors in age reporting. We trace each individual's age through every available register, and then based on the age reported for them at their first appearance, adjust all their subsequent ages. Table B.1 identifies the common errors for the registers in our possession. In any given register between one-tenth and one-fifth of the population reported an age inconsistent with the one reported when they first appeared. One-third of these mistakes, however, are a difference of plus or minus one year and may be due to variations in the date of reporting. The remaining errors are as likely to be the result of poor transcription (both in the original data and in our conversion of them to machine-readable form) as incorrect reporting.

Overall, the net error in age reporting was slight. Once we organize the population into five-year age groups most errors cancel each other out. Table B.2 contrasts the net error between the recorded age and the adjusted age by five-year age groups. The mean error for almost all age groups was below 3 or 5 percent. The worst discrepancies occur among the older age groups (above 50) with net errors around 5–10 percent. These results compare favorably with population registration elsewhere, even in modern times.[30] Even uncorrected ages may, therefore, be sufficiently precise for most demographic analysis. Our registers, if they are representative of all banner population registers, place these Chinese demographic data among the more accurate examples of world historical data.

Having closed the population and corrected the age structure, we trace each live person from one register to the next by five-year age cohort. We divide the number of deaths recorded in the second register by the person-years at risk between the two registers to calculate the central death rates over three years.[31] We adjust these rates for

---

[29] We have done our calculations for males both with and without including these unannotated disappearances as deaths. The results are very similar. They are slightly smoother in the oldest age groups with the procedure whose results we present. A similar assumption could not be made for females because young women could also exit through marriage, thus female disappearances could also reflect unrecorded out-marriages.

[30] According to a comparison with figures on US data presented in Ewbank 1981, our data are apparently almost as accurate as the 1960 US census for non-whites.

[31] To perform this calculation, we assign each person alive in the second register three

five year intervals and then calculate $_5q_x$, the probability of dying before age $x + 5$ conditional upon surviving to age x, according to a conventional method known as the Reed—Merrill technique (Shryock *et al.* 1971, 443).[32] From these death probabilities we then derive the full range of life table functions including life expectancy and the standard deviation of life expectancy (Chiang 1968, 209-211).[33] The result is an abridged life table by five-year age intervals based on the distribution of deaths during specific three-year periods.

Logistic regression

In the course of our analysis, there are many times when we wish to analyze the effects of "independent" variables on a dichotomous "dependent" variable, that is, a variable that can only take on one of two values.[34] Commonly, such a variable will be an indicator of whether or not an event has occurred during a specified time period, for example, whether or not a cancer patient being given an innovative new treatment survives. In some cases, it will be an indicator of an outcome, for example, which party a voter has cast his or her ballot for in a two-party election. In our own analysis, we often want to determine how the chances of a demographic event such as birth or death occurring over a given three-year period are affected by individual age, sex, household position, and banner occupation.[35] In

person-years of risk, distributed according to reported age in the first register, with one person-year of risk added to each of the three single-year age groups passed through during the intercensal period. As we do not know the exact year of death, we assign 1/3 of a death to each of the three years in the intercensal period. Similarly, we distribute the one and a half person-years assumed to have been lived by the people who died during the intercensal period to each of the three years in the period by 4/6, 3/6, and 2/6 per year of age. We would like to thank Tom Pullum for suggesting this method of calculation.

[32] We would like to thank Richard Barrett for suggesting the Reed—Merrill method to us. In Lee, Anthony, and Suen 1988 we have life expectancy by the rates of survival according to the methods suggested in Hill and Trussell 1983. The results are approximately the same.

[33] We would also like to thank Ronald Lee for introducing us to Chiang's 1968 and 1984 analyses on how to calculate the standard deviation of life expectancy.

[34] In a regression, the "dependent" variable is normally on the left-hand side of the equation, and "independent" variables are on the right. The labeling of the variable on the left as "dependent" reflects the implicit assumption that it can be expressed as a function of the variables on the right-hand side.

[35] Because we have linked observations of individuals at three year intervals, we can construct variables that are equal to 1 if the individual dies during an intercensal period, and equal to 0 otherwise. Similarly, we can construct variables that are equal to 1 if an individual has any children during an intercensal period, and equal to 0 otherwise.

some cases we analyze how the sex of a registered birth is affected by the social and economic circumstances of the parents.[36]

The goal is to estimate coefficients for independent variables in an equation that relates them to a dichotomous dependent variable. We would like to estimate an equation such as (1), where Y is an indicator of whether or not an event occurs, or the outcome of an event, $x_1 \ldots x_n$ are numeric representations of the independent variables, and e is an error term.

(1) $$Y = a_1x_1 + a_2x_2 + \ldots + a_nx_n + e$$

In such situations, however, a key assumption necessary for linear regression does not hold. Linear regression assumes that the error term is normally distributed.[37] When such an assumption is valid, standard statistical tests can be used to determine whether or not the coefficients estimated for the independent variables are statistically significant or not. When the dependent variable is discontinuous and the error is no longer normally distributed, such tests are no longer valid. Calculated coefficients can give misleading estimates not only of the relative importance of the independent variables, but also of whether or not their apparent effects can be ascribed to random fluctuation.

We can attempt to resolve the problem with the distribution of the error term by transforming the dependent variable to make it continuous. To transform, we may choose one of the two outcomes that the dependent variable represents, and compute the probability P that each combination of independent variables results in that outcome. The result is the following equation, (2), where the dependent variable Y has been replaced by the probability of the outcome of interest, $P(Y = 1)$. In the case of mortality that we mentioned earlier, P (Y=1) would be the probability of dying within the next three years for each combination of circumstances.

(2) $$P(Y = 1) = a_1x_1 + a_2x_2 + \ldots + a_nx_n + e$$

We still cannot use standard linear regression, however, because of its implicit assumption that the effects on the dependent variable of changes in the independent variables are linear. Under this assumption, for example, increasing the value of one of the independent variables by one-half should have twice as much of an effect on the

---

[36] In such situations, we construct a variable that is equal to 1 if most of the births in an intercensal period are male, and 0 otherwise.

[37] The normal distribution is often referred to as "a bell curve" because of its symmetry and its resemblance to the silhouette of a bell.

dependent variable as increasing their values by one-quarter. This cannot be the case when a dependent variable is dichotomous, and corresponds in some way to the probability of an event taking place. For example, if the chances of the event of interest occurring are 0.75, there is no way that doubling the value of the independent variables can double the chances of its occurring, because a probability of 1.5 would be for all practical purposes impossible.

Through further manipulation of the dependent variable, however, the situation may be resolved. Performing the logistic transformation $Z = \log(P/1-P)$ on the probability creates a new dependent variable for which the linearity assumption holds. The result is (3). In this new equation, the independent variables are untransformed. Regression coefficients are estimated using maximum-likelihood estimation. The coefficients $a_1...a_n$ may be tested for significance. Moreover, measures of goodness-of-fit equivalent to the R^2 in linear regression may also be calculated.

$$(3) \qquad log(P/1 - P) = a_1x_1 + a_2x_2 + ... + a_nx_n$$

In this equation, the coefficients $a_1...a_n$ represent the change in the log-odds of the event of interest associated with a one-unit change in the value of the independent variables. Increasing the value of x_1 by 1, for example, would increase the log-odds of the event of interest by a_1. Alternatively, it would multiply the odds of the event of interest by $exp(a1)$. Thus if a_1 were 1 and the event of interest were death during a three-year period, changing x_1 from 1 to 2 would multiply the odds of dying by 2.718. Through further algebraic manipulation the effect on the probability of dying of changing a_1 can also be approximated, and in the text of the chapters we often present the results of such approximations.

The interpretation of the coefficients on categorical independent variables requires further explanation. For categorical independent variables, for example, banner occupation, we usually create a dichotomous dummy variable for every category except one, which becomes the reference category. Each dummy variable is coded true or false (1 or 0) according to whether or not the corresponding category is indicated for that observation. The coefficients estimated for each category represent its effect on the odds of the event of interest relative to the omitted reference category. The effect of changing categories can be calculated by subtracting coefficients.

Appendix C

Household division contract of Lang Zhongqing and Lang Wenlin

Because of their many family tasks they find it hard to live together. From today on all their familial possessions, with the exception of land, housing, and grain, including all furniture and household objects shall be equally divided such that each side is in agreement. If there is any disagreement, the lineage representatives and the intermediaries should adjudicate.

This document of property division is created to provide written proof of this agreement as oral agreements may prove unreliable.

- Land: Lang Zhongqing should receive 24 *mu*: 6.2 *mu* of land west of Xigang kao, 10 *mu* of land in Changlong kao, 3.2 *mu* of land in Liuyuanwen, and 4.6 *mu* of land in Fenlu kou.

- Housing: Lang Zhongqing should receive the eastern room and the rooms on the eastern side of the courtyard.

- Land: Lang Wenlin should receive 14.3 *mu*: 5.3 *mu* east of Xigang kao, 9 *mu* in Changlong.

- Housing: Lang Wenlin should receive the western room and 2 smaller rooms on the west side of the courtyard.

Lineage representatives (*zuzhong ren*): Lang Zhirong, Lang Zhiqiang.

Intermediaries (*zhongjian ren*): Guo Songyi, Ding Yizhuang, Sha Qimin.

Secretary: Zhang Caisan.

March 11, 1956 Signed Lang Zhongqing and Lang Wenlin.

Translation note: The entire text was written by one person, but the two parties, their representatives, and intermediaries each affixed their chops below their names. We have, of course, changed the names to preserve confidentiality.

Glossary

Baqi	八旗	dou	斗
bainian haohe	百年好和	dutong	都統
baizong	百總	duozi duofu	多子多福
bangding	幫丁	faqian ding	發遷丁
Baodao tun	包道屯	feiding	廢丁
baojia	保甲	fengnian	丰年
baoyi	包衣	fengshou	豐收
bazi	八字	fenjia	分家
bingding	兵丁	fenjia dan	分家單
bitieshi	筆帖史	Fengtian	奉天
bo	伯	gaiyun	改運
bomin	撥民	gaoliang	高粱
caifeng jiang	裁縫匠	getui	革退
caimai	采買	gongjian	貢監
changming baisui	長命百歲	gongjiang	弓匠
chen	陳	gongsheng	貢生
chuding	初丁	gu[a]	故
cuizhang	催長	gu[b]	姑
da	大	guan xuesheng	官學生
dadou	大豆	guanfu	官夫
dagong	大功	guoyuan	果園
Daoyi tun	道義屯	Hanjun	漢軍
Daoyi xiang	道義鄉	Hanyu	漢語
daxilin	打細鱗	houbu	侯補
di	弟	hu	戶
ding	丁	hujun	護軍
dingdai	頂帶	huaerjiang	花兒匠
Dingjia fangshen	丁家房身	huang	黃

jiading	甲丁	muding	牧丁
jiansheng	監生	muzhang	牧長
jiazhang[a]	家長	nikan	尼堪
jiazhang[b]	甲長	niru	牛彔
jie	姐	pijiang	皮匠
jijiang	机匠	pinchu	聘出
jinshi	進士	Ping'an qiao	平安橋
jiuli	舊例	Puhe	蒲河
juanna	捐納	qi	齊
juren	舉人	qianfeng	前鋒
kang	炕	qidi	旗地
kaoxuan	考選	qin	親
kezi jiang	鍬子匠	Qing	清
kushi	庫史	ranjiang	染匠
lao	老	rending hukou ce	人丁戶口冊
laoding	老丁	sao	嫂
laozheng	癆症	shaolian	稍廉
lianbo	廉薄	shen	嬸
liangzhang	糧長	shenhao	甚好
lingcui	領催	Shenyang	沈陽
linghu	另戶	Shengjing	盛京
maimai	買賣	shengyuan	生員
Manyu	滿語	shi	石
mei	妹	shu	叔
menpai	門牌	siku	司庫
mi	米	sima	緦麻
ming	命	sugu	粟穀
mu	畝	sumi	粟米
mu yizi gui	母以子貴	sui	歲
		taoding	逃丁

tiejiang	鐵匠	yuan	院
tongchi	同吃	yuding	魚丁
tongju	同居	zaosheng guizi	早生貴子
tongxing buzong	同姓不宗	zili	側例
tuiding	退丁	zhan	斬
tun	屯	zhenghu	正戶
tuntian	屯田	Zheng huangqi	正黃旗
Wangba Miao	王八廟	zhengshen qiren	正身旗人
weisuo	衛所	zhinü	侄女
wufu[a]	五服	zhishiren	執事人
wufu[b]	無服	zhizao ku	織造庫
wulun	五倫	zhizi	侄子
xiao[a]	孝	zhong	中
xiao[b]	小	zhongjian ren	中間人
xiaogong	小功	zhuangding[a]	庄丁
xiaomai	小麥	zhuangding[b]	壯丁
xiaoqi wei	驍騎衛	zu	族
xinbu	新補	zuo maimai	作買賣
Xincheng qu	新城區	zuoling	佐領
xinfang	新放	zupu	族譜
xinzeng ding	新增丁	zuren	族人
xiong	兄	zuzhang	族長
yimin	移民	zuzhong ren	族中人
youding	幼丁		

References

Aldrich, John H. and Forrest D. Nelson. 1984. "Linear probability, logit and probit models. Sage University Paper series on Quantitative Applications in the Social Sciences, series no. 07–045. Beverley Hills: Sage Publications.

An Shuangcheng. 1983. "Shun Kang Yong sanchao baqi dinge qianxi" (A preliminary analysis of the Eight Banner quotas under the Shunzhi, Kangxi, and Yongzheng emperors). *Lishi dang'an* (Historical Archives). 2: 100–103.

An Zuozhang. 1985. *Qin Han guanzhi shigao* (A draft history of civil administration during the Qin and Han). Qilu shushe.

Arriaga, Eduardo E. and Peter O. Way. 1988. "Determinants of excess female mortality." *Population Bulletin of the United Nations.* 21/22–1987: 45–54.

Ashton, Basil, Kenneth Hill, Alan Piazza, and Robin Zeitz. 1984. "Famine in China, 1958–1961." *Population and Development Review.* 10.4(December): 613-645.

Ba Jin. 1978. *Family.* Sidney Shapiro, tr. Beijing: Foreign Language Press.

Baker, Hugh. 1979. *Chinese Family and Kinship.* New York: Columbia University Press.

Baqi Zeli (Rules and Regulations of the Eight Banners). Qianlong (1736-1795) edition. Beijing National Library.

Barclay, George W. 1954. *Colonial Development and Population in Taiwan.* Princeton: Princeton University Press.

Barclay, G. W., A. J. Coale, M. A. Stoto, and T. J. Trussell. 1976. "A reassessment of the demography of traditional rural China." *Population Index.* 42.4 (Winter): 606–635.

Basu, Alaka Malwade. 1989. "Is discrimination in food really necessary for explaining sex differentials in childhood mortality?" *Population Studies.* 43.2 (August): 193–210.

Bellah, Robert, *et al.* 1991. *The Good Society.* New York: Knopf.

Bengtsson, Tommy, Gunnar Fridlizius, and Rolf Ohlsson, eds. 1984. *Preindustrial Population Change: The Mortality Decline and Short-term Population Movements.* Stockholm: Almquist and Wiksell.

Berkner, Lutz. 1972. "The stem family and the development cycle of the peasant household: an eighteenth century Austrian example." *American Historical Review.* 77 (April): 398–418.

——— 1975. "The use and misuse of census data for the historical analysis of family structure: a review of household and family in past time." *Journal of Interdisciplinary History*. 4 (Spring): 721-738.

Berkner, Lutz and Franklin Mendels. 1978. "Inheritance systems, family structure, and demographical patterns in Western Europe 1700–1900." In Charles Tilly (ed.) *Historical Studies in Changing Fertility*, 209–224. Princeton: Princeton University Press.

Bhatia, Shushum. 1983. "Traditional practices affecting female health and survival: evidence from countries of South Asia." In Alan Lopez and Lado T. Ruzicka, eds., 165–178.

Blayo, Yves. 1975. "La mortalité en France de 1740 à 1829." *Population*. (November–December): 138–139.

Bonfield, Lloyd, Richard Smith, and Keith Wrightson, eds. 1986. *The World We Have Gained: Histories of Population and Social Structure*. Oxford: Basil Blackwell.

Bongaarts, John. 1980. "Does malnutrition affect fecundity? A summary of evidence." *Science*. 208: 564–569.

Bongaarts, John and Robert G. Potter. 1983. *Fertility, Biology, and Behavior*. New York: Academic Press.

Boulais, Le P. Guy. 1924 (1966 reprint). *Manuel du Code Chinois*. Taipei: Ch'eng-wen.

Brunnert H. S. and V. V. Hagelstrom . 1910. *Present-day Political Organization in China*. Shanghai: Kelly and Walsh.

Buxbaum, David, ed. 1978. *Chinese Family Law and Social Change: in Historical and Comparative Perspective*. Seattle: University of Washington Press.

Campbell, Cameron. 1995. "Chinese mortality transitions: the case of Beijing, 1700–1990." PhD dissertation. University of Pennsylvania, Department of Sociology and Graduate Group in Demography.

Campbell, Cameron and James Lee. 1996. "A death in the family: household structure and mortality in rural Liaoning, life event and time series analysis 1792–1867." *History of the Family*. 1.3: 297–328.

Forthcoming. "Gender patterns of mortality in rural Liaoning: infanticide, neglect, and the Far East mortality pattern, 1774–1873." In Lee and Saito, eds.

Chaffee, John. 1985. *The Thorny Gate of Learning in Sung China: A Social History of Examinations*. Cambridge: Cambridge University Press.

Chao, Kang. 1986. *Man and Land in Chinese History*. Stanford: Stanford University Press.

Chen, B. H., C. J. Hong, M. R. Pandey, and K. R. Smith. 1990. "Indoor air pollution in developing countries." *World Health Statistics Quarterly*. 43.3: 127–138.

Chen, Guangsheng. 1989. "Songdai shengzi buyu fengsu de shengxing jiqi yuanyin" (The reasons for the rise of infanticide during the Song). *Zhongguo shi yanjiu* (Research in Chinese History). 1: 138–143.

Chen, Jiahua. 1985. "Baqi bingxiang shixi" (A preliminary analysis of Eight Banner finances). *Minzu yanjiu* (Ethnic Studies). 5: 63–71.

Chen, Jiahua and Fu Kedong. 1988a. "Baqi jianli qian Manzhou niulu he renkou chutan" (A preliminary study on the population size and the number of *niru* before the establishment of the Eight Banner system in Manchuria). In Wang Zhonghan, ed., 259–280.

1988b. "Baqi Hanjun kaolue" (A short study on the Han martial banners). In Wang Zhonghan, ed. 281–306.

1988c. Zuoling shulue (A short discussion on the Eight Banner company commander). In Wang Zhonghan, ed. 307–336.

Chen, Lincoln and A. K. M. A. Chowdhury. 1977. "The dynamics of contemporary famine." In *International Population Conference, Mexico.* 1: 409–426. Liege: International Union for the Scientific Study of Population.

Chen, Lincoln, Emdadul Huq, and Stan D'Souza. 1981. "Sex bias in the family allocation of food and health care in rural Bangladesh." *Population and Development Review.* 7.1 (March): 55–70.

Chiang Chin Long 1968. *Introduction to Stochastic Processes in Biostatistics.* New York: Wiley.

1984. *The Life Table and its Applications.* Miami: Robert Krieger Publishing Company.

Chikusa, Tatsuo. 1978. "Succession to ancestral sacrifices and adoption of heirs to the sacrifices: as seen from an inquiry into customary institutions in Manchuria." In Buxbaum, ed. 151–175.

Chu T'ung-tsu. 1961. *Law and Society in Traditional China.* Paris and The Hague: Mouton & Company.

1962. *Local Government in China Under the Ch'ing.* Cambridge: Harvard University Press.

Chuan Hansheng, and Richard A. Kraus. 1975. *Mid-Ch'ing Rice Markets and Trade: An Essay in Price History.* Cambridge: Harvard University Press.

Claude, Richard P., eds. 1976. *Comparative Human Rights.* Baltimore: the Johns Hopkins University Press.

Coale, Ansley. 1986. "The decline of fertility in Europe since the eighteenth century as a chapter in human demographic history." In Ansley Coale and Susan Cotts Watkins, eds. *The Decline of Fertility in Europe.* Princeton: Princeton University Press, 1–30.

Coale, Ansley and Paul Demeny. 1966/1983. *Regional Model Life Tables and Stable Populations.* Princeton: Princeton University Press.

Cohen, Myron. 1976. *House United, House Divided: The Chinese Family in Taiwan.* New York: Columbia University Press.

Cole, James. 1986. *Shaohsing: Competition and Cooperation in Nineteenth Century China.* Monographs of the Association of Asian Studies, no. 44. Tucson: University of Arizona Press.

Confucius (551–479 BC). 1979. *The Analects.* D. C. Lau, tr. London: Penguin Books.

Crossley, Pamela. 1989. "The Qianlong retrospect on the Chinese-martial banners." *Late Imperial China.* 10.1 (June): 63–107.

1990. *Orphan Warriors.* Princeton: Princeton University Press.

D'Souza, Stan and Lincoln C. Chen. 1980. "Sex differentials in mortality in rural Bangladesh." *Population and DevelopmentReview*. 6.1 (June): 257–270.

Da Qing huidian shili (Collected statutes of the Qing Dynasty with cases and precedents). 1818 ed., Zhonghua shuju edition 1994 reprint.

Daoyi xiangzhi (Daoyi District Gazetteer). 1984. Mimeograph edition.

Das Gupta, Monica. 1987. "Selective discrimination against female children in India." *Population and Development Review*. 13.1 (March): 77–100.

Davis, Kingsley. 1955. "Institutional patterns favouring high fertility in underdeveloped areas." *Eugenics Quarterly*. 2: 33–39.

Dennerline, Jerry. 1986. "Marriage, adoption, and charity in the development of lineages in Wu-hsi from Sung to Ch'ing." In Patricia Ebrey and James Watson, eds. *Kinship Organization in Late Imperial China, 1000–1900*. Berkeley: University of California Press, 170–209.

Ding Yizhuang. 1992. *Qingdai baqi zhufang zhidu yanjiu* (Research on the Eight Banner Garrison System during the Qing). Tianjin: Guji chuban she.

Ding Yizhuang and Liu Xiaomeng. 1988. "Shishu Qingchao Qianlong nianjian di dongbei liumin jiqi dui qiren shengji wenti" (A preliminary discussion of migration to northeast China during the Qianlong reign and its impact on banner livelihood). *Heilongjiang minzu congkan*. 1: 50–57, 63.

Dongbei qu ziran dili ziliao (Materials on the natural geography of northeast China). 1957. Beijing: Kexue chuban she.

Dyson, Tim. 1991. "On the demography of South Asian famines, parts I and II." *Population Studies*. 45.1 (March): 5–25, and 45.2 (July): 279–297.

E'Ertai (1680-1745). *Baqi tongzhi* (General History of the Eight Banners). Changchun: Dongbei shifan daxue chuban she, 1985, punctuated edition.

Elliott, Mark 1993. "Resident aliens: the Manchu experience in China, 1644–1760." PhD dissertation. University of California, Berkeley, Department of History.

Elo, Irma and Samuel Preston. 1992. "Effects of early-life conditions on adult mortality: a review." *Population Index*. 58.2 (Summer): 186–212.

Elvin, Mark. 1973. *The Pattern of the Chinese Past*. Stanford: Stanford University Press.

Esherick, Joseph and Mary Rankin, eds. 1990. *Chinese Local Elites and Patterns of Dominance*. Berkeley: University of California Press.

Ewbank, Douglas. 1981. *Age Misreporting and Age-selective Underenumeration: Sources, Patterns, and Consequences for Demographic Analysis*. Washington DC: National Academy Press.

Feeney, Griffith and Hamano Kiyoshi. 1990. "Rice price fluctuations in fertility in late Tokugawa Japan." *Journal of Japanese Studies*. 16.1 (Winter): 1–30.

Fei Hsiao Tung (Fei Xiaotong). 1939. *Peasant Life in China*. London: Routledge and Kegan Paul Ltd.

1946/1983. "An interpretation of Chinese social structure and its changes." Reprinted in *Chinese Village Close-up*. Beijing: New World Press, 124–157.

1953, "Basic power structure in rural China." In Margaret Redfield, ed. *China's Gentry*. Chicago: University of Chicago Press, 75–90.

Fei Hsiao-tung and Chih-i Chang. 1945. *Earthbound China: A Study of Rural Economy in Yunnan*. Chicago: University of Chicago Press.

Feng Han-chi. 1937. "The Chinese kinship system." *Harvard Journal of Asiatic Studies*. 2: 142–289.

Feng Peizhi, Li Cuijin, and Li Xiaoquan. 1985. *Zhongguo zhuyao qixiang zaihai fenxi, 1951–1980* (An analysis of the major climatic disasters in China 1951–1980). Beijing: Qixiang chuban she.

Fengtian Tongzhi. 1934/1982. Shenyang: Dongbei wenshi congshu reprint.

Finegan, Michael. 1988. "Inheritance and family structure in Qing China: Evidence from Taiwan and Fujian." Unpublished manuscript.

Finegan, Michael and Ted Telford. 1988. "Chinese archival holdings at the Genealogical Society of Utah." *Late Imperial China*. 9.2 (December): 86–114.

Flinn, Michael W. 1981. *The European Demographic System, 1500–1820*. Baltimore: Johns Hopkins University Press.

Freedman, Maurice. 1966. *Chinese Lineage and Society: Fukien and Kwangtung*. New York: Humanities Press Inc.

Frisch, Rose. 1975. "Demographic implications of the biological determinants of female fecundity." *Social Biology* 22.1: 17–22.

1978. "Population, food intake, and fertility." *Science*. 199: 22–30.

Fu Kedong. 1983. "Baqi zhidu huji chutan" (A preliminary study of the Eight Banner household registration system). *Minzu yanjiu* (Ethnic Studies). 6 (December): 34–43.

Fu Kedong and Chen Jiahua. 1980. "Baqi zhidu zhong de Man Meng Han guanxi" (Manchu–Mongol–Han relations inside the Eight Banners). *Minzu yanjiu* (Ethnic Studies). 6 (December): 24–39.

Fuge (c. 1850). 1984. *Tingyu congtan*. Beijing: Zhonghua shuju 1984.

Furth, Charlotte. 1987. "Pregnancy, childbirth and infancy in Ch'ing dynasty China." *Journal of Asian Studies*. 46.1 (January): 7–35.

Galloway, Patrick R. 1988. "Basic patterns in annual variation in fertility, nuptiality, mortality, and prices in pre-industrial Europe." *Population Studies*. 42.2 (July): 275–303.

1994. "Secular changes in the short-term preventive, positive, and temperature checks to population growth in Europe, 1460 to 1909." *Climatic Change*. 26: 3–63.

Gamble, Sidney. 1921. *Peking: A Social Survey*. New York: George H. Doran Company.

1933. *How Chinese Families Live in Peiping*. New York: Funk and Wagnalls.

1954. *Ting Hsien, a North China Rural Community*. New York: Institute of Pacific Relations.

Gautier, Etienne and Louis Henry. 1958. *La population de Crulai, paroisse*

Normande: etude historique. Institut National d'Etudes Démographiques, cahier 33. Paris: Presses Universitaires de France.

Geertz, Clifford. 1959. "Form and variation in Balinese village structure." *American Anthropologist* 61.6: 991-1012.

Ginsburg, Caren and Alan Swedlund. 1986. "Sex-specific mortality and economic opportunity: Massachusetts, 1860–1899." *Continuity and Change.* 1.3 (December): 415–445.

Gjerde, Jon, Anita Tien, and James Lee. 1987. "Comparative household processes of stem, joint, and nuclear household systems: Scandinavia, China, and the United States." Manuscript presented to the 1987 Annual Meeting of the Social Science History Association.

Gold, Diane R. 1992. "Indoor air pollution." *Clinics in Chest Medicine.* 13.2 (June): 215–29.

Goldman, Noreen. 1980. "Far Eastern patterns of mortality." *Population Studies.* 34.1 (March): 5–22.

Goode, William J. 1971. *World Revolution and Family Patterns.* New York: The Free Press.

Gray, Ronald. 1983. "The impact of health and nutrition on natural fertility." In R.A. Bulatao and R.D. Lee, eds. *Determinants of fertility in Developing Countries.* New York: Academic Press, 139–162.

Grigg, E. N. R. 1958. "The arcana of tuberculosis." *The American Review of Tuberculosis and Pulmonary Disease.* 78: 151–172, 426–453, 585–603.

Guan Jialu, Tong Yonggong, and Wang Zhonghan. 1987. *Yong Qian liangchao xianghongqi dang* (Archival documents from the Bordered Red Banner during the reigns of the Yongzheng (1723–1735) and Qianlong (1736–1795) emperor). Shenyang: Liaoning renmin chuban she.

Guo Songyi. 1982. "Qingdai guonei de haiyun maoyi" (Qing coastal trade). *Qingshi luncong* 4: 92–110.

_____ 1991. *Qingdai quanshi* (The complete history of the Qing dynasty). Vol. 3. Shenyang: Liaoning renmin chuban she.

Guo Yunjing. 1984. *Qingdai jingji shi jianbian* (A short economic history of the Qing dynasty). Zhengzhou: Henan renmin chuban she.

Hajnal, John. 1965. "European marriage patterns in perspective." In D. V. Glass and D. E. C. Eversley, eds. *Population in History.* London: Edward Arnold Publishers, 101-146.

_____ 1982. "Two kinds of preindustrial household formation system." *Population and Development Review.* 8.3 (September): 449–494.

Hammel, Eugene and Peter Laslett. 1974. "Comparing household structure over time and between cultures." *Comparative Studies in Society and History.* 16: 73-111.

Han Guanghui. 1988. "Qingdai jingshi baqi rending de zengzhang yu dili qianyi" (The growth and geographical mobility of the Eight Banner population in the capital region during the Qing). *Lishi dili* (Historical Geography). 6: 197–208.

Hanley, Susan B. and Arthur P. Wolf, eds. 1985. In *Family and Population in East Asian History.* Stanford: Stanford University Press.

Hareven, Tamara ed. 1978. *Transitions: The Family and the Life Course in Historical Perspective*. New York: Academic Press.

Harrell, Steven. 1985. "The rich get children: segmentation, stratification, and population in three Chekiang lineages, 1550–1850." In Hanley and Wolf, eds., 81–109.

　1987. "On the holes in Chinese genealogies." *Late Imperial China* 9.1 (June): 52–87.

　Editor. 1995. *Chinese Historical Micro-Demography*. Berkeley: University of California Press.

Harrell, Steven and Tom Pullum. 1995. "Marriage, mortality, and the developmental cycle in three Xiaoshan lineages." In Harrell, ed., 141–162.

He Xingzhou, Wei Chen, Ziyuan Liu, and Robert S. Chapman. 1991. "An epidemiological study of lung cancer in Xuan Wei County, China: current progress. Case-control study on lung cancer and cooking fuel." *Environmental Health Perspectives*. 94: 9–13.

Heligman, Larry. 1983. "Patterns of sex differentials in mortality in less developed countries." In Alan Lopez, and Lado T. Ruzicka, eds., 7–32.

Henry, Louis. 1961. "Some data on natural fertility." *Eugenics Quarterly*. 8.2 (June): 81-91.

　1989. "Men's and women's mortality in the past." *Population. English Selection*. 44.1 (September): 177–201. (English translation of "Mortalite des hommes et des femmes dans le passe." *Annales de Demographie Historique*. 1987: 87–118.)

Hill, Kenneth and James Trussell. 1983. *Manual X: Indirect Techniques for Demographic Estimation*. New York: United Nations Population Studies, No. 81.

Ho, Ping-ti. 1959. *Studies on the Population of China, 1368–1953*. Cambridge, Mass.: Harvard University Press.

　1962. *The Ladder of Success in Imperial China: Aspects of Social Mobility (1368–1911)*. New York: Columbia University Press.

　1975. *Cradle of the East*. Hong Kong: Chinese University of Hong Kong Press.

Hout, Michael. 1983. *Mobility Tables*. Sage University Paper Series on Quantitative Applications in the Social Sciences, 07-031. Beverly Hills: Sage Publications.

Hsieh Jih-chang and Chuang Ying-chang, eds. 1985. *The Chinese Family and its Ritual Behavior*. Taipei: Institute of Ethnology, Academia Sinica.

Hsiung Ping-chen. 1994. "Constructed emotions: the bond between mothers and sons in late imperial China." *Late Imperial China*. 15.1 (June): 87–117.

　1995a. "To nurse the young: breastfeeding and infant feeding in late imperial China." *Journal of Family History*. 20.3: 217–238.

　1995b. *Youyou: chuantang Zhongguo de chiangbao zhi dao* (Childhood: traditional Chinese infant care). Taipei: Lianjing.

　Forthcoming. "More or less: Chinese medical and cultural traditions of fertility control." In Lee and Saito, eds.

Hsu, Francis. 1943. "The myth of Chinese family size." *American Journal of*

Sociology. 48.5: 555–62.

Hu Yuanreng and Noreen Goldman. 1990. "Mortality differentials by marital status: an international comparison." *Demography.* 27.2 (May): 233–50.

Huang, Philip. 1985. *The Peasant Economy and Social Change in North China.* Stanford: Stanford University Press.

—— 1990. *The Peasant Family and Rural Development in the Yangzi Delta, 1350–1988.* Stanford: Stanford University Press.

Hulsewe, A. F. P. 1985. *Remnants of Ch'in Law.* Leiden: E.J. Brill.

Humphries, J. 1991. "Bread and a pennyworth of treacle: excess female mortality in England in the 1840s." *Cambridge Journal of Economics.* 15.4 (December): 451–73.

Hymes, Robert. 1986. *Statesmen and Gentlemen: The Elites of Fu-chou, Chiang-hsi in Northern and Southern Sung.* Cambridge: Cambridge University Press.

Isett, Christopher. 1996. "Social change and rural development in Manchuria, 1644–1945." PhD dissertation. University of California, Los Angeles, Department of History.

James, William. 1985. "The sex ratio of Oriental births." *Annals of Human Biology.* 12: 485–487.

Jiang Liangqi (1723-1789). *Donghua lu* (The Donghua Records). Beijing: Zhonghua. 1980 punc. ed.

Jiang Tao. 1993. *Zhongguo jindai renkou shi* (Modern population History of China). Hangzhou: Zhejiang renmin chuban she.

Jin Dechuan (c. 1700). *Qijun zhi* (Banner army gazetteer). Liaohai congshu edition.

Johansson, S. Ryan. 1991. "Welfare, mortality, and gender. Continuity and change in explanations for male/female mortality differences over three centuries." *Continuity and Change.* 6.2 (August): 135–177.

—— 1994. "Food for thought: rhetoric and reality in modern mortality history." *Historical Methods.* 27.3 (Summer): 101–125.

Kennedy, R. E. 1973. *The Irish: Emigration, Marriage, and Fertility.* Berkeley: University of California Press.

Kim, Jae-on and Charles Mueller. 1978. *Factor Analysis: Statistical Methods and Practical Issues.* Quantitative Applications in Social Sciences, no. 14. Beverley Hills: Sage Publications.

Kito Hiroshii. 1991. "Zen kindai Nihon no shush-ryoku: Koshosusho-ritsu wa jijitsu dataka." *Jyochi keizai ronshu.* 36, 83-98.

Knodel, John. 1988. *Demographic Behavior in the Past: A Study of 14 German Village Populations in the Eighteenth and Nineteenth Centuries.* Cambridge: Cambridge University Press.

Kong Jingwei. 1986. *Dongbei jingii shi* (Economic history of northeast China). Chengdu: Sichuan renmin chuban she.

Lai Huimin. 1994. "Guoji yu Qingdai huangzu" (Adoption among the imperial lineage). In Lee and Guo, eds., 60–89.

Lam, David A. and Jeffrey A. Miron. 1991. "Seasonality of births in human populations." *Social Biology.* 38: 51–78.

1994. "Global patterns of seasonal variation in human fertility." *Annals of the New York Academy of Sciences.* 709 (February 18): 9–28.

Lamson, Herbert. 1935. "Differential reproduction in China." *Quarterly Review of Biology.* (September): 308-321.

Lang, Olga. 1946. *Chinese Family and Society.* New Haven: Yale University Press.

Lao She. 1979. *Rickshaw.* Jean James, tr. Honolulu: University of Hawaii Press.

Laslett, Peter and Richard Wall. 1972. *Household and Family in Past Time.* Cambridge: Cambridge University Press.

Lau, Joseph. 1985. "Duty, reputation, and selfhood." In Robert Hegel and Richard Hessney, eds. *Expressions of Self in Chinese Literature.* New York: Columbia University Press, 363–383, 428–432.

Lavely, William, James Lee, and Wang Feng. 1990. "Chinese demography: the state of the field." *Journal of Asian Studies.* 49.4 (November): 807–834.

Lee, James. 1978. "Migration and expansion in Chinese history." In William H. McNeill and Ruth S. Adams, eds. *Human Migration: Patterns and Policies.* Indiana University Press, 20-47.

1991. "Homicide et peine capitale en Chine à fin de l'empire: analyse statistique preliminaire des données." *Etudes Chinoises.* X.1–2 (Autumn): 113–134.

(Li Zhongqing). 1994. "Zhongguo renkou zhidu: Qingdai renkou xingwei jiqi yiyi" (The Chinese demographic system: Qing population behaviors and their implication). In Lee and Guo, eds., 8–24.

Lee, James and Robert Eng. 1984. "Population and family history in eighteenth-century Manchuria: preliminary results from Daoyi 1774–1798." *Ch'ing-shih wen-t'i.* 5.1 (June): 1–55.

Lee, James and Jon Gjerde. 1986. "Comparative household morphology of stem, joint and nuclear household systems: Norway, China, and the United States." *Continuity and Change.* 1.1 (May): 89–112.

Lee, James (Li Zhongqing) and Guo Songyi, eds. 1994. *Qingdai huangzu renkou xingwei he shehui huanjing* (The Qing imperial lineage: population behavior and social setting). Peking: Peking University Press.

Lee, James and Osamu Saito, eds. Forthcoming. *Abortion, Infanticide, and Reproductive Culture in Asia: Past and Present.* Oxford: Oxford University Press.

Lee, James and Wang Feng. 1995. "Male nuptiality and male fertility among the Qing imperial lineage: polygyny or serial monogamy." Manuscript presented to the IUSSP Conference on Male Fertility. Zacatecas, Mexico.

1996. "Nuptiality among the Qing nobility: implications for two types of marriage systems." Manuscript presented to the IUSSP Conference on Asian Population History. Taipei, China.

Lee, James, Lawrence Anthony, and Alice Suen. 1988. "Liaoning sheng chengren siwang lu, 1796–1819" (Adult mortality in Liaoning, 1796–1819). In *Qingzhu diyi lishi dang'an guan liushi zhounian lunwen ji* (Proceedings of the Symposium on the Occasion of the Sixtieth Anniversary of the

References

First Historical Archives). Beijing: Zhonghua shuju, Vol. 2, 885–898.

Lee, James, Cameron Campbell, and Lawrence Anthony. 1995. "A century of mortality in rural Liaoning." In Steven Harrell, ed., 163–182.

Lee, James, Cameron Campbell, and Guofu Tan. 1988. "Qingdai zhongye Fengtian Daoyi tun liangjia yu renkou bianhua" (Grain prices and population in Daoyi during the mid-Qing). *Dongbei difang shi yanjiu* (Studies on the Local History of Northeast China). 3: 29–36.

———. 1989. "1772–1873 jian Fengtian diqu liangjia yu renkou bianhua" (Grain prices and population in Liaoning from 1774 to 1873). In Liu Ts'uijung, ed. *The Second Conference on Modern Chinese Economic History*. Taipei: Academia Sinica, Institute of Economics, 511–542.

———. 1992. "Infanticide and family planning in late imperial China: the price and population history of rural Liaoning, 1774–1873." In Rawski and Li, eds., 145–176.

Lee, James, Cameron Campbell, and Wang Feng. 1993. "The last emperors: an introduction to the demography of the Qing (1644–1911) imperial lineage." In Roger Schofield and David Reher, eds. *Old and New Methods in Historical Demography*. Oxford: Oxford University Press, 361–382.

Lee, James, Wang Feng, and Cameron Campbell. 1994. "Infant and child mortality among the late imperial Chinese nobility: implications for two kinds of positive check." *Population Studies*. 48.3 (November): 395–411.

Lee, Ronald. 1987. "Population dynamics of humans and other animals." *Demography* 24.4 (November): 443-467.

Legge, James (1815-1897). 1971 reprint of 1887 edition. *The Chinese Classics: An English translation by James Legge*. Taipei: Wenshizhe.

Lennox, William. 1919. "Some vital statistics based on the histories of 4,000 Chinese families." *Chinese Medical Journal*. (July): 325–345.

Leridon, Henri. 1977. *Human Fertility*. Chicago: The University of Chicago Press.

Levy, Marion. 1949. *The Family Revolution in Modern China*. Cambridge, Mass.: Harvard University Press.

Li Bozhong. 1994. "Kongzhi zengzhang, yibao fuyu: Qingdai qianzhongqi Jiangnan de renkou xingwei" (Controlling population to guarantee wealth: population behavior in Jiangnan during the Mid-Qing). *Xin shixue* (New History). 5.3 (September): 25–71.

Li Chi: Book of Rites; An Encyclopedia of Ancient Ceremonial Usages, Religious Creeds, and Social Institutions. 1967. James Legge Tr. Ch'u Chai and Winberg Chai eds. New Hyde Park, New York: University Books reprint of Oxford University Press 1885 edition with new material added by the editors.

Li, Lillian. 1982. "Introduction: food, famine, and the Chinese state." *Journal of Asian Studies*. 41.4 (August): 687–707.

Li Lin. 1988a. *Manzu jiapu xuanbian* (Selected Manchu Genealogies). Shenyang: Liaoning minzu chuban she.

———. 1988b. *Benxi xian Manzu jiapu yanjiu* (Research on the Manchu Genealogies of Benxi County). Shenyang: Liaoning minzu chuban she.

1989. "Baqi hanjun" (The Eight Banner Man army). Unpublished manuscript.

1992. *Manzu zongpu yanjiu* (Research on Manchu Genealogies). Shenyang: Shenliao shushe.

Li Qiao. 1985. "Baqi shengji wenti shulue" (A short discussion of the problems of Eight Banner livelihood). *Lishi dang'an* (Historical Archives). 1: 91–97, 47.

Li Shutian. 1993. *Qingdai Manzhou tudi zhidu yanjiu* (Research on the System of Land Tenure in Manchuria during the Qing). Changchun: Jilin wenshi chuban she.

Liang, Fangzhong. 1980. *Zhongguo lidai hukou tiandi tianfu tongji* (Statistics on China's Historical Population, Cultivated Land and Land Tax). Shanghai: Renmin chuban she.

Liang Xixin, *et al.* 1985. *Liaoning sheng jingji dili* (Economic Geography of Liaoning Province). Beijing: Xinhua chuban she.

Liaoning gonglu jiaotong shi (History of roads in Liaoning). 1988. Beijing: Renmin jiaotong chuban she.

Liu, Jingzhen. 1994a. "Songren shengzi buyu fengsu shitan: jingjixing liyou de tansuo" (A preliminary study of the Song practice of infanticide and neglect: the economic rationales). *Dalu zazhi*. 88.6: 1–23.

1994b. "Shazi yu niying: Songren shengyu wenti de xingbie chayi" (Killing sons and drowning daughters: sex differentials in Song fertility). *Zhongguo lishi xuehui shixue jikan*. 26: 99–106.

1995a. "Cong juanzi huaitai de baoying chuanshuo kan Songdai funu de shengyu wenti" (Song female fertility issues: Abortion and its consequences). *Dalu zazhi* 90.1: 1-15.

1995b. "Han Sui zhijian de `shengzi buju' wenti: Liuchao shengyu lisu yanjiu zhiyi" (Infanticide and neglect between the Han and Sui dynasties: a study of human fertility during the Six Dynasties). *Dalu zazhi*. 89.00–00.

Liu, Ts'ui-jung. 1978. "Chinese genealogies as a source for the study of historical demography." *Studies and Essays in Commemoration of the Golden Jubilee of the Academia Sinica*. (June): 849–870.

1985. "The demography of two Chinese clans in Hsiao-shan, Chekiang, 1650–1850." In Hanley and Wolf, eds., 13–61

1986. "Agricultural change and population growth: A brief survey on the case of China in historical perspective." *Academia Economic Papers*. 14.1 (March): 29–68.

1992. *Ming Qing shiqi jiazu renkou yu shehui jingji bianqian* (Lineage Population and Socio-economic Changes in the Ming and Qing Periods). Taipei: Institute of Economics, Academia Sinica. 2 vols.

1995a. "Historical demography of South China lineages." In Harrell, ed., 94–120.

1995b. "Demographic Constraint and Family Structure in Traditional Chinese lineages, ca. 1200-1900." In Harrell, ed., 121–140.

Lopez, Alan and Lado T. Ruzicka, eds. 1983. *Sex Differentials in Mortality:*

Trends, Determinants, and Consequences. Camberra: Australian National University, Department of Demography. Miscellaneous Series No. 3.

Lunn, Peter G. 1991. "Nutrition, immunity and infection." In Roger Schofield, David Reher, and Alain Bideau, eds. 1991. *The Decline of Mortality in Europe*. Oxford: Clarendon Press, 131–145.

Luo Ergang. 1984 rev ed. *Lüying bingzhi* (The Green Standard Military System). Beijing: Zhonghua.

Macfarlane, Alan. 1978. *The Origins of English Individualism: Family, Property, and Social Transition*. Oxford: Oxford University Press.

———. 1987. *The Culture of Capitalism*. Oxford: Oxford University Press.

Malthus, Thomas R. 1872. *An Essay on the Principle of Population, Seventh Edition*. London: Reeves and Turner.

Mason, William and Herb Smith. 1990. "Age-period-cohort analysis and the study of deaths from pulmonary tuberculosis." In William M. and Stephen E. Fienberg, eds. *Cohort Analysis in Social Research: Beyond the Identification Problem*. New York: Springer-Verlag, 151–227.

McKeown, Thomas. 1976. *The Modern Rise of Population*. New York: Academic Press.

McKeown, T. and R. G. Record. 1962. "Reasons for the decline of mortality in England and Wales during the 19th century." *Population Studies*. 16: 94–122.

Mencius (371-289 BC). 1970. *Mencius*. D. C. Lau, tr. London: Penguin Books.

Menken, Jane, James Trussell, and Susan Watkins. 1981. "The nutrition fertility link: an evaluation of the evidence." *Journal of Interdisciplinary History*. 11.3 (Winter): 425–441.

Miyazaki Ichidsada. 1976/1981. *China's Examination Hell*. Conrad Schirokauer, tr. New Haven: Yale University Press.

Mosk, Carl and S. Ryan Johansson. 1986. "Income and mortality: evidence from modern Japan." *Population and Development Review*. 12.3 (September): 415–440.

Muhuri, Pradip K. and Samuel H. Preston. 1991. "Effects of family composition on mortality differentials by sex among children in Matlab, Bangladesh." *Population and Development Review*. 17.3 (September):415–434.

Mumford, J. L., X. Z. He, R. S. Chapman, S. R. Cao, D. B. Harris, X. M. Li, Y. L. Xian, W. Z. Jiang, C. W. Xu, J. C. Chuang, W. E. Wilson, and M. Cooke. 1987. "Lung cancer and indoor air pollution in Xuan Wei, China." *Science* 235: 217–220.

Nathanson, C. A. 1984. "Sex Differences in Mortality." *Annual Review of Sociology*. 10:191–221.

Park, Chai Bin and Nam-Hoon Cho. 1995. "Consequences of son preference in a low-fertility society: imbalance of the sex ratio at birth in Korea." *Population and Development Review*. 21.1 (March): 1–26.

Parrish, William and Martin Whyte. 1978. *Village and Family in Contemporary China*. Chicago: University of Chicago Press.

Pasternak, Burton. 1983. *Guests in the Dragon: Social Demography of a Chinese*

District, 1895–1946. New York: Columbia University Press.

Pebley, A. R., S. L. Huffman, A. K. M. A. Chowdhury, and P. W. Stupp. 1985. "Intrauterine mortality and maternal nutritional status in rural Bangladesh." *Population Studies.* 39.3 (November): 425–440.

Perkins, Dwight. 1969. *Agricultural Development in China, 1368–1968.* Chicago: Aldine Publishing Company.

Pope, C. 1989. "Adult mortality before the twentieth century: current evidence and new sources." Manuscript presented to the UCLA Von Gremp Workshop in Economic History.

Preston, Samuel. 1976. *Mortality Patterns in National Populations.* New York: Academic Press.

Qiu Jun (1420–1495). *Daxue yanyi bu* (The Supplement to the Exposition of the Great Learning). (Japanese fascimile of 1792 edition).

Rawski, Evelyn. 1979. *Education and Popular Literacy in Ch'ing China.* Ann Arbor: University of Michigan Press.

Rawski, Thomas and Lillian Li, eds. 1992. *Chinese History in Economic Perspective.* Berkeley: University of California Press.

Rindfuss, R. and P. Morgan. 1983. "Marriage, sex, and the first birth interval: the quiet revolution in Asia." *Population and Development Review.* 9.2 (June): 259–278.

Saito, Osamu. 1992. "Infanticide, fertility, and population stagnation: the state of Tokugawa historical demography." *Japan Forum.* 4(2): 369–381.

Schofield, Roger. 1986. "Did the mothers really die? Three centuries of maternal mortality in 'The World We Have Lost'." In Lloyd Bonfield, Richard Smith, and Keith Wrightson, eds. *The World We Have Gained: Histories of Population and Social Structure.* Oxford: Basil Blackwell, 231–260.

Schofield, Roger and David Reher. 1991. "The decline of mortality in Europe." In R. D. Schofield, D. Reher, and A. Bideau, eds., 1–17.

Schofield, Roger and E. A. Wrigley. 1979. "Infant and child mortality in England in the late Tudor and Early Stuart Periods." In C. Webster, ed. *Health, Medicine and Mortality in the Sixteenth Century.* Cambridge: University Press, 61–96.

Schofield, Roger, David Reher, and Alain Bideau, eds. 1991. *The Decline of Mortality in Europe.* Oxford: Clarendon Press.

Shang Hongkui, Liu Jingxuan, Ji Yonghai, and Xu Kai. 1990. *Qingshi manyu cidian* (A Manchu Language Dictionary of Qing Historical Terms). Shanghai: Shanghai Guji chuban she.

Shapiro, Ian. 1986. *The Evolution of Rights in Liberal Theory.* Cambridge: Cambridge University Press.

Shiga Shuzo. 1978. "Chinese family law and social change." In Buxbaum, ed. 109–150.

Shirokogoroff, S. M. 1926. *Social Organization of the Manchus.* Extra Volume of the North China Branch of the Royal Asiatic Society.

Shorter, E. 1982. *A History of Women's Bodies.* New York: Basic.

Shryock, Henry, Jacob Siegel, *et al.* 1971. *The Methods and Materials of*

Demography. Washington: US Department of Commerce Bureau of the Census.

Skinner, William G. 1976. "Mobility strategies in late imperial China: A regional analysis." In Carol Smith, ed. *Regional Analysis*. New York: Academic Press, 327–364.

1987. "Sichuan's population in the nineteenth century: lessons from disaggregated data." *Late Imperial China*. 8.1 (June): 1–79.

1993. "Infanticide as family planning in Tokugawa Japan." In Barbara Miller, William Skinner, and eds. *Sex and Gender Hierarchies*. Cambridge: Cambridge University Press, 236–270.

1993. "Family systems and demographic processes." Manuscript to be published in David Kertzer and Thomas Fricke, eds. *Anthropological Demography: Toward a New Synthesis*. Chicago: University of Chicago Press.

Smith, Thomas C. 1977. *Nakahara: Family Farming and Population in a Japanese Village, 1717-1830*. Stanford: Stanford University Press.

Tang huiyao (Important documents of the Tang AD 618-905 dynasty). Shanghai: Zhonghua shuju, 1955 edition.

Tang Xianglong. 1931. "Daoguang chao juanjian zhi tongji" (Statistics on the sale of official degrees during the Daoguang Emperorship). *Shehui kexue zazhi*. (December): 437–444.

Telford, Ted A. 1986. "Survey of social demographic data in Chinese genealogies." *Late Imperial China*. 7.2 (December): 118–148.

1990. "Patching the holes in Chinese genealogies: mortality in the lineage populations of Tongcheng County, 1300–1880." *Late Imperial China*. 11.2 (December): 116–136.

1992. "Covariates of men's age at first marriage: the historical demography of Chinese lineages." *Population Studies*. 46.1 (March): 19–35.

1995. "Fertility and population growth in the lineages of Tongcheng County 1520–1661." In Harrell, ed. 48–93.

Todd, Emmanuel. 1982. *La Troisieme Planete*. Paris: Seuil. Published in English as *The Explanation of Ideology: Family Structures and Social Systems*. London: Blackwell, 1985.

Tong Yonggong, Guan Kexiao, Shen Hui, Guan Jialu, and Wang Peihuan. 1984. *Sanxing fudutong yamen Manwen dang'an yibian* (Translations from the Manchu Language Archives of the Sanxing Lieutenant General's Office). Shenyang: Liaoshen shushe.

United Nations Model Life Tables for Developing Countries. New York: United Nations Department of International Economic and Social Affairs Population Studies No. 77.

Van de Walle, Etienne. 1992. "Fertility transition, conscious choice, and numeracy." *Demography*. 29.4 (November): 487–502.

Wakefield, David. 1992. "Household division in Qing and Republican China: inheritance, family property, and economic development." PhD dissertation, University of California, Los Angeles, Department of History.

Wakeman, Frederic Jr. 1985. *The Great Enterprise: The Manchu Reconstruction of Imperial Order in Seventeenth Century China.* Berkeley: University of California Press.

Waldron, Ingrid. 1983. "The role of genetic and biological factors in sex differences in mortality." In Alan D. Lopez and Lado T. Ruzicka, eds., 141–165.

1986. "What do we know about causes of sex differences in mortality? A review of the literature." *Population Bulletin of the United Nations.* 18-1985: 59–76.

1987. "Patterns and causes of excess female mortality among children in developing countries." *World Health Statistics Quarterly.* 40: 194–210.

Wall, Richard. 1981. "Inferring differential neglect of females from mortality data." *Annales de demographie historique.* 119–140.

Wall, Richard and Peter Laslett. 1983. *Family Forms in Historic Europe.* Cambridge: Cambridge University.

Walter, John and Roger Schofield. 1989. *Famine, Disease, and the Social Order in Early Modern Society.* Cambridge: Cambridge University Press.

Waltner, Ann. 1991. *Getting An Heir: Adoption and the Construction of Kinship in Late Imperial China.* Honolulu: University of Hawaii Press.

Wang Feng and Nancy Tuma. 1993. "Changes in Chinese marriage patterns during the twentieth century." *Proceedings of the XXII General Conference of the International Union for the Scientific Study of Population.* Liege: IUSSP, 3: 337–352.

Wang Feng, James Lee, and Cameron Campbell. 1995. "Marital fertility control among the late imperial Chinese nobility: implications for two types of preventive check." *Population Studies.* 49.3 (November): 383–400.

Wang Feng and Yang Quanhe. 1996. "Age at marriage and the first birth interval: the emerging change in sexual behavior among young couples in China." *Population Development Review* 22.2 (June): 299-320.

Wang Gungwu. 1979. *Power, Rights, and Duties in Chinese History.* Canberra: Australian National University.

Wang Shaowu. 1988. "Jin sibai nian dongya de lengxia" (Cold summers in East Asia during the last four hundred years). Manuscript.

1990. "Gongyuan 1380 nian yilai woguo huabei qiwen xuli de chongjian" (Reconstruction of temperature in north China since 1380). *Zhongguo kexue Series B.* (May): 553–560.

Wang Yuquan, Guo Songyi, Lin Yongkuang, *et al.* 1991. *Zhongguo tunken shi* (History of State Land Cultivation). 2 vols. Beijing: Nongye chuban she.

Wang Zhonghan. 1985. "Shixi Kangxi zhi nongben sixiang" (A preliminary analysis of the Kangxi emperor's emphasis on agriculture). Manuscript presented at the Conference on Ming-Qing History, Hong Kong University.

1988 (ed.). *Manzu shi yanjiu ji* (Research Collection in Manchu History). Beijing: Zhongguo shehui kexue chuban she.

1990. "Guanyu Manzu xingcheng zhong de jige wenti" (Several questions on the origins of the Manchu people). *Qingshi xinkao* (New Studies of Qing History). Shenyang: Liaoning daxue chuban she, 44–58.

1990. "Qingdai qidi xingzhi chutan" (A preliminary investigation in to the nature of banner land during the Qing). *Qingshi xinkao* (New Studies of Qing History). Shenyang: Liaoning daxue chuban she, 71–86.

1990. "Qingdai baqi zhong de Man Han minzu chengfen wenti" (The ethnic composition of the Manchu and Han Eight Banner population during the Qing). *Minzu yanjiu.* 3: 36–46, 4: 57–66.

Editor. 1995. *Zhongguo minzu shi* (History of China's Ethnic Peoples). Beijing: Shehui kexue chuban she.

Wang Zongyou, ed. 1990. *Guangzhou Manzu jianshi* (A Short History of the Cantonese Manchus). Guangzhou: Guangdong renmin chuban she.

Watkins, Susan Cotts and Jane Menken. 1985. "Famines in historical perspective." *Population and Development Review.* 11.4 (December): 647–673.

Weir, David. 1984. "Rather never then late: celibacy and age at marriage in English cohort fertility, 1574–1871." *Journal of Family History.* 9 (Winter): 340–354.

Wilson, Chris. 1984. "Natural fertility in preindustrial England, 1600-1799." *Population Studies.* 38.2 (July): 225-240.

Wolf, Arthur. 1984. "Family life and the life cycle in rural China." In Robert Mc C. Netting, Richard Wilk, and Eric Arnould, eds., *Households: Comparative and Historical Studies of the Domestic Group.* Berkeley: University of California Press, 279–298.

1985a. "Fertility in prerevolutionary rural China." In Hanley and Wolf, eds., 154–185.

1985b. "Chinese family size: a myth revitalized." In Hsieh Jih-chang and Chuang Ying-chang, eds., 30–49.

1985. "Introduction." In Hanley and Wolf, eds., 1–12.

Wolf, Arthur and Chieh-shan Huang 1980. *Marriage and Adoption in China, 1845–1945.* Stanford: Stanford University Press.

Wolf, Margery. 1968. *The House of Lim: A Study of a Chinese Farm Family.* New York: Appleton-Century.

Wrigley, E. A. and R. S. Schofield. 1981. *Population History of England 1541–1871.* Cambridge, Mass.: Harvard University Press.

Wu Chengming. 1985. *Zhongguo ziben zhuyi yu guonei shichang* (Chinese Capitalism and the Chinese Domestic Market). Zhongguo shehui kexue.

Wu-Williams, A. H., X. D. Dai, W. Blot, Z. Y. Xu, X. W. Sun, H. P. Xiao, B. J. Stone, S. F. Yu, Y. P. Feng, A. G. Ershow, J. F. Fraument, Jr., and B. E. Henderson. 1990. "Lung cancer among women in north-east China." *British Journal of Cancer.* 62: 982–987.

Xi Qing (c. 1810). 1984. *Heilongjiang waiji* (Travels in Heilongjiang). Harbin: Heilongjiang renmin chuban she.

Xu Xiping and Lihua Wang. 1993. "Association of indoor and outdoor particulate level with chronic respiratory illness." *American Review of Respiratory Diseases.* 148: 1516–1522.

Xu Zhao-yi, William J. Blot, Han-Ping Xiao, Anna Wu, Yi-Ping Feng, J. Stone, Jie Sun, Abby G. Ershow, Brian E. Henderson, Joseph F. Fraumeni, Jr. 1989. "Smoking, air pollution, and the high rates of lung cancer in Shenyang, China." *Journal of the National Cancer Institute.* 81: 1800–1806.

Yang, C. K. 1959. *The Chinese Family in the Communist Revolution.* Cambridge: The Technology Press.

Yang, Martin C. 1965. *Chinese Village: Taitou, Shantung Province.* New York: Columbia University Press.

Yang, Xiangkui and James Lee. 1990. "Lun youbiao zhui yu jietan" (The origins of local administration during the Han). *Gu Jigang jinian lunwen ji* (Essays in Commemoration of Gu Jigang). Chongqing: Bashu, 228-240.

Zeng Yi, Tu Ping, Gu Baochang, *et al.* 1993. "Causes and implications of the recent increase in the reported sex ratio at birth in China." *Population and Development Review.* 19.2 (June): 283–302.

Zhang Zuofeng, Shun-Zhang Yu, and Guo-Dong Zhou. "Indoor air pollution of coal fumes as a risk factor of stroke, Shanghai." *American Journal of Public Health.* 78(8): 975-976.

Zhao Lian (1770-1829). *Xiaoting zalu* (Essays by Zhao Lian). Beijing: Zhonghua shuju, 1980.

Zhao Wenlin and Xie Shujun. 1988. *Zhongguo renkou shi* (Population History of China). Beijing: Renmin chuban she.

Zhao Zhongwei. 1994. "Demographic conditions and multi-generation households in Chinese history: results from genealogical research and microsimulation." *Population Studies* 48.3 (November): 413–426.

——— 1996. "Demographic conditions and household formation in Chinese history: a simulation study." Presented at the IUSSP Conference on Asian Population History, January 4-8, Taipei, Taiwan.

Zheng Chuanshui. 1981. "Xinghai geming yu baqi zhidu de bengkui" (The 1911 revolution and the destruction of the Eight Banner system). *Liaoning daxue xuebao.* 5: 30–35.

Zheng Qin. 1988. *Qingdai sifa shenpan zhidu yanjiu* (Research in Qing legal history). Changsha: Hunan jiaoyu chuban she.

Zhongguo Shejui Kexueyuan Jindai Shi Yanjiusuo Fanyishi. 1981. *Jindai lai Hua waiguoren ming cidian* (Contemporary Dictionary of Foreigners in China). Zhongguo shehui kexue chuban she.

Zhongguo ziran dili tuji (A Collection of Maps on the Natural Geography of China). 1984. Beijing: Ditu chuban she.

Zhou Yuanlian. 1981. *Qingchao kaiguo shi yanjiu* (Research on the Founding of the Qing State). Shenyang: Liaoning renmin chuban she.

——— 1982. "Guanyu baqi zhidu di jige wenti" (Some problems on the banner system). *Qingshi luncong* (Essays in Qing History). 3: 140–154.

Zhu Jiefan. 1974. *Zhongguo yaoyan congkan diyi ji* (The First Collection of Chinese Folk Sayings). Taiwan: Shangwu yinshu guan.

——— 1989. *Zhonghua yanyu zhi* (A Compendium of Chinese Folk Sayings). Taiwan: Shangwu yinshu guan.

Zhu Yong. 1987. *Qingdai zongfa yanjiu* (Studies on Qing Family Law). Changsha: Hunan renmin chuban she.

Zi, Etienne. 1896. *Pratique des examens militaires in Chine.* Varietes Sinologiques, Vol. 9. Shanghai.

Index

Titles available in paperback are marked with an asterisk